Already Ours

Betty McCutchon

Already Ours

Every Day of the Year

Betty McCutchan

Providence House Publishers
Franklin, Tennessee

Copyright 1999 by Betty McCutchan

All rights reserved. Written permission must be secured from the publisher to use or reproduce any part of this book, except for brief quotations in critical reviews or articles.

Scripture and commentary: 1) King James Version. Copyright © 1976 by Thomas Nelson, Inc., Nashville, Tennessee; 2) The Open Bible, Expanded Edition, Copyright © 1985 by Thomas Nelson, Inc., Nashville, Tennessee.

Printed in the United States of America

03   02   01   00   99   1   2   3   4   5

Library of Congress Catalog Card Number: 99-70373

ISBN: 1-57736-146-6

Cover design by Gary Bozeman

PROVIDENCE HOUSE PUBLISHERS
238 Seaboard Lane • Franklin, Tennessee 37067
800-321-5692
www.providencehouse.com

Dedicated with deep love and affection to

Richard
the light of my life and the joy of my soul for forty-three years

Richard Jr., Jan, and Anne
cherished children of our union

Terry, Dave, and Kerry—
treasured children-in-love

and

James, John, Megan, Katie, and the one-on-the-way—
adored angels of incalculable value

Preface

You wake up in the morning, yawn, and bend down to put on your house slippers. On the floor beside them is a small box, one containing a blessing from God. You have a busy day ahead of you, so you shove the box aside and head for a bowl of cereal instead. On the drive to work another small gift floats your way, but you're absorbed in business thoughts, so you ignore the blessing it contains. At work a colleague greets you with alarming news regarding your work performance. Again God drops a blessing box at your feet, this time a huge one, but you're too terrified to open it. Throughout your workday, blessing after blessing rests at your fingertips, but you don't take time to reach out for them and study them and gain insight and Godly help from them. By the end of your workday, you enter the turnpike, once again headed homeward. Traffic crawls at a snail's pace, motorists' tempers flare, and a major pile up causes you to have to detour. You gripe and complain, not taking note of gift box after gift box raining down from heaven. God's blessings remain unopened where they've fallen because you're too exhausted to pick them up, much less open them up. By the time you reach home, all you want is for God to send some peace and quiet and perhaps even a little solitude.

It's time to pick up *Already Ours, Every Day of the Year*, sit down in a quiet spot and rediscover something you've known all along: God loves you, His blessings surround you and they are free. God is everywhere and He is in everything. *Already Ours, Every Day of the Year* is an affirmation of God's blessings, the ones He gives us every moment of every day. Far too often, we simply don't see them, and I think this is because we're not looking for them. Not many of us would take a gift from a giver and then never open it, but I have ignored many of God's gifts, and I imagine

Already Ours, Every Day of the Year

you have too. These gifts are the blessings God pours out on us by the bucketsful every moment of every day. Time and again, we get so caught up in the happenings of the moment that we miss what that moment holds, and we're left with an exquisite package in our hands, one we never open.

The essays, devotionals, and vignettes in *Already Ours, Every Day of the Year* are laid out in such a way that readers can begin at Day 1 and continue reading daily through to Day 365 or Day 366 in a leap year. It is my prayer and hope that nestled somewhere in a daily reading you will find something of what you might need for your daily walk with the Lord. It is also my prayer that you will come to the realization that all of God's bountiful blessings are already yours. None of us have to wait until we see our Lord face to face to experience all God has to offer us. He has given everything to us now. It belongs to us. Open His gifts, explore them, and extract from them what God has put there for you.

My love to you in Christ,
Betty McCutchan

Already Ours

1 IN THE SUMMER OF 1998 MY HUSBAND AND I VISITED ST. PETER'S Basilica, the Vatican Museum, the Sistine Chapel, and the Colosseum in Rome, Italy. We even threw coins in Trevi Fountain. In preparation for the coming of the year 2000, scaffolding surrounded some of these structures, with workers putting finishing touches on them, getting them ready for a new millennium which will also usher in a year of jubilee.

In Old Testament times, every fiftieth year the trumpet of the jubilee blared throughout the land, and those who had become indentured slaves were freed. God gave them a new beginning. Today is a new beginning for us. It signals a new start, a time for us to begin to see God everywhere and in everything. God reaches down to us and speaks to us every moment of every day, pouring out blessing after blessing on us. "For it is the jubile; it shall be all for you alone" (Lev. 25:12, OPEN BIBLE). This year is for you and for me, and it is a gift from God. Let us pray that we use it wisely.

2 WHEN I WAS A CHILD GROWING UP IN GEORGIA, MY BIGGEST fantasy was of my father confounding all manner of obstacles and delivering me from the hands of hopeless situations and harmful people. Of course in my whimsical view of him, he was decked out in a knight's shining armor, mounted atop the most handsome steed ever to come down the tube. A fantasy is a fantasy is a fantasy of course, and my father, one whom I saw precious little as I grew up, never darkened the door of reality. Not only did he not snatch me from danger, but he played no major role in my life—ever—for my parents divorced when I was four and I saw little of him during my formative years. My father, my imagined knight in shining armor, never showed up. Plight after plight came and went, but he was nowhere in sight.

It wasn't until many years later that I learned the Knight had always been there and not only had redeemed me, but had formed a lifeline between us, one that set me free to be all that He wants me to be. This Knight was not my earthly father and never would be; instead he was and is my heavenly Father, and as such there is no need for a magnificent white horse. Instead, zillions of golden chariots of hope are at His command, and these chariots swoop down from heaven filled with His presence, His healing words, and His heavenly beings—those creatures charged with the responsibility of keeping my feet safe and on solid ground.

It took years for me to understand the wealth contained in God's magnificent chariots so abundantly filled with His richest blessings—His love; His concern; His approval; His help in times of stress, anguish, and despair when I had nowhere to turn and no human to take me by the hand and lead me into untroubled waters.

Nestled in the arms of our Savior, our Lord and our King, God invites us to ride in His golden chariots of hope and meditate on His words, soothing words of love, nurture, and encouragement, words to heal our broken hearts and spirits.

3 RECENTLY, WHEN MY HUSBAND AND I PLANNED A CRUISE vacation for ourselves, many people, on hearing our news, questioned our rationale for doing such a thing in light of the movie, *Titanic*. I can't count the number of times someone said to one or the other of us, "Have you seen *Titanic?*" My reply was, "Not yet, but I will when we return from vacation." The movie was high on my priority list, but I didn't want to see something of this nature before we embarked on our trip. I did feel compelled to defend our actions to others on occasion, however.

"What if you hit an iceberg?"
"In the middle of the Caribbean Sea?" I'd respond.
"What if the ship sinks?"
"Well, then, I guess it would just sink," I'd say.
"Aren't you afraid to get on a ship?"
"Why should I be?" I'd ask.
"There's no way on God's green earth I'd ever do such a thing."
"Well, I'm not you," I'd admit.

We received our ticket packet in the mail about two weeks before we sailed. I must admit that with all the questioning I had allowed myself to become somewhat apprehensive. My uneasiness subsided, though, as I scrutinized the contents of the packet. Our flight departure times and their numbers were listed along with other information. The number of our homebound flight was 555. Five is the biblical number symbolic of God's grace. Triple grace! And I had wasted precious moments giving our safety a second thought? We were going on the vacation of a lifetime, and God was with us every step of the way. He always had been, and He always would be.

I did see *Titanic* soon after our return home. And still my husband and I look forward to the next time when we might be able to afford such a glorious excursion. Far too many of us do not look to God as we look to the future, but focus on the negatives the future might bring us. Look to the hills, my friend. Look upward. God is ever there, and He is forever watching over His children and taking care of them regardless of the road they are on.

4 ON A RECENT CRUISE TO THE CARIBBEAN, MY HUSBAND AND I became intrigued with the other sea vessels we encountered. Many were cruise ships of various sizes. Some were sailboats or tugboats or fishing boats. We even encountered several freighters. Docked at port one morning, I noticed several ships tied up to the pier. One of them was much smaller than the others. As my husband and I talked, I referred to that ship as the lesser vessel, and then an epiphany occurred. It matters little whether God's children are great or small. He watches over us all. After that, I viewed all the sea vessels differently. Regardless of their size or the jobs they performed, they are all precious in His sight because aboard each one are some of God's children.

Whatever your station in life, my friend, God cares for you.

5 MY HUSBAND AND I HAD THE GOOD FORTUNE TO BE SEATED AT A table aboard ship with four lovely ladies. They were all in their early eighties, and they were absolutely charming and delightful. Each one in her own way contributed to our growth. One brought us wisdom, another kindness, another a heavy heart, and the other energy and zest for living. We fell in love with them and thanked our Lord for allowing them to cross our paths and enrich our lives.

Let us look around us each day and become aware of the people God places in our paths. There are no coincidences with our Lord. He plans our lives carefully. It is up to us to open ourselves to His plans and embrace what is there for us and learn from those whose lives intersect our own.

Already Ours, Every Day of the Year

6 AS WE DOCKED BY THE ISLAND OF DOMINIQUE, A NATIVE GREETED those who went ashore by playing "Auld Lang Syne" and "Amazing Grace" on his steel drum. I had never heard those two melodies played back-to-back, and I'm so glad he presented me with such an opportunity. It is God's amazing grace that keeps remarkable memories of days gone by in our hearts and in our minds. It is His grace that enables us to continue on when life seems so bleak and lifeless. "Should old acquaintance be forgot and never brought to mind?" No, never forgotten. Always remembered. His amazing grace keeps them ever with us and heals us from whatever pain and suffering they might bring our way. Something good is always around the corner. Look to the hills, my friend, from whence comes our help — God's amazing grace — which is always there, always leading and directing and healing and saving us, even from ourselves.

7 WHEN WE ARRIVED AT THE ISLAND OF ST. THOMAS, ALL NON-U.S. citizens had to have a pass to go ashore. We had the proper blue piece of paper in hand, of course, and were able to disembark at will. How glad I am to be a child of God, where the only pass needed to be in His presence or to approach Him is one of relationship. There is no standing in line waiting to see Him or to talk with Him. He is ever available to us. We are blessed indeed to be children of the King and citizens of His country.

8 ABOARD SHIP WE MET A COUPLE FROM ENGLAND WHOSE American granddaughter now resides with them. They talked of her homesickness for America, and they sounded as if they couldn't relate to it or understand it. Their motto seemed to be: "Get on with it." I understood the granddaughter's homesickness quite well because I've been there. I know this entity, and it is well named. It really is a sickness — a longing for a place and people no longer a part of our lives. This is what the apostle Paul felt and wrote about regarding heaven. He longed to be at home with his God and his Lord, but he knew his work on earth wasn't finished yet. He set his sights on the race at hand, and he continued on until he completed his work.

All of us are in a race of sorts. There is something there for you to do, and there is something there for me to do. In the doing of it, we often become homesick for heaven just as the apostle Paul did. But we, too, continue until we finish the course God has laid out before us. We are indeed blessed to be honored with such a task.

9 ON THE ISLAND OF ST. THOMAS WE HAILED A TAXI TO TAKE US back to our ship. A native driver picked us up in town, and we made our way back to the dock as his passengers. Try as we might, we couldn't get this man to talk with us. I figured he'd either just about had his fill of tourists for the day, or he was just in a bad mood. Our encounter with him, however, wasn't without benefit. It served to remind me that our God not only is willing but always quite able to receive us into His presence and listen to us and commune with us hours and hours on end. Blessed indeed is the person who avails himself of such an honor.

10 ONE AFTERNOON WHILE TAKING MY DAILY TWO-MILE WALK aboard ship, I passed a lady sitting in one of the deck chairs. She glanced up from her book and asked me for the time. I gave it to her, knowing she was taking in my deep Texas drawl. She thanked me in a very proper English way of speaking. I chuckled to myself and wondered if she had actually understood what I had said. And then my thoughts turned heavenward. How thankful I am our Lord knows His children. Even the hairs of our head are numbered. No matter what we say to Him, He understands us, and the extraordinary thing about all this is that He not only understands, but He knows what we're going to say before we even say it.

Never fear to talk with the Lord, my friend. He knows who you are and He hears every word. There's no mistaking your nationality. He knows exactly where you live and He knows exactly what you need from Him. And it doesn't matter at all to Him if you have a Texas twang.

11 WHILE VISITING IN THE CITY OF CARACAS, OUR TOUR GUIDE pointed out the houses of the squatters dotted throughout the mountainside. He told us how they got to be where they now are and what brought these people to his country. He went on to inform us that many other countries try to hide these kinds of things from tourists, but there was no way the squatters could be hidden from view, so he just pointed them out and got it over and done with. I admired his openness and honesty. It gave me the opportunity to really see what the capital city of Venezuela was all about, and I very much liked what I saw. Being fully informed served only to whet my appetite to see all there was to see and to experience all there was to experience.

This is the way it is in almost everything that comes our way in life. To get to the really good stuff or the really good part and soak it in, sometimes we have to squat in the low, lonely valleys that get us to the place of being able to view the whole. Never despair of unlovely and crushing circumstances. They frequently come into our lives. But, so too, comes that which is pleasant, that which makes life such a joy. Did not our Lord tell us our lines are fallen unto us in pleasant places, and that we have a good heritage? And did He not tell us He would show us a path of life in which in His presence there is fullness of joy? And did He not say at His right hand are pleasures evermore?

When the going gets rough, my friend, look heavenward. Our Lord will show you the right path, the one that lands you in a pleasant place.

12

On a recent airline flight, we had marvelous traveling weather. I had a window seat and was able to see the land below. We were flying at 35,000 feet, and I had a good view. I wondered what the lives of the people on the ground were like and in what activities they were engaged. Of course I had no way of knowing, but this didn't prevent my curiosity from surfacing. And then, while scanning the landscape, I suddenly realized that God is not only aware of the lives of the people below, but of all people everywhere on earth.

God is omnipotent. He is everywhere and He knows everything about us. He knows when we rise in the morning and He knows when we sleep at night. He knows when we're happy and when we're sad. He collects our tears and He rejoices in our happiness. Nothing about us escapes His notice. How blessed are we to have such a magnificent Being to care so much about us.

"Casting all your care upon him; for he careth for you" (1 Pet. 5:7, KJV). God cares for you and He cares for me. We are indeed blessed creatures.

13 Even though we had relished every moment of our Caribbean cruise, we looked forward to going home. We missed our children and grandchildren and our friends. We wanted to see our dogs and even wanted to return to our work. We longed to sleep in our own bed and eat from our own table. It was time to return home. I think something like this happens for all of us when we're away on vacation. We know before we leave for our journeys that the time will come to return to everyday life.

If we feel this way about returning to an earthly home, then imagine how much more excitement we will feel for our return home to be with our Lord in heaven. Just as we enjoy strange and exotic and exciting places to visit here on earth and look forward to going home once again, so too, do we look toward that magnificent time when we will return to our eternal home and see our Lord face to face.

14 Each time we disembarked from our ship and set foot on shore, my husband and I had the sensation that the ground beneath us was swaying, and we felt as we did when we were aboard ship and moving on the sea. It took us a day on shore to lose our sea legs. Humans are prone to become acclimated to their habitats. We get used to anything, and whether it is normal or abnormal, we grow to accept it.

"If a man love me, he will keep my words; and my Father will love him, and we will come unto him, and make our abode with him" (John 14:23, KJV). Just as it isn't normal for our bodies to sway on land, so too it isn't normal for us to be able to live effectively for God outside His habitat for us. We must remain grounded in Him if we want Him to make His abode with us.

15 We sat on the runway at San Juan, Puerto Rico, for almost an hour before taking off. Many passengers grumbled at the delay because their connecting flights in other airports were tight, and there was no room for dallying. How I wanted to reach out and touch them and tell them there are no coincidences with God. We were delayed for a reason. Yes, we were waiting for clearance from the tower to take off, but there were individual reasons for the holdup. I didn't know what they were, but I didn't have to know, and neither did they. All I had to do was trust God to see what unfolded. Nothing else.

For me, the holding pattern meant that I would have a fantastic opportunity to see Atlanta, Georgia, decked out in her evening splendor because we would be over an hour late arriving there. Had we arrived at that airport earlier, I would have missed it. The delay also meant fatigue for me, which encouraged me to sleep during flight, something I seldom do. Rest meant a cheerier spirit with my mate and those whom I encountered on the plane and at the airport.

Most of us rush too much. We don't take time to rest in God and see what He has in store for us. It's like Christmas in that presents are everywhere beneath His tree, but we're so busy rushing about that we don't open the gifts to see what marvelous things are waiting inside.

16

COMING HOME, WE APPROACHED THE AIRPORT IN ATLANTA, Georgia. Once again, I had a window seat, and I could look out over the city. Familiar lights dotted the landscape below, and with each light I claimed a memory of my growing up years in such a splendid place. I had not lived in Atlanta in over forty years, but as I caught a glimpse of the downtown skyline, sad longings crept into my heart. How I wished I could be going for a visit to see my deceased mother, grandparents, and brother. Uncles and aunts used to live there, but now only a few relatives remained.

Someone once told me, "Life is not a dress rehearsal." Too often we act as if we're rehearsing for a play rather than experiencing the actual event itself. Once a moment is gone, it never returns again. Margaret Mitchell captured the essence of this thought in the title of her book, *Gone With the Wind*.

"So teach us to number our days, that we may apply our hearts unto wisdom" (Ps. 90:12, KJV). Yes, Lord. Teach us to number our days.

17

GOD GAVE MANKIND THE GIFT OF MUSIC. ALL KINDS OF SOUNDS and all kinds of words are uttered through musical notes. Most of us gravitate toward particular types of melodies, rhythms, and the like. Few of us are not emotionally stirred by music. In fact, many of us would like to be able to reproduce what we hear, hoping when or if we do, it will sound as wonderful as what we're trying to imitate from a CD, tape, TV, movie, or live performance. Mostly, we fall far short of our efforts and then, perhaps, allow ourselves to become envious of the performers' talents, wishing we'd been blessed with such ability.

We often forget, however, that had not the creators of symphonies, concertos, jazz, modern music, and the like, or performers of such creations not used the talent given them, we would not be blessed with their work. In the same sense, if each of us does not use our own God-given talents and abilities, others will not be blessed through us. We often tell ourselves we have little to offer others because what we have seems so little to us—so tiny, so minuscule. What nonsense! You and I may not be a Beethoven or a Bach or have the beautiful voice of the lady who sang in church last Sunday or the sound of the fiddler at the last country music festival we attended, but all of us have been given talents. Either we can use them like the great performers do, or we can complain we got shortchanged because what we have been given doesn't seem spectacular to us. God doesn't make mistakes. He created ants as well as elephants. Both are important in His eyes, and both have unique work to do, as do all creatures created by the living God.

18

One morning I awakened with a painful and swollen area beneath my left armpit. Realizing I could have some sort of infection, I called my physician and arranged for an appointment that day. She confirmed my suspicions and prescribed an antibiotic—double the usual dosage. Twenty-four hours into taking the medication, I became extremely nauseated, which led to regurgitation. These symptoms prompted me to call my doctor once again, assuming she would change the medication. She didn't. Instead, she ordered another medication for the new symptoms of nausea and vomiting, and insisted I continue the original regime. I wasn't too happy with her, but I complied. Needless to say, I was well and free of all symptoms long before the antibiotic ran out.

My doctor has an excellent reputation, and she knows what she's doing. She is more than very good at her job. Later, as I pondered my hesitation to follow her orders explicitly, I inwardly chuckled. This woman had invested enormous time and effort to perfect her craft. Of

Already Ours, Every Day of the Year

course she is aware of any side effects to any medication she prescribes. Nausea and vomiting occur in a certain percentage of patients taking the drug I was given. All I needed to do was take the medicine and report any side effects I might develop from it and leave the rest to her.

And this is the way we often react when our Lord offers a cure for what ails us. We go to Him with a complaint. He listens, and then He either sends or allows a circumstance to come into our lives to deal with our problem, which usually means He's set about growing us into the image of Christ. Often that which comes appears to us to be much worse than our original problem, and so we go to Him once again to report the awful consequences of His treatment. Our Lord then silently urges us to keep on keeping on, and if we're wise, we do so. Later and somewhere along the line, healing comes; our problem is resolved. And then along comes another situation when we'll need to consult our Great Physician once again for whatever new it is that distresses us. And do you know what? Something new will present itself. It always does. Our Great Physician will once again come to our aid with another "prescription," one that will heal us once again. Our part in this process is simple—just follow the Doctor's orders.

19

Last Sunday a lovely family sat in front of us in church. The mother and father had two children, a boy of about four and a girl of about six. Halfway through the service, the mother left with the boy, leaving the girl sitting next to her father on the pew. The innocence of this child captivated me and I wondered how she would survive a world that isn't necessarily a good and safe place in which to live. Far too often children are robbed of their purity and innocence. "This child will need strength," I kept telling myself over and over again. I began praying for her, wondering what life would bring her and what she would have to endure for Christ's sake. I prayed she would be given whatever she needed, be it strength or endurance or love, to live a life that would be pleasing to the Lord.

Then revelation came. I am one of those people who have always felt the presence of the Lord within me, and I have felt blessed because of it. I've often pondered who it was who prayed for me as I was growing up because I have had a sense of an awesome power guiding me to made good choices and decisions during those years. I've also always known I was not wise enough to make those good choices for myself. So, who prayed for me as I had prayed for this child? Was it my mother? My grandparents? A Sunday school teacher? I know from God's Word that while Jesus was in the garden He prayed for me as well as for all those God gave Him. But I also know from the depths of my being someone unknown to me also prayed for me. Is this not what Christians do for each other and strangers? Look around you. Someone you know or a total stranger might be in need of intercessory prayer.

20

When I was growing up in one of America's large cities, no one questioned the purity of the water I drank. When I was thirsty, I simply went to the kitchen sink, turned on the faucet, drew up a glass of water, and gulped it down. In those days, I don't recall seeing bottled water in grocery stores. I would have guffawed wildly if I'd come across an individual bottle of purified water in a soft drink dispensing machine and probably asked myself, "What is this?" This is not the case today. Almost everywhere one looks one can find bottled water, water that is good for us, water that is without impurities floating around inside it.

Are we Christians not blessed indeed to have the Living Water available to us, residing in us, always there to quench our thirst? How many of us avail ourselves of this Living Water? How many of us even go to His fountain to drink? We don't have to pay God for it. It's free. The next time you see a bottle of purified water on a store's shelf or reach for one from a dispensing machine, thank God that He is indeed your Living Water—that which quenches your thirst and that which is utterly pure.

21

One of our children and her family live fairly close to us, so we often drive down to see her family on a Saturday afternoon. It's not quite a three-hour drive there and back, and the time passes quickly. Not long ago, as we were traveling the roads of East Texas to her house, it occurred to me how long it would take us to get there if we had lived a century ago and had to travel by horse and buggy or covered wagon. Posing this question to my husband (he's the mathematician in our family), he calculated we would proceed at about five miles an hour, and so it would take a good twelve hours for us to get to our destination. I gulped and I gasped and a giant light bulb went off above my head. How blessed are we to have such contraptions as the automobile at our disposal. What about washing machines and clothes dryers and dishwashers and vacuum cleaners? I could go on and on with airplanes and computers and the like, but I think you get my point.

And then a great revelation came. What have I personally done with all that God has given modern man? Maybe we all need to ask ourselves this question.

22

When I was growing up in Georgia, people didn't own a passel of shoes to wear, at least not the people I knew. I always had one pair of shoes at a time, and this meant I wore the same shoes on Sunday that I wore to school each day. I took very good care of that pair of shoes, polishing them often to keep them looking good. And I frequently visited the shoe shop for repairs. I loved going there, and I guess it might be because the ones I frequented had what I called little cubicles to sit in while my shoes were being reheeled or resoled. I sort of felt like some kind of sovereign walking through that small swinging door and sitting down on a built-in seat in a mini-stall. I whiled away my time inhaling the odor of shoe polish and studying the people who came in.

I seldom frequent such places anymore. I don't take as good care of the many shoes I now own, either. I haven't seen one of those shoe stalls in eons because the few shoe repair shops I now go into don't have them. I do remember, though, that I was rough on shoes, especially "running over" my heels, which meant that if I didn't take care of my shoes, pretty soon they would begin to look rough and scuffy, and no matter how well dressed I thought I might have been, I really wasn't because of my shoes.

In a sense, shoes are like God's Word—the Bible. Shoes take us to where we want to go, get us to where we want to be. The Bible takes us to where we want to go, too, and also gets us where we want to be. "Thy word is a lamp unto my feet, and a light unto my path" (Ps. 119:105, KJV). Often when we're new in the faith, we polish it up, so to speak, and keep it in good repair. As time goes on and we move upward in the world, however, frequently we neglect prayer and the reading of God's Word the way we once did. Maybe it's time we all return to God's mini-stall, take a seat and study His Word, drink in the sweet aroma of what it says, and converse with Him. We could return to that delightful feeling of being a child of the King and, as His child, a sovereign indeed.

23

We have two dogs who live in our fenced-in backyard. Whenever I round the curve in our driveway, they run to the gate, vigorously wagging their tails, with one of them making dog sounds that cause me think he's saying, "She's here! She's here. Oh, good. She's here." He also runs to his mama and almost knocks her over licking her ear, reminding me of football players giving each other a high five after a tremendous play. It matters little to them whether I've been gone two minutes, a day, or overnight. Their greeting is the same each time I drive up. I never doubt their excitement at seeing me and lovingly welcoming me home once again.

Is this not our Lord's reaction each time we approach Him in prayer? It matters little whether we've just gotten off our knees communing with Him and once again return to add a comment or make a request. In my mind's eye, I see Him brighten and light up with joy, love, and excitement at my return home to Him. How blessed we are that we have One who loves us so unconditionally and expresses His delight in us as He sees us draw near to Him.

24

When our three children were growing up and the family was in the car traveling to someplace or other, inevitably one of them would begin calling out, "How long till we get there?" Another would chime in, "How much further do we have to go?" Once these questions got verbalized, it was difficult if not impossible to quell them. Pretty soon, all three children took up the cause and badgered their father and me with their questions of how long it would be before they could be freed from the car. Sometimes their questioning drove me nuts.

Is this not the way we are with our Heavenly Father? We're on an earthly pilgrimage with multitudes of events occurring along the way, and most of the time we have a long way to go. Sometimes what is in our life is pleasant, and sometimes it isn't. And sometimes what is happening seems like it will take forever to be over and done with.

"How long will I have to endure this?"

"Lord, graduation is so far down the road."

"Lord, don't you think it's about time I delivered this child? I'm so full of baby and my back is killing me."

"Lord, will I ever get that promotion?"

Already Ours, Every Day of the Year

"Lord, will it ever rain again?"

The list could go on and on, but I think you get my point. We behave toward our Heavenly Parent much as children act toward their earthly parents.

Our children are now grown. We no longer hear these questions. Do we miss them? No. We're just grateful the kids are grown and now mature and patient enough that these questions no longer need to be asked. I often wonder if God gets weary of all our impatient questions, even knowing as I do that our Heavenly Parent never wearies of anything we ask of Him. I do believe, however, He is mighty glad when we begin to grow spiritually, and we ask fewer and fewer questions and just sit back with Him and enjoy the ride.

25 Have you ever commanded your child to wipe his nose, or stand up straight, or close her mouth while eating? Usually, parents issue these directives from a loving heart because parents want children to grow into polite, respectful little creatures and thus lay down the law when they believe the law needs to be laid down. Often, however, the child does not feel or hear the love in the order, and when this happens, the child can get the notion he is acceptable only if he obeys. If he chooses not to comply, he might assume he is not loved. He also might imagine he can never please and then quit trying altogether.

Not so with our Lord God. As we walk with Him, we know His love is unconditional. If we slip and fall into sin, He forgives us. If we refuse to do something he's asked us to do, He forgives us. If we're lazy, He loves us. When we're angry, we're still acceptable to Him. Nothing can separate us from God's love. We don't have to be anything or do anything to receive His love. It is always there, and it is unconditional. We are blessed indeed to be His children and to have such a loving Parent.

26 There are few things more dreary than the bare limbs of winter trees silhouetted against an even more bleak and gloomy winter sky. Fortunately for me, I live in the southern part of our country, and I don't have to endure extended times such as these. But when it does occur, I somehow come to believe I will never see the sun shining again or feel her rays bathing my body with her soothing warmth. And then I realize a truth. The sun is shining. Only the clouds or a weather front prevent my being able to see it. Regardless of whether I see it in the sky or feel its warmth radiating down on me, the sun is there, and it's doing what God designed it to do.

Sometimes the circumstances of life are like the dismal, cheerless winter skies. We come to believe the anguish and pain of our hearts blot out the rays of God's goodness and grace to the point that we cannot behold His light that is forever there. Whether I can or cannot see the sun in the sky, it is there. It is always shining. Whether I feel God's presence within me and the inherent warmth it brings, His presence is always there, always shining. Like clouds that eventually give way to bright skies, so too does heavy heartedness give way to joy and brightness and the ability to see what has been there all along.

27 WHEN I WAS GROWING UP IN GEORGIA, I OFTEN TOOK THE BUS in my part of town, transferred to another bus downtown, and continued my journey until arriving at my best friend's house for an overnight visit. My family didn't own a suitcase, so I carried my belongings in a brown paper sack. Looking back on that scene now brings tears to my eyes and sorrow for that poor creature of a child I once was.

But, do you know what? On thinking deeper, I realize that child really wasn't deprived or poor at all. She knew within her heart that the Lord God was with her. She understood He would always take care of her, no matter what. And He did. She was never a poor creature. How could she have been? God walked along beside her every step of the way. Her riches were beyond measure.

28 IN RECENT YEARS, I'VE DISCOVERED THE ADVANTAGES OF exercise. Not only does walking on a treadmill cause my heart to beat faster and my breathing to come quicker, but it also makes me feel just plain good. I used to think I was going nowhere when I did this, because when I got back to where I started I really hadn't been anywhere at all or seen anything different from what my eyes beheld at the beginning of my so-called journey. I often told others that walking on a treadmill was boring because I didn't go anywhere, and I didn't see interesting things along the way.

Already Ours, Every Day of the Year

This is the way many of us are in our daily lives. We often believe we're going nowhere and accomplishing nothing because what we are doing seems to us so minuscule, so small. We content ourselves with looking at the small picture instead of focusing on the big one. Just as my weight dropped and my spirits soared from my daily walk, so too will joy come for us as we trudge along the treadmill of life. All we ever have to do is keep on keeping on. Much will happen in the interval of our journey, and it will come so slowly we won't comprehend it until it has long been in our hands, and we one day decide to take a gander at it. Then we know. Our trip has not been in vain. In fact, it's been downright adventuresome and lovely, and we see such awesome benefits from it.

29 WE HAVE A LARGE MIRROR THAT IS ABOVE THE SINK AND counter in our hall bathroom, the one we call the guest bath. As I busily cleaned the countertop one day, I glanced upward into the mirror and caught a reflection of the breakfast area and sunporch behind me. I gasped at the beauty my eyes beheld. Blues, mauves, and greens all intermingled with deep cherry woods that were topped off with copper-laden bowls dotted generously with gorgeous greenery and flowers tucked inside. It was the same room I had just left, but it didn't look like the same room.

As I marveled at this, it slowly sank in that I had recaptured the room's original charm because I was now looking at it from another angle. I had closed my eyes to what they drank in on a daily basis because I was accustomed to it. I took the room's loveliness for granted. I had allowed myself to become blind to what was before my eyes because I continued to view the room the way I always had, never thinking to look at it in a new and fresh and different way.

How many times do we miss out on what is really there because we won't risk looking from a new perspective or from a different viewpoint? Open our eyes, Lord, that we might see.

30 WHEN I WAS GROWING UP, WINTER WAS MY FAVORITE SEASON of the year. I think this was so because summers were so miserably hot and humid in the part of the South where I lived. I tolerate cold better than heat. With the advent of air-conditioning, however, winter no longer charmed me.

Today, while driving home for lunch, I changed my mind once again about winter. I took note of a sports-utility vehicle rumbling down a trail on the side of the road. I studied the beaten path beneath its wheels and the trees and vegetation dotting its passageway. The sun was shining on the scene in such a way that I envisioned sun diamonds bouncing off not only the vehicle, but the grass, bare tree limbs, shrubbery and even the sky itself. I wanted to stay and linger awhile and drink in the beauty, but I couldn't. I had to get home. On the way there, however, epiphany came: I had been so caught up in my own perception of the season I had allowed myself to miss its treasures and its very core. I translated this insight into my life, and the season in which I am now. Have I focused so much on the glory of other days and other times that I've neglected to revel in and take in the awe and wonder of the treasures this season of life has in store for me? Are there seasonal diamonds within my reach, ones I'm neglecting to harvest?

31

A WEATHER FRONT MOVED INTO OUR AREA WHILE I WAS home for lunch, and the sun vanished. Again, the sky took on that familiar dreary look, the one I associate with winter. But, as I drove down the road heading back to work, something was different. Winter no longer meant to me what it had only moments before. True, the sun diamonds had vanished, but other jewels dotted the landscape, ones just as precious as those of the sun. Here and there along the way, vibrant blooming red flowers teased my eyes, urging me to take a gander at them. Patches of dormant grasses coaxed me to give them a nod, indicating they were lovely, and I had ignored them. Several red vehicles winked at me, not wanting me to give them the cold shoulder either. True, cars aren't seasonal, but they are most lovely when they embellish a somewhat lackluster landscape.

Passing by the middle school, a group of boys played catch. They were oblivious to my passing vehicle, but I did not block them out. They frolicked with each other, their laughter and joy bouncing off the walls of the gray sky I once thought was nothing less than gloomy. Even their jackets and coats shouted at me to pay attention to them, noting their texture and fine interwoven coloring.

Already Ours, Every Day of the Year

Whatever had I been doing to think winter was without dynamic wonder, in nature or in me? It had been there all along right beneath my nose. I had allowed the wrinkles, graying hair, diminishing physical endurance, and the prospect of whatever other age-related disasters might be out there, to cloud my vision. Embrace the winter of your life, my friend. Nothing is like it. In fact, nothing is like the season you are presently in.

32 DRIVING TO WORK THIS MORNING, I PASSED BY A GROUP OF middle school boys running a trail on the field next to the school. They were all dressed alike in gray sweat suits, and I assumed they were either in physical education class or in an athletic program. There were about fifteen to twenty of them, and they were of various heights, weights, and body builds. Some of them held their heads erect, arms at a ninety-degree bend moving in time with their feet, breathing easily, obviously enjoying the exercise, while others huffed and puffed along the way, having a difficult time.

This is a commentary on people, I mused. This is the way we are. Some of us get into the program and vigorously get on with it, extracting from it its benefits, while others of us struggle along the way, making even simple tasks more difficult than they really are. I prayed for the lagging boys and for all of us who wrestle with life's uphill events. May we be granted strength for the tasks at hand, but may we also be endowed with the endurance and insight we need to be faithful to that task to which our Lord has called us, not making more of a thing than is really there.

33 WE'VE ALL SEEN MOVIES OR TELEVISION SHOWS OR READ books in which the main character or characters board a ship for a cruise to somewhere or other. Paper confetti floats in the air, the ship's horn lets out a deep-throated blast, and passengers dot the railings aboard the ship waving good-bye to those on shore. People shout, "Bon voyage" to their departing family or friends. Good voyage! Have a good trip! A flurry of excitement begins for the passengers. Everyone on board looks forward to having the time of their lives.

Wouldn't it be wonderful if each of us could awaken to a new day dawning in our lives with such expectations? Wouldn't it be fantastic if we viewed each new day with such enthusiasm? Why can this not be so? The sun has risen. A new day is beginning. Bon voyage, my friend. Have a good trip. Whatever happens today, no matter what it might be, may you find joy in it. This day will be worth the trip. You are not alone. God is with you.

34 A NUMBER OF YEARS AGO, I FOOLISHLY GOT INTO OUR Volkswagen bug and drove out on a snowy highway to go see about my mother-in-law. At the time, she was a widow. Cars whizzed past me on the road, and I wondered at the wisdom of my driving as slowly as I was, so I decided the other drivers were right in passing me, and I was wrong in dawdling. I went a little faster. Soon afterward, I hit an icy patch on the road. My car spun out of control, and I shouted, "I don't know what to do! I don't know what to do!" I had heard to steer in the direction of the spin, and I wrongly assumed this meant in the direction in which the car was traveling. This route led me toward the side of the road, and I knew if I didn't do something fast, I would end up in the ditch. Once again, I shouted, "I don't know what to do!"

A voice from within said, "Do not be afraid of sudden fear" (Ps. 8:25, KJV). I jerked the steering wheel around, heading back for the road. When I did this, I also put on the brakes—all wrong choices, I later learned. I ended up with my car traveling sideways down the side of the road, collecting a bank of snow as I came to a stop.

I found myself stuck on an isolated road. "What do I do now?" I said aloud.

"Be strong and of a good courage" (Josh. 1:6, KJV), my mind whispered, "and be thankful you're in a stick shift vehicle. Just rock it out." With a grateful heart I did, thanking my God that He had brought to my memory His words from the Bible. Indeed, His words are a light unto my path and a lamp unto my feet.

35 WHEN ONE IS ABOARD AN OCEAN LINER, ONE NEVER KNOWS what is over the horizon. Perhaps another ship will pass us and we can wave to strangers in the night. Maybe a storm lurks ahead, even a hurricane. It could be that a fabulous sunset is about to burst forth. Or we might spot a whale or a school of porpoises or dolphins. We might even see an island or a small fishing craft. The sky might hold an airplane. One never knows what is over the horizon until one reaches it and then looks out further to the never-ending horizon just ahead.

A dedicated sailor never fears what is out of his range of vision on the sea. He just sets his course and heads into it. Would that we could do the same. None of us knows what lurks just ahead for us. But we do know who our Captain is. He will keep us safe, no matter what is out there. Keep sailing, dear friend, keep sailing.

36

WE ARE IN THE PROCESS OF CONVERTING A LARGE STOREroom in our garage into a small study. There are all kinds of junk stored in that room. It's been a major undertaking to sort through it, deciding what to throw away, what to keep, and where to put what is kept. In the process of all this, I came across some boxes that contained items from my mother's home. I had put them there after Mother's death many years ago. I originally had planned to go through what I'd packed up from her apartment at some point—a time when I felt I could do something of this nature without its taking an emotional toll on me. I never got around to it, however. First one thing came along and then another, and I finally forgot about the boxes altogether.

Going through them, I came across my mother's scissors. They were, like everything else my mother owned, in perfect shape. Sharp. In excellent working order. I took them in my hands, examined them thoroughly, and snapped them briskly. And then I broke down sobbing. My sorrow was for the loss of my mother—a grief I seldom acknowledged much less openly displayed.

My mother was a stiff-upper-lip kind of person. She did not indulge in weepy emotions, and she forbade me to do so. She often told me she didn't want me to cry when she died. I complied. But, my mother is no longer here on planet Earth. I felt deep sorrow that she no longer was. There was no reason not to express it. Now, each time I take her scissors to cut something or other, I think of her, and in my mind's eye I cut her free from the bondage of suppressing her emotions, and in so doing free myself to grieve my losses openly.

37 THIS MORNING I AWAKENED TO THE NEWS OF AN ESCAPED lioness from a zoo in Kissimee, Florida. Newscasters informed us it is the female of this species who does the hunting. I shuddered, for I knew this area is very close to Disney World. "Help them to recapture her," I asked of God. "Keep those people safe."

I shivered once again, but this time at the thought of there being a more sinister and furious being out there who stalks all of God's children, waiting to devour them, and his name is Satan. The Bible tells us he paces up and down the earth, seeking those whom he might devour. Just as newscasters warned residents in Kissimee to take care and be vigilant, so too must we be careful of this invisible demon who wants to get his hands on us and do as much harm to us as possible.

38 LAST NIGHT MY HUSBAND AND I STOPPED AT A CONVENIENCE store to fill up our gas tank. As he went inside to pay for his purchase, I sat in the car watching people go in and out of the store. A man drove up, got out of his running car, and went inside the building. It was very cold, and I assumed he would be in and out of the store very quickly, and this was his reason for leaving his car motor running. In my mind's eye, I calculated how easy it would be for anyone to jump inside his vehicle and take off with it. I wondered at this man's wisdom, almost sending an engraved invitation to a would-be robber. And then I paused and took stock of my own actions. How many times have I opened the door to Satan, almost inviting him into my world by my foolish actions? I paused for a long time and then prayed to God in heaven to help me live my life more carefully.

39 EARLY IN OUR MARRIAGE, MY HUSBAND AND I LIVED IN A house that had been converted into three apartments—two upstairs and one downstairs. We lived in one of the upstairs apartments. No one lived below. My husband was in school, and one day I was off work from my job as a scrub nurse. I set about cleaning our tiny three-room apartment. Suddenly, a memory crept in and captured my attention. I had lived in a similar house during one of the happiest times of my childhood. I lived downstairs, and my best friend lived upstairs. I often played a game with her, and it went like this: Sometimes when I went up to see her, I would sneak up the inside stairs leading to her apartment. I made sure I made no noise doing this because my objective was to pounce out of nowhere and frighten the living daylights out of her. Double French doors led from the landing above into her apartment, and I knew she frequently sat on the sofa at those doors. Scaring her was an easy thing to do, and we both enjoyed this game. I don't know what her parents thought of it.

Suddenly, I quit sweeping the floor and glanced toward the door leading into our apartment. I could see the sun shining on the wall adjacent to the lattice door, and I saw the shadow of a figure. The front door was the only entrance or exit to our apartment. The only other outside door was one that led to a tiny balcony. I froze when a face appeared at the bottom of the door. It was a man, and I asked him what he wanted. He ordered me to let him in. I felt trapped. Without thinking, I walked to the balcony door, went outside and yelled, "Help!" A black man was kneeling beside the driveway next door, digging in the dirt. He looked up to me, but said nothing. The stranger at the door made plenty of noise getting back down the stairs. I looked as I saw him run down the street, get in a car, and back his vehicle all the way down the street. When I looked below again, no one was there. The man planting the flowers was gone. All of this happened in a matter of seconds, and I never understood who the man below was or how he vanished so quickly.

I don't know if that man below was ever there. All I know is I saw him when I yelled, and my would-be attacker fled. Why did I think of my childhood prank when I did, and who was that man on his knees? God has mysterious and wonderful ways of taking care of His children.

40 YESTERDAY, DRIVING HOME FROM WORK I PASSED A FLOCK of pigeons who were very close to the edge of the pavement. They busied themselves pecking at the ground. As I approached them, I thought they would quickly disperse and fly into the evening sky. They never moved. Not one inch. They just continued doing what they had been doing before my one-ton vehicle and I came rumbling down the street. Surely my wind wake would disturb them, I thought. Not so. Spying on them further in my rearview mirror, the pigeons remained as they had been. They did not fear me or my approaching vehicle, and I marveled at this.

And then I understood why they ignored me. This was their home. They were accustomed to people like me dashing here and there to get wherever it is they were going. They felt safe, and because they did, they had no fear of everyday happenings. Would that we were like these pigeons. Would that we would rest in the ever-loving arms of our Lord, knowing that He is watching over us and taking care of us. There is no reason to fear.

41 My husband just called me on the phone to inform me of the death of a dear elderly lady in our church. On Christmas day he had tried to visit her in the nursing home where she resides, but she was at her daughter's house, and he didn't get to see her. I could tell by the tone of his voice that he regretted missing a last visit with her. And then I thought about heaven and her home going, and I became excited. She now was in the presence of her Lord, and she saw Him face to face, and I knew her face would be one of the many familiar ones there welcoming us to heaven when the time came for God to call us home.

How thankful I am for the opportunity to have known such a wonderful person. May my life touch others in the way that hers did.

42 Do you see your glass as being half full or half empty? This is how many people gauge whether a person is a pessimist or an optimist. There may be something to this. I don't know. I think it's more important, if we're going to measure anything at all, to put a plumb line alongside our beliefs about God. Is He who He says He is? A plumb line never lies. It's ninety degrees perpendicular to whatever it is we're plumbing. God the Holy Spirit walks along beside us every step of the way. Look to your right or your left. Look in front of you and behind you. If you look hard enough and long enough, you'll sense His very presence. He is there. And do you know what? It matters little to Him whether you're an optimist or a pessimist. He loves both kinds of people.

43 Several years ago, we hired a professional to landscape our yard. He planted a young red maple tree in a flower bed adjacent to our garage. Over time the tree grew, of course, and in so doing began to bend away from the house so that it could soak up

Already Ours, Every Day of the Year

more sun. Recently, redoing the complete yard, the nurseryman replanted this tree into another flower bed surrounding a large pine tree. He tied a rope to the tree, securing the other end of the rope to a stake that he hammered into the ground. Braced in this way, the bent tree would eventually straighten itself and be upright as it searched for light above it.

The nurseryman warned me to keep the tree well-watered, as it could wither and die if it dried out as a result of transplantation. I heeded his advice and added something of my own. Several of the tree's leaves began to turn brown and drop to the ground, and I became concerned the tree wouldn't make it, so I began talking to the tree and encouraging it, telling it how pretty it was and how much pleasure it brought me.

"Now, don't worry," I'd croon, "you'll get use to this spot soon. It's a lovely place to stand. I'm here, and I'll take care of you. You're going to be okay. You won't always have to wear that noose around you. Look. See. It isn't tight at all."

Sometimes, we feel as bound as my tree was, struggling to survive in our environment, maybe thinking we're not getting whatever it is that will keep us from going under. Our Heavenly Father also speaks to us, urging us onward and encouraging us. What binds us is the very thing that straightens us out and causes us to search for God's light. We are blessed indeed to have the master nurseryman watching over us and taking care of us.

44

This morning as I drove out of the driveway, I noticed our transplanted maple tree. It's winter, the tree's limbs are bare, and it's been ten months since it's been moved to its present location. The tree isn't standing completely upright yet, but I noticed the rope tied to the stake in the ground is no longer taut. In fact, it's sagging quite a bit in the middle. I suspect before the summer is gone, the tree will be well on its way to standing tall and almost uncurved.

Loving hands and a willing heart saved the tree's life. I firmly believe that had I not taken care of it as I did, nurtured it and babied it, it would not have survived and certainly wouldn't have thrived and struggled to grow upright as it almost is.

If such can happen in the world of trees, and it does, then how much more can come to pass in the lives of those people whose burdens have become so great their spirits are sagging, perhaps even threatening to destroy them. Look around you today, my friend. Bent and weakened spirits are there, probably surrounding you on every side. Reach out to them. Talk to them. Lend a helping hand. Watch them grow upright, able to stand on their own two feet.

45 I KNOW MANY THINGS ABOUT MY HUSBAND, BUT THE ONE thing about him that is dearest to me is his selflessness. He is a selfless creature. Seldom have I seen him put himself first in anything. My work requires I do continuing education credits in order to be relicensed. Each year I travel to Dallas for a three-day stint for this purpose. This means I travel alone and stay in a hotel alone. I don't like doing this. Last year, my husband took time off from his work to accompany me on this mission. This meant long days for him with nothing to do but hang around a hotel, twiddling his thumbs.

Jesus said no man has a greater love than to lay down his life for his friends (John 15:13). I do not doubt, if circumstances called for it, my husband would lay down his life for me. Yet, even greater than this, he lays down his life for me every moment of every day, and he does this by being the selfless person he is. God has wonderfully blessed me by giving me such a stupendous mate. Think about your spouse today. What has he or she done for you that makes your life more than it could be without him or her?

46 I HAVE AN OFF-WHITE BLOUSE THAT I WEAR WITH A DEEP green wool suit. The blouse has a fluffy tie at the neck, one that hangs down well over the top button of the two-breasted suit's jacket. More often than not, as I busy myself about whatever it is I'm doing, the bow creeps inside the jacket, and I somehow believe I look unkempt when it does this. Most of the time when I'm wearing this outfit, I look down at the bow and bring it back to the position I want it to be in. It never stays put, so I don't wear these clothes often, and when I do, I battle with it all day.

Not long ago I wore this outfit and once again struggled with the bow. I soon got tired of doing this and just decided to leave it alone and let the bow fall where it would. That day, four separate people commented on how pretty I looked in that green suit. One of the people was a complete stranger who approached me in the grocery store to tell me how much she liked my outfit. Three others, also complete strangers—one of them even touching my elbow—smiled at me and expressed their liking for my clothes.

Then I understood. I had been sweating the small stuff, and when I did this I robbed myself of blessings. This is the way it is when we prioritize minor things. It's when we let little things go that we get ourselves in position to receive the good stuff, the things that brighten our day and make life such a joy.

47 WE'RE HAVING SOME WORK DONE ON THE STOREROOM IN our garage. There are three men at the house sawing and hammering and laying wallpaper and painting. Our dogs, who are fenced in the backyard, have gotten used to the men coming and going and being at the house. I've noticed they wag their tails when they see them coming. However, when I drive up after being away from the house, or walk out of the house to leave it, it's a different matter altogether. At such times, their hair bristles, and they growl at the men. They are fiercely loyal to me, and they don't want anyone to mess with me or even give a hint that they might do so. At such times, it's difficult for them to distinguish between friend and foe, because they're so caught up in their love for me and in their job of watching after me and taking care of me.

I wonder if parents aren't somewhat like my dogs in this regard. We see our childrens' peers come and go, even from our own homes, and we become friendly with them. Yet, we're ever mindful of our responsibilities for our children's safety and our job of watching over them and taking care of them. It's sometimes difficult for a parent to be able to distinguish friend from foe, because we're so caught up in our love for our children.

Think about parents today and the awesome responsibility that rests on their shoulders. Pray for them as you see them along the way. Their tasks are demanding.

48 YESTERDAY, THE RAINS CAME, AND THEY FIERCELY HUNG around all day. The workers at my house had to quit working because of the dampness and the inability of the paint to dry. They could go no further until it did. Of course I was disappointed, and so were they. But neither of us could do anything about it.

At any given moment, circumstances can come along that can wreak havoc on our schedules. What do you do when you have to shift course in midstream? Do you fuss and complain or fret and stew? Or do you let yourself feel the disappointment and then move on to other tasks? Far better to go with the flow of events than to let events overflow you.

49 DURING YESTERDAY'S STORM, A FEW THUNDERBOLTS CRASHED earthward, leaving a resounding clamor of thunder in their wake. I was at work, busy at my computer. I had to make a choice: keep working, taking a chance of an outage of electricity and thereby losing my present computer work, or shutting it down and doing something else instead. I didn't want to do something else. I wanted to continue with my work, but I knew better than to take the chance. It clips my wings to lose words already set in sentences, and derailing already-laid plans is also quite frustrating. The best laid plans, however, can and do go awry. Yes, I lost valuable time on this project, but I gained something far greater. Patience. Isn't it just fantastic how God wills and works in us of His good pleasure to bring us into the image of Christ?

50 THE WEATHER IS PERFECTLY BEAUTIFUL TODAY. THERE'S hardly a cloud in the sky, and the sun warms the ground, giving off the illusion of spring rather than winter. Who would have thought we experienced a tornado warning yesterday? Who would have thought yesterday's gullywasher that produced dangerously high levels of water in the streets would turn into today's spectacular display of God's handiwork?

It has been said, "It's always darkest before dawn." Today, however, doesn't make yesterday's memories evaporate. Yesterday's low-hanging, menacing clouds still seep through. That chilling blast of the fire station horn lingers in the air. The memory of scanning the southwest sky, listening intently for the sound of a freight train, hangs on. Just because the sun is out today and the weather is spectacular doesn't make yesterday's uneasiness go away. It never does. It matters not if we're talking about the weather or life itself. Everyone experiences hard times, times when we don't think we're going to make it. It's also been said, "Time heals all wounds." Perhaps. I've yet to see a wound, however, that didn't produce a scar, whether that scar was physical, emotional or spiritual. Wounded people surround us. Reach out today and touch someone with love, remembering yesterday's heartaches may have vanished, but the damage from them remains. Perhaps it would be better to say, "Time plus love heals all wounds."

51 Last week as I drove to the grocery store I passed a house with a sign in front of it. It said: "It's a girl!" "Bless this house, Lord," I mumbled, "and bless this family. Bless this child whom You have sent here to live. May her parents be wise in Your wisdom. May they look to You for guidance. May they lead this child into a knowledge of You, and may they raise her in Your nurture and admonition. Amen."

Family, friends, and strangers, people everywhere, need intercessory prayer. Let us look around us today and pray for them.

52 Grandma was a worrier. About everything. She worried about the weather, finances, one of her children or grandchildren, the next meal. She just plain worried. I took after her in this regard, until I learned how not to do this. How did I learn this? By taking God's word seriously. "Be careful for nothing but in everything by prayer and supplication with thanksgiving let your requests be made known unto God" (Phil. 4:6, KJV). This means what it says. Everything can be taken to God and left there for Him to take care of, to see about. I just need to notify Him and thank Him ahead of time and then just go on about my business. Too simple, you say. Not so, my friend, because I've experienced "the peace of God which passeth all understanding" (Phil. 4:7, KJV), keeping my heart and my mind on Christ Jesus when I do this. What God has done for me, He will and can do for you. Try it. Tell Him this moment what it is that causes you to fret and worry. He's an excellent listener, and He's the Supreme Helper.

53 A few months ago, my husband and I babysat our two small grandsons who are very close in age. They were a handful, and I looked forward to the afternoons when they would be napping. To my chagrin, their rest periods seldom coincided, one of them going down before the other and getting up sooner than the other. I wanted them both quiet and sleeping at the same time, but it seldom happened that way, and I'm glad it didn't. If it had, I would have missed out on a very important conversation with the older boy.

He seemed to be hot-wired that day, giving no hint of wanting to hit the sack. He wanted first one thing and then another, and I wearied of his ever calming down and giving his old grandma a break. Inspiration came.

"How about a popsicle?" I asked him.

His eyes lit up, and he led the way to the freezer. I got him a stick of purple ice, and he took me by the hand and led me to his small table, where he sat down, urging me to sit opposite him. I did. As he chomped on his frozen sweet, he propped a hand beneath his chin and had a little chat with me. It was as if we were having afternoon tea and discussing trivial things, just doing nothing but enjoying each other's company and what the moment brings.

My grandson taught me a valuable lesson that day. In our haste to discharge a duty or complete a chore, we can miss a precious moment, one begging to be savored and treasured. That stolen moment is tucked safely in my memory and is one I often take out and relive.

54

I AM BY NATURE AN IMPATIENT PERSON. I HAVE NEVER LIKED waiting, and I have never liked this quality in myself, but I can now take heart. I'm not nearly as impatient as I was when I was twenty. I'm better at it than I was at thirty. By forty, I'd come a long way. By the time I reached my fifties, I struggled with impatience less, and it didn't rear its ugly head as often.

I began asking God for patience when I was in my thirties. He granted my request. Wait, you say. I just read that by the time you were forty you thought you'd come a long way, and by fifty the problem didn't plague you as much. What do you mean God granted you patience in your thirties? What I mean is, God began willing and working in me to bring about that for which I prayed, and He did this by either sending or allowing circumstances into my life that called for patience. This, my friend, is how we learn anything worth learning. We learn through experience. So be careful for what you pray. In His time and in His way, God will give it to you.

Already Ours, Every Day of the Year

55 WHEN I FIRST SAT DOWN TO PEN THESE ESSAYS, DEVOTIONALS, and vignettes, I didn't understand the enormity of what I'd undertaken. I just began writing, never second-guessing what would come next from my fingertips. A month into my work, I began to question my ability to complete that which I had begun. Then I remembered a dream I'd had several months before beginning this project.

In the dream there was a shelf above some furniture in a house. All kinds of beautiful knickknacks adorned this shelf. The problem was, the bric-a-brac were just lined up in a row in such an ordinary fashion that I wasn't aware of what treasures they were. I began taking each piece down, one by one, dusting it off and rearranging it on the shelf. This improved its aesthetic value and my appreciation of it, so much so that I was stunned and taken aback at what beauty I had when I completed the job. My dream ended here, and I came away from it with uplifted spirits.

Whenever I doubt what will come next in this project, I just remember the dream, take each item off the shelf once again, polish and dust it, and then rearrange it in a more attractive manner. And then I am reminded of the parable of the two fish and five loaves of bread. Jesus fed multitudes with so little and what little He had never ran out. Everyone ate, and there was food left over. What a silly goose I am. All I have to do is keep on writing. The words won't run out; neither will the stories. If this is true for me, my friend, then it is true for you too. Whatever you're doing, keep on keeping on. God is with you. "If God be for us, who can be against us?"

56 MY GRANDMOTHER WAS A WOMAN WHO HAD A SAYING FOR everything that happened. I remember her telling me one day as I complained about something or other, "You have to take the bitter with the sweet." It stopped me in my tracks, and I quickly left off with my grumblings, knowing if I proceeded any further with my topic I'd only hear another pithy statement leading to yet another catchy phrase and on and on. There never seemed to be an end to them.

I think this is one of the reasons why I'm so fond of pecans. I like picking them out of their shells and popping their meat into my mouth and crunching down, savoring every bite. Seldom do I eat these nuts without eventually encountering one of those pieces of that brown stuff inside the shell that tastes so bitter. Whenever I do this, I mumble, "You have to take the bitter with the sweet," think fondly of Grandma, and then continue eating. Then I add, "C'est la vie." Grandma didn't speak French, and neither do I except for a few phrases, but what can I say? I've exhausted all her hackneyed sayings. I don't think she would mind one bit my adding to her list. The apple seldom falls far from the tree. Grandma used to say that too.

57 I'VE NOT ALWAYS KNOWN A LOT ABOUT DOGS. IN FACT, WHEN I was growing up, dogs terrified me. One of them even treed me up a telephone pole one day. I'm sure I looked pitiful holding on to a pair of metal foot rests with my hands and balancing the rest of me with my feet planted firmly atop some wooden stubs about two feet from the bottom of the pole. Some kind soul finally came along and rescued me from that ferocious beast, who seemed to be grinning broadly as he lapped at my feet, vigorously wagging his tail.

Early in our marriage, my husband had to struggle to keep from guffawing wildly as I related the story of my being "attacked" by a neighborhood boxer as I walked home from work. That creature snuck up behind me, jumped up, put his paws on my shoulders, and lapped my face when I turned my head to see what it was that hit my back. Mr. Boxer had a hilarious time chasing me all the way home.

Soon after this, my husband bought me a Boston bull terrier—at least this was what the dog was supposed to be. Pepper turned out to be a cross between a Boston bull and just plain old mutt, and I fell in love with her after I got over my fear of her. It took some time and some doing, but I finally managed to leave my dog phobia behind, nestled closely with other trinkets of my childhood.

It wasn't until Pepper died, however, that I understood what she had done for me. She rescued me from myself, my preoccupation with a fear and trembling of that which I didn't understand—the love of a dog for its master. At the time of her death, I wished I'd never known her, never loved her. I mourned her leaving me.

Throughout the years, my husband replaced her with another dog and then another and another. Dogs are precious creatures to me. If they're not mistreated, they love unconditionally. And I am grateful to the Lord God that he put them on earth. It's really true: Dog is man's best friend. And it is equally true that God loves unconditionally and He is an even greater friend to man.

Already Ours, Every Day of the Year

58 I ALWAYS SEEM TO MISPLACE BELTS. NO MATTER WHAT scheme I devise to keep this from happening, some belt or other manages to elude me, burrowing itself in some obscure place, daring me to find it if I can. It's frustrating, especially when I'm in a hurry, or I've become exhausted from the hunt and mumble a quick prayer, "Lord, lead me to where this belt is." Most of the time, within seconds, I spot the missing belt. Sometimes the belt continues its disappearing act. When this happens, I quickly change my clothes and tell myself the Lord hasn't led me to the missing object for a reason. Sometimes I figure out the reason, and sometimes I don't. It doesn't matter. What does matter is God's hidden truth in this. If He leads me to solving a minor problem, why on earth would I doubt His ability and desire to help with the big stuff when it comes along? Whether our problem is little or enormous, God sees, He knows, He helps, and He solves. All we have to do is wait on Him. "But they that wait upon the Lord shall renew their strength; they shall mount up with wings as eagles; they shall run, and not be weary; and they shall walk, and not faint" (Isa. 40:31, KJV).

59 I'VE NOTICED ONE OF THE FIRST THINGS MOST MOTHERS encourage their children to say is, "Thank you." The other day my grandson brought me the newspaper, and I thanked him for it. He said, "You're welcome." His words so delighted me that I thanked him once again, knowing he would repeat what he had just said. I tried to think of a way to get him to say "Thank you" to me, but I couldn't, so I just settled for his "You're welcome."

And just so, I know it must bring great delight to our Heavenly Father to hear us voice our appreciation for the many things He does for us. When was the last time you looked heavenward and thanked your Heavenly Father for all His many blessings?

60 WHEN I WAS IN THE THIRD OR FOURTH GRADE, THERE WAS A girl in the grade above me who had the biggest heart and kindest spirit of anyone I had ever known. Whenever the class received a food treat from the teacher or a parent, this girl willingly shared hers with whoever asked. If she were on a swing or the monkey bars on the playground, and another kid wanted to play where she was, she relinquished her position. If someone needed a piece of paper, they went to her. The same was true for pencils or crayons. She even volunteered help with others' schoolwork. One would have thought this girl was popular with her classmates, but she wasn't. The only time any of the students paid her any attention at all was when she was doing something for them. I've often wondered what became of her because we moved during that school year. I wondered if she continued to be the giving person I knew her to be. Somehow, I think she did. With all of my heart I believe she had been taught about this kind of giving at home and had put the lessons into practice at school.

"Let us not be weary in well doing for in due season we shall reap, if we faint not. As we have therefore opportunity, let us do good unto all men, especially unto them who are of the household of faith" (Gal. 6:9–10, KJV). Yes, somehow I believe this girl kept on giving to unthankful people, and the thought of it causes a warm spot to well up in my heart. Somewhere in the world there is an older lady or was an older lady who is reaping the rewards of that which she has sown.

61

Each Saturday as I'm out and about running errands, I make a point to drive by my church to check on the progress of our Family Life Center that is under construction. In my heart, I applaud the men who laid the concrete foundation, and I mentally do a high five with myself when steel beams stretch heavenward from that foundation. I am beside myself with joy as I see a stack of bricks on the ground waiting for the mason's touch. The building is still in progress, but I know there will come a time when it's completed.

God is willing and working in us of His good pleasure, and He too is building something of lasting value in each of us. He's shaping us into the image of Christ. Perhaps it would serve us well if we made a periodic check on that work in us. "Look!" we might shout, "is that gentleness I see? How beautiful this meekness is. Oh, Lord, how sweet Your fruit in us is becoming." Of course God completes His work in us only when we see him face to face, but what a glorious event to look forward to that completion of His work in us.

Already Ours, Every Day of the Year

62 "But we have this treasure in earthen vessels, that the excellency of the power may be of God, and not of us" (2 Cor. 4:7, KJV). Have you ever thought about that treasure in you? Have you ever wondered what it was? I have. Many times. It wasn't until I experienced troubles on every side, however, and walked through these distresses without losing hope that I began to comprehend the immensity of that treasure and what it is. "For our light affliction, which is but for a moment, worketh for us a far more exceeding and eternal weight of glory; While we look not at the things which are seen, but at the things which are not seen; for the things which are seen are temporal; but the things which are not seen are eternal" (2 Cor. 4:17–18, KJV). God, the Holy Spirit, is that treasure, and He resides in the hearts and spirits of those who call Him Heavenly Father. All of us who belong to Him are rich beyond our wildest imaginings. Do you see the treasure dwelling in you?

63 Have you ever been so troubled and feeling down and out that you've commented to a friend, "I'm so low, I have to look up just to see bottom." I think we've all experienced this from time to time as we've trudged down this road of life. Whenever I feel this way, I say to myself: "I will lift up mine eyes unto the hills, from whence cometh my help. My help cometh from the Lord which made heaven and earth" (Ps. 121:1–2, KJV). And then I remember it is the Lord God, who never sleeps, who keeps me from slipping. It is God who keeps me safe. It is God who wrestles with whatever is there that might trouble me by day or by night, and that it is He who keeps me from all evil and who watches over my soul. "The Lord shall preserve thy going out and thy coming in from this time forth, and even for evermore." (Ps. 121:8, KJV). I no longer look up just to see bottom. I look up to see the Lord whom I know is looking down on me. God is ever there for you and for me.

64 A number of years ago, my husband and I were traveling through a strange city. It was early afternoon, at the height of rush hour, and it was misting. We were in the inside lane of a four-lane highway, and an eighteen-wheel truck in the outside lane was ahead of us by about two car lengths. Without warning, a red vehicle pulled over in front of us, apparently to get around the eighteen-wheeler. He immediately slammed on his brakes after doing this, which meant we had to stop our car, and we had to do it in a hurry. When my husband applied his brakes, our car began to swerve in the direction of the eighteen-wheeler. We came so close to hitting the side of the truck that I could almost see underneath the truck bed. Realizing braking made us skid, my husband began pumping the brakes, and each time he did, I got another good look beneath the truck's trailer. Immediately I cried, "Help us, Lord. Help us!" And of course He did. I don't know how we stopped without hitting the big truck or the car in front of us, but we did. "I cried unto God with my voice, even unto God with my voice; and he gave ear unto me" (Ps. 77:1, KJV). Did I say that I didn't know how we stopped without hitting either vehicle? I correct that. I know exactly how we stopped, and I know Who stopped us.

God is there for you today, my friend, whatever it is that this day might bring to you. God is there.

65

Several months ago, I left my office to go home for lunch. Passing our UPS man along the way, I reminded myself to look on the front porch when arriving home, as I was expecting a package. As I neared our house, I noticed the outside corner floodlight was on, and this puzzled me. The dogs weren't at the gate when I drove up, and I thought this odd. I became uneasy as I unlocked the door, and the apprehensive feeling intensified when I noticed a light shining from our bedroom at the other end of the house. The light switch there turned on power to that room and the floodlight. I didn't throw my car keys on the fireplace the way I usually do, but instead gripped them in my hand as I made my way to the sun porch. Once there, I saw one side of the outside door frame lying on the floor and wondered, "What on earth happened to this?" My heart began to beat fast, and my breathing came in short gasps as I opened the door and commanded Bailey to come inside and go search. She came to my side but would move no further. I put her back outside and retraced my steps to where I had come in the house. Looking to my left, I noticed one of the drawers to our china cabinet lying in the floor. We had been robbed, and for all I knew the robber was still inside our house.

Already Ours, Every Day of the Year

Once outside, I got back into the car and backed it out of the garage. With the motor still running, I called my husband on the car phone to tell him what had happened. We lost all but a teaspoon of our sterling silver and all of my costume jewelry, but most of all, I lost the sense of security I once had. To this day, I sometimes become anxious when entering the house alone. It is then that I remind myself I am never alone. God is always with me. Thieves might take my possessions and damage my sense of security, but they can never take God away from me. For this, I am eternally grateful.

66 WHEN I WAS A CHILD, I WAS USUALLY ONE OF THE LAST KIDS chosen for a game of softball or any other kind of sport. It was humiliating. No one seemed to want me on their team, but I wanted to play badly enough that I put up with my athletic lot in life. I even toughed it out and cried as little as possible when I got hit behind the ear with a baseball bat. I wish I had known then what I know now. God was on my side. Others may not have wanted me on their team, but He did. He was there with me every step of the way, and He collected my tears that day and every other day before then and since then. My tears are tucked away along with your own in God's tear bottle, where they remain even unto this very day, because our tears are precious to our Lord.

Fret not when your child hangs on the sidelines, hoping to hear his or her name called for a team, if it's called at all. Comfort your child with the knowledge that God sees and He understands and He's more than happy to issue a call for His team, the best team to be on.

67 SEVERAL YEARS AGO WE REMODELED OUR HOUSE, AND WHEN we finished, I learned the value of using a squeegee on the shower walls right after bathing. If a showerer put the old squeegee to use at the conclusion of each shower, then a big scouring job wouldn't lay just around the corner waiting to pounce on me. I made it the responsibility of the user of the shower (excluding company, of course) to mop up the walls after bathing. This routine works wonders on accumulating soap scum, mildew, and mold formation. A good scouring seldom is needed because a little work is done each day.

This reminds me of staying current in my Bible readings and talks with God. When I take the Bible off the shelf each day, open its pages, and allow God's spirit to commune with me, and when I commune with the Lord through prayer, not too much of life's unpleasantness clings to my spirit. Distasteful things are there; that's the way life is. Unsavory things will always come along, and when they do, daily reading of the Bible and communing with God keeps these events at bay. And so, when we stay in touch with God each day, we're better prepared when the time comes for a good scouring in our lives.

68 YESTERDAY A CHILD ASKED ME MY FAVORITE SONG. I replied with a question of my own: "Can I pick a gospel song?" Her eyes lit up, and her face brightened.
"Of course," she said.
"'Great Is Thy Faithfulness,'" I told her.
Her face brightened even further. "That's one of my favorite hymns too."
"Why do you ask me this?" I inquired. "And all the other questions you've been shooting my way? Is this some sort of test?"
"I just wanted to see how much alike we are," she replied.
"Well, how much alike are we?"
"Very much," she replied. "We are very much alike."
I had passed her test, and then I began wondering about the greatness of God's faithfulness, and I marveled at it. People have come and gone in my life, and some of those people have let me down, as I'm sure I've let some of them down. God has never let me down. He's never failed me. I can trust Him with anything.
My little friend wanted to know how much in synch we were, and I'm so glad I passed her test and grateful to her that her questions reminded me of God's faithfulness.

69 WE HAVE A CAMELLIA BUSH IN THE BACKYARD, A RATHER large one, almost bordering on what I would classify a tree, but I've been so busy this winter I've had little time to pay attention to anything which is not absolutely essential. I've flitted here and there and lost no time letting grass grow under my feet as I've scurried

Already Ours, Every Day of the Year

about accomplishing first one thing and then another, completing one chore only to move to another more demanding one.

As I stood at the kitchen sink one day in the midst of all my activity, gulping down a glass of water, trying to get it down as fast as I could so I could move on, I glanced out the window. Outside, hundreds of breathtakingly elegant and brilliant crimson petals from the camellia bush lay at its feet, literally covering the ground beneath it with a blanket of scarlet gracefulness. The sight almost took my breath away, and I stood motionless, entranced by what lay in front of me. And then wakening came swiftly.

If I had been too busy to see the first petals fall to the ground, and certainly I had not even taken note of them until almost all the petals were gone from the tree, then I had been too busy, and I needed to do something about it, and I did. I kicked off my shoes, took my water, went into the sunroom, sat down, and rocked in the chair, gazing at the tree and drinking in its message to me: "I'm here! I'm here! Aren't I spectacular? And look. I've provided such a magnificent sight for you. Thank you for noticing."

And thank you, tree, for bringing me back down to earth so I can sort out that which is essential from that which is not. Our Lord uses absolutely splendid ways to get our attention and cause us to prioritize people, places, events, and other activities in our lives.

70 SEVERAL YEARS AGO WHILE DRIVING HOME FROM WORK after a thunderstorm, I spied twin rainbows in the sky. I'd never seen anything like that before. One kaleidoscope of colors hovered above the one beneath it. As often as I could, I glanced skyward, absolutely awed by what I saw. To me, a rainbow is symbolic of God's promises, His faithfulness to keep that which we've committed to Him. I figured I'd never see something of this nature again.

I was wrong. Just today I looked out the sunporch window. And guess what I saw? The last hurrah of yesterday's camellia bush and also the dance of our tulip tree surrounded by blooms on our peach and plum trees. Magnificent. Absolutely gorgeous. God's promises literally surround us. It doesn't matter what season it is—whether it's the brilliance of fall, the majesty of spring, the purity of winter, or the dazzling rays of the sun in summer. I don't need to see another twin rainbow. God's revealed glory in nature shouts His faithfulness and His love. I don't need any more than this.

71 MANY PEOPLE COME AND GO IN OUR LIVES. SOME ARE THERE for a long time and have a great influence on us and some are there for a moment and touch us only briefly. We are fortunate, indeed, if we don't outlive our children and if we manage to maintain a loving relationship with them throughout their adulthood. I think the greatest blessing, though, is that of a loving mate, one who walks with us everyday, one who sees us at our best and at our worst and still loves us, and one who we come to know we can depend on. How blessed we are to have a God who understands it is not good for man to be alone and provides the perfect person to walk along beside us as we travel throughout life.

Let us thank our God for providing a "better half" for us, and let us thank Him for the time, however short or long, He gives us with this precious one.

72 THERE ARE TIMES WHEN WHILE VACUUMING THE FLOOR I inadvertently disconnect the cord from the electrical outlet. Of course, when this happens, my work comes to a standstill. Is this not the way it is in our relationship with our Lord? In order for us to keep going, to keep trudging along in life, we too, must remained connected to our source of power—the Almighty God, the Everlasting Father, the Prince of Peace. Pick up that cord. Plug it in. None of us go anywhere when we're disconnected from Him.

73 SEVERAL DAYS AGO I WAS SEARCHING FOR AN ITEM THAT WAS supposed to be in the top drawer of my dresser. In my haste and in a frenzy at not being able to find that for which I was looking, I began tossing first one thing and then another on top of the dresser. Halfway through the process I abandoned the search there and began investigating several other areas of the bedroom, thinking I could have left the item other than where I usually put it. Finally, in desperation I mumbled aloud, "Lord, please lead me to the scarf." Then I walked back to the dresser and the mess I'd made on top of it, and there, right under my nose, was that which had earlier eluded me. The scarf had been in its normal place all along.

Is this not the way it so often is for us regarding our knowledge of the presence of God? He is always there. He is always with us. In our eagerness and haste to solve many of life's problems, we go scurrying here and there searching for answers when they have been right under our noses all along. God is ever present, and He is ever ready to solve our problems. Most often He waits, however, for us to seek His face, reach out to Him, and request His assistance.

74

When I was a small child, I remember lying on the lawn at my paternal grandparents' house and searching the evening sky. My grandparents would be stretched out in lawn chairs talking about first one thing and then another. Sometimes there would be other family members present, and animated and lively conversation would fill the air. My grandparents provided many things for me as I grew up, but the one thing I remember most are those delicious evenings sprawled on the grass, investigating the stars, listening to a cricket singing, taking in a lightning-bug show, and luxuriating in pure delight and happiness.

Such a small and insignificant gift to give to a child, yet such a magnificent one. What are we giving our children and grandchildren? The best things in life are free.

75

It's windy outside, and our yardman is out in it raking and collecting pine straw, limbs, and pine cones. I sat at the window during lunch and watched him as he worked. He's a quiet man and sets about to do his job as quickly and efficiently as possible. Every now and then a big rush of wind came along, snatched up a handful of leaves and pine straw, tossed it about, and dropped it once again on the ground. Usually, the droppings landed on what already had been raked and cleaned. This happened over and over again, but our yardman persisted. He simply retraced his steps and gathered up the new mess the wind had made. He didn't make a production of it, and he didn't seem perturbed by it. He just took the situation for what it was and continued on.

Would that we were as unswerving in our daily walk with the Lord. Would that we were as diligent to the tasks He has assigned us. Were we as uncomplaining and willing to deal with the havoc left by the winds in our life. Lord, help me see a situation for what it is and then go on—without fanfare, complaint, or irritation. And thank You for this good man who works so diligently in our yard and the lesson he brought my way today.

76 GRANDMA WAS THE KIND OF PERSON WHO BELIEVED IN TAKING care of those charged to her keep. Money was scarce when she was raising me, and she often allowed the coal-burning fire to dwindle during the nighttime so that we could have enough coal to keep warm the next day. Many times, that dear woman got up out of her own bed, took a cold towel-wrapped iron from my feet, put the iron back on the stove to reheat, rewrapped it and placed it beneath my feet again. She couldn't keep the cold out of the house, but she could try and break its hold on her grandchildren.

This grandmother gave me what little she had of the world's goods, but she also gave me something far more precious than gold and silver. She gave me love, and I don't know where I would be today if she had not been so generous with it.

Love never fails. "And now abideth faith, hope, charity, these three; but the greatest of these is charity" (1 Cor. 13:13, KJV).

77 WHEN MOST OF US WERE GROWING UP IN OUR FAMILIES OF origin and extended families, we probably believed a cousin or an aunt and uncle, siblings, or even parents and grandparents would always be close by. It takes a little living for many of us to come to the realization that as time moves on, so do circumstances. Cousins grow up, and aunts and uncles age, as do parents and grandparents. Family members move away, and before long those faraway days of our youth are gone. Someone may be in Seattle, somebody else might be in New York. Marriages occur and sisters and brothers move away. Deaths occur. It often becomes an impossible task to get all the family together in the same place at the same time. It often takes a death in the family to accomplish this.

King Saul wrote in the book of Ecclesiastes, "To every thing there is a season, and a time to every purpose under the heaven: a time to be born,

Already Ours, Every Day of the Year

and a time to die; a time to plant, and a time to pluck up that which is planted; a time to kill, and a time to heal; a time to break down, and a time to build up; a time to weep, and a time to laugh; a time to mourn, and a time to dance; a time to cast away stones, and a time to gather stones together; a time to embrace, and a time to refrain from embracing; a time to get, and a time to lose; a time to keep, and a time to cast away; a time to rend, and a time to sew; a time to keep silence, and a time to speak; a time to love, and a time to hate; a time of war, and a time of peace."

Our task is not one of rekindling the past but one of becoming wise regarding the use of time. Life is seasonal. A foolish man or woman prances barefoot around in the snow dressed in summer clothes. A wise man or woman dresses appropriately for the season. We cannot embrace the present, living it as God intended, unless we let go of the past. Become aware of time. Use it wisely and let go that which is gone. All any of us have is the present moment.

78 On one of the tables in my office is a frosted dish which holds scented pebbles and stones and bits and pieces of broken glass. It intrigues many people who visit me. Quite often, someone reaches over and takes a piece of glass or a small pebble to examine it closely, often bringing it to the nose and taking a whiff of it.

This is my cue to make the observation of the dish's contents being like a broken spirit. Were I to take all those pebbles and stones and glass pieces and put them together, I'm not quite sure I'd have a thing of exquisite beauty. But, as they now are, each piece in its own kaleidoscopic glory, what assaults the eye is more than just something pretty. They are the building blocks of brokenness, that which is so burdensome to bear but which makes us so much more than we could ever be without it.

"The sacrifices of God are a broken spirit: a broken and a contrite heart, O God, thou wilt not despise" (Ps. 51:17, KJV).

79 Yesterday, I visited a lady who has been diagnosed with a terminal illness. She is aware of her limited time to walk on planet Earth. I've known her for many years, and she has a tendency to be of a watchful and anxious nature. She talked easily of her impending death and what she wanted done with what she would leave behind. To have heard our conversation, one would have thought we were discussing a brief trip or a longed-for vacation. No stress lines or marks crossed her brow, and she smiled readily and easily.

None of this surprised me. This woman has walked a long distance with the Lord, and she knows she is not alone on this her final trip before she meets her Lord and Master and sees Him face to face.

God grant her strength and grace as she makes her way toward Him, and grant me the ability to hold her up in prayer until she waves her final goodbye to those whom she loves and who love her.

80 My husband is in the retail business and for many years we've gone to market to replenish his stock. There is a fishpond behind the lobby of the Dallas Trade Mart where we sometimes parked our two oldest children as we went into several nearby showrooms to order merchandise. The children were well behaved, and I never worried they would do anything more than watch the fish swim around and talk to each other. We were never far from where they were, and they were always in our eyesight. It never occurred to me an unsavory person would come along and harm them. I was at peace with this procedure.

I would not feel as confident today. It seems a child is not safe alone, even in his own backyard. Just so, our Heavenly Parent knows the safety of our individual environments. He knows where we are every moment of every day. He would never place us in danger, but if danger comes, and it will, He is there walking along beside us every inch of the way. Bad things do happen to God's people, but we must remember when these things come, they are there only because God allows them there, and the operative word here is allows. Trust Him for the outcome of that which tears your life asunder.

81 Job was an extraordinary man. He lost all his possessions, oxen, sheep, and camels, and before he'd even had time to digest this, news came of the death of his sons and daughters. He said at this time: ". . . the Lord gave, and the Lord hath taken away; blessed be the name of the Lord" (Job 1:21, KJV). Then Job suffered with boils from the soles of his feet to the top of his head. He then said: "What? shall we receive good at the hand of God, and shall we not receive evil?" (Job 2:10).

Then three friends came along to comfort him with wise and holy admonitions, but comfort it was not. His wife even encouraged him to curse God and then die. There's no doubting Job's deep anguish of soul and spirit. Through it all, however, Job was able to say: "Though he slay me, yet will I trust in him . . . He also shall be my salvation" (Job 13:15–16, KJV).

You might be tempted to say, "Well, why wouldn't he? God gave him twice as much as he had before, and He blessed his latter days, even giving him seven sons and three daughters." Yes, the Lord did bless Job's latter days, and He did give him more children. But, do you think those seven sons and three daughters erased his longings and memories of his other children and became a balm of forgetfulness for his heart? Look at the words above. The "slay me" words were recorded in the thirteenth chapter of Job, and it isn't until the forty-second and last chapter that we are told of God's blessings on him in his latter days.

"Though he slay me, yet will I serve him." May this become our motto, Lord.

82 THERE HAVE BEEN TIMES IN MY LIFE WHEN GRIEVOUS events have occurred, and I've turned heavenward and cried to the Lord, "Why? I don't understand. Just tell me why." I've felt guilty after doing this because well-meaning Christians have chastised me for questioning God. And then I am reminded of our Lord's question as He hung from the cross: "My God, my God, why hast thou forsaken me?" (Matt. 27:46, KJV).

Just as Jesus didn't get a response to His question, neither will I, and neither will you. Nevertheless, it is human nature to want answers to the disquieting and distressful events in life. It is human to seek our Heavenly Father's face, asking Him to explain that which so often is unexplainable. So, my friend, when you ask our Lord to tell you why, never despair. Even though an answer doesn't immediately come, He hears and He understands our turmoil. He knows all too well our "whys" will eventually turn into "hows" as He makes a path for us through the valley of the shadow of death. It is perfectly permissible to ask our Heavenly Parent why.

83   This morning I listened as a television news commentator announced a list of the country's forty most generous philanthropists. I gasped at the generosity of these Good Samaritans and wished I, too, had large sums of monies to give. And then insight slowly made a path to my brain. Jesus told us to give as we are able (Luke 11:41). He said it is more blessed to give than to receive (Acts 20:35). And the apostle, Peter, said, "Silver and gold have I none: but such as I have I give thee" (Acts 3:6, KJV).

It matters little whether we have all of the world's wealth or none of it; all of us have something to give, and more than likely it isn't money. It is up to us to decide what that something is and then offer it to others. The Good Samaritan chose his role. It didn't fall to him by lot.

84   A good friend of mine is agonizing over a crucial decision she must make. Since it involves quite a sum of money, she is unsure of what to do. She laid her fears and anxieties before me, hoping I could help her in her dilemma. I could only point out her alternatives, and in so doing pray she would make a wise decision.

"I will lift up mine eyes unto the hills, from whence cometh my help. My help cometh from the Lord, which made heaven and earth" (Ps. 121:1–2, KJV). God is ever there, and He is ever willing to help us with whatever is before us or behind us or beneath us or above us. The clear path to any decision begins with lifting our eyes to the hills and listening to the voice of our Lord. He will always lead us to the right path. All we have to do is go through the doors He opens for us.

85   Recently, at the World Trade Center in Dallas, my husband and I encountered an older couple waiting as we were for the market to open. The woman was well past retirement age, and I marveled at her enthusiasm and eagerness to get on with the process of replenishing her business stock. Talking with her, I learned she had been in business only ten years and apparently ran a thriving establishment. Her face brightened and her eyes sparkled as she talked about the lines she carried and how well she had done with them. I thanked God for her and prayed God would continue to bless her in her business ventures.

Already Ours, Every Day of the Year

It's never too late, and we're never too old to begin a new venture. The only thing holding us back is us.

86 AFTER KING SOLOMON OFFERED A THOUSAND BURNT offerings to the Lord, God appeared to him in the night and said, "Ask what I shall give thee" (2 Chron. 1:7, KJV). Solomon responded, "Give me now wisdom and knowledge, that I may go out and come in before this people: for who can judge this thy people that is so great?" (2 Chron. 1:10, KJV).

Can you imagine God asking you such a question? What would your request be? Silver? Gold? Land? Houses? Boats? Fame? Solomon could have asked for and received anything he wanted, yet he asked for wisdom.

"And God said to Solomon, Because this was in thine heart, and thou hast not asked riches, wealth, or honour, nor the life of thine enemies, neither yet hast asked long life; but hast asked wisdom and knowledge for thyself, that thou mayest judge my people, over whom I have made thee king: Wisdom and knowledge is granted unto thee; and I will give thee riches, and wealth, and honour, such as none of the kings have had that have been before thee, neither shall there any after thee have the like" (2 Chron. 1:11–12, KJV).

You might say, "God hasn't asked me what I wanted?" Hasn't He? His question is so subtle and His voice is so soft that often we don't hear the question, but nevertheless, my friend, God has asked you, and He's asked me. What is our response?

87 KING DAVID WAS GUILTY OF ADULTERY AND MURDER, YET the Bible tells us he was a man after God's own heart. Incest and murder occurred in his household, and little time elapsed without his having to fight a war. A son rebelled against him. Problems surrounded him. They were on every side. Even one of his wives scorned him after seeing him dance unto the Lord. Yet, David remained a man after God's own heart, and he remained faithful to God.

David said, "The law of the Lord is perfect, converting the soul; the testimony of the Lord is sure, making wise the simple. The statutes of the Lord are right, rejoicing the heart; the commandment of the Lord is pure, enlightening the eyes. The fear of the Lord is clean, enduring forever: the judgments of the Lord are true and righteous altogether. More to be desired are they than gold, yes, than much fine gold: sweeter also than honey and the honeycomb" (Ps. 19:7–10, KJV).

We are indeed blessed that our Heavenly Father looks not at what's on the outside of man but into his heart. Let us with this mighty king of old say, "Let the words of my mouth, and the meditation of my heart, be acceptable in thy sight, O Lord, my strength, and my redeemer" (Ps. 19:14, KJV).

88

Through the inspiration of the Holy Spirit, David penned many songs in the book of Psalms. In so doing, he gives us not only words to live by but a glimpse into his heart and soul. We see a man who loved God and served him. We also see a man who traveled down many of the same sorrowful paths we have trod. We see a king humble himself and freely ask his Lord for forgiveness, comfort, guidance, help, and strength.

How grateful I am a man by the name of King David once lived on earth and chose to serve God and to live by His statues. David helped me to know, "The Lord is my shepherd," and he caused me to realize "goodness and mercy shall follow me all the days of my life: and I will dwell in the house of the Lord for ever" (Ps. 23:1, 6, KJV).

89

A number of years ago, I began each day reading from the book of Psalms. I would read five chapters a day, completing the entire book each month. In this way, I learned many things about God. He is my light. He is my salvation. He is my shepherd. The earth is His, and the people on it belong to Him. Weeping may endure for a night, but joy comes in the morning. A man is blessed whose transgression is forgiven and whose sin is covered. Everything I know about trusting, delighting, committing, and resting in God comes from bathing myself in these Holy words. I don't know what my life would be without knowing God is my refuge and my strength and an ever present help in trouble, and I don't want to know either. I'm just grateful to the Lord that He has planted within my heart and mind a desire to avail myself of His Holy Book, the one His Spirit inspired so many men to write.

Praise God for His written Word, for it indeed is a light unto our path and lamp unto our feet.

Already Ours, Every Day of the Year

90 WHEN I WAS A SMALL CHILD, I REMEMBER MY GRANDFATHER coming home with a loaf of bread under his arms. He had spent the morning waiting in line for it. These were the days following the Great Depression and shortly before the outbreak of World War II. There was little food to go around, and for me to sit at a table for a meal of blackeyed peas and cornbread was nothing short of a miracle. Yet, through it all, God provided for us. He did not forsake us or turn His back on us. My grandfather did not beg for bread, but he wasn't too proud to stand in line waiting for it.

"Ask, and it shall be given you; seek, and ye shall find; knock, and it shall be opened unto you" (Luke 11:9 KJV). Ask, seek, knock.

91 MY GRANDFATHER FINALLY LANDED A JOB AS A MACHINIST with National Biscuit Company. As such he was able to bring home broken pieces of chocolate for us kids to eat. I didn't eat mine, however. I found a better use for it. I bartered with neighborhood kids for rides on their scooters, bikes, and skates. Broken pieces of chocolate brought much joy into my life. How grateful I am for a grandfather who provided the best he could for his family, and for a man who understood a child's need to taste that which other children had.

Today might be a good day to call parents or grandparents and thank them for the small blessings they brought our way as we were growing up.

92 ZACCHAEUS WAS A TAX COLLECTOR AND A RICH MAN. WHEN Jesus passed through Jericho, the town where Zacchaeus lived, Zacchaeus rushed out to get a look at the man everyone was talking about, but since he was of short stature, he couldn't see over the heads and shoulders of the crowd. He spied a fig tree and climbed up into it, so he could get a better look. Jesus glanced up to where Zacchaeus perched himself and said to him, "Zacchaeus, make haste, and come down; for today I must abide at thy house" (Luke 19:5, KJV). Before anyone could bat an eyelash, Zacchaeus jumped from the tree and walked away from the crowd with Jesus.

Stunned onlookers mumbled and complained and exclaimed, "he [Jesus] was gone to be guest with a man that is a sinner" (Luke 19:7, KJV). They probably wagged their heads, thinking, "What is the world coming to?" The despised tax collector, however, rejoiced in his encounter with Jesus and enlightened Him regarding new methods of collecting taxes: "Behold, Lord, the half of my goods I give to the poor; and if I have taken any thing from any man by false accusation, I restore him fourfold" (Luke 19:8, KJV).

The onlookers saw and judged. Jesus saw and loved. "For the Son of man is come to seek and to save that which was lost" (Luke 19:10, KJV).

93

Grandma led a hard life. She was a quiet woman, and she was a strong woman. I never heard her raise her voice or complain. If I try hard, I can conjure up an image of her — blue eyes, gray hair, a sweater covering her dress, probably one made from flour sacks. Even though she died when I was sixteen, I've carried a portion of her spirit with me throughout my life. I wish she were here so that I could tell her how much I appreciate what she did for me, but of course that isn't possible.

If I could live my life over again and have a choice of what family to belong to, I would choose that which God already gave me. Deprivation became my strength. Perhaps, after all, I've honored my grandmother and let her know my appreciation and love for her by the kind of life I've lived. I hope so.

94

My best childhood friend's mother and father became sort of surrogate parents for me. My mother was a single mom and worked hard to make a living for us. She didn't have time to do a lot of baking and cooking, and I spent much time with my feet beneath the kitchen table of my friend's house. Her mother reminded me of my grandmother in that she was a quiet and gentle woman, never complaining.

It's remarkable and awe inspiring to me that God reaches down and takes care of us in such a splendid way. How blessed I was to have had a good childhood friend with parents who had the ability to love one who was not their own. Is not our Lord extraordinary?

Already Ours, Every Day of the Year

95 I've often wondered where I get my love for classical music. I wasn't brought up on it, nor was I exposed to it. Yet, when I hear the works of the old masters, my heart reaches out, grasps the notes, and soaks them up. Very little touches the innermost parts of my being as does this kind of music.

The same is true for God's Word. I wasn't brought up on that either, and my exposure to it was almost nil. Yet, God reached down from the heavens above, grabbed hold of me, and brought me up to Him. What a glorious union that has been.

Nothing touches my heart like God's unconditional love for me. His love is everywhere I look. It's in the petal of a rose, on a child's face, in the wind and the rain and the snow and the sunshine in the calm waters and storm-tossed waters as well. God's love is everywhere. How grateful I am for it, and how blessed I am because of it.

96 Sammy Bear, our dog, who is a cross between a chow and a Labrador, is skittish. It's difficult to pet him or touch him, because in his eagerness to get attention, he often falls over his own four feet, ducking his head and dancing about, not sitting still and just reveling in the attention you're offering him. He acts this way with everybody except one good friend. With her, Sammy Bear is different. He comes to the gate, pokes his nose through it, and allows my friend to stroke his head and touch his neck. He sits still while lapping her fingers. I wonder at his strange and unusual behavior.

And then I know. He senses her inwardly heavy heart and deep sorrow, for she lost her thirteen-year-old son years ago in a tragic accident and the remains of her loss follow her every step of her way. He doesn't know this about her, of course, but it seems he senses something about her that needs him in a special way, a way others do not. And so he sits still and focuses his attention on her in a way that he doesn't do with others. Would that we were like Sammy Bear in this regard. Would that we honed in on those special unspoken needs of those around us, those whose hearts are heavy.

97 There are times when I long to see my mother again and to talk with her. Mother wasn't a very happy person, and she lived a difficult life. We became estranged for a portion of my young adulthood, but at the time of her death, we had managed to get past our differences, and I'm glad we did.

In her last days, Mother suffered congestive heart failure, and one of her greatest fears was of dying alone. Try as I might, I couldn't convince her she would not be alone when death came, regardless of whether a human was present or not. As it turned out, no human was there. She was in a hospital, and she died when my brother and sister-in-law left to go eat supper. To my knowledge, no one was with her.

But, it calms my spirit and brings great joy to my heart to know that angels escorted her to heaven. Perhaps what I want to tell my mother most is, "I told you so," and yet perhaps what I want to tell her even more is, "I love you, and I know you did the very best you could for me. Thank you. See you later, Alligator."

And I can hear her say, "In a while, Crocodile."

98 I NEVER KNEW MY FATHER WELL. MY PARENTS DIVORCED when I was four, and my mother took my brother and me and moved back home with her parents. Before long, Mother sent Buddy to my other grandparents to live. I can count on one hand the times in my formative years I saw or visited with my father. He remarried and began a new life, and our paths seldom crossed.

For reasons I'm unable to explain, I've always carried a sense of God's presence in me. Except for sporadic visits to Sunday school as I was growing up, I didn't receive much religious training. Yet, throughout all this, I knew God was with me, and in my teens He literally reached down from heaven and drew me to Him. Finally and at last I had a Father, and what a wonderful and perfect father He has been. I don't have to do or say or be anything other than what I am. My heavenly Father loves me, and I belong to Him. Nothing is greater than God's love and His gift of eternal life to His children.

99 WHEN I WAS SEVENTEEN, I ALMOST GOT HIT BY A TRAIN. AT that time, Mother and I lived in a house with her two sisters and their families. After riding public transportation home from school, I had to cross a set of about eight railroad tracks to get to my aunts' house. Atlanta, Georgia, was known then as the rail center of

Already Ours, Every Day of the Year

the South, and trains traveled up and down those tracks all the time. The tracks ran close to the National Biscuit Company, and frequently workers from there crossed over them to reach their bus stops. On this particular day, my mind must have been off in la-la land, because when the northbound train cleared the tracks, I proceeded to cross without looking northward. I heard a group of people on the other side of the tracks screaming, and I wondered what in the world was going on. It wasn't until I cleared the tracks, however, that I looked up and spied a southbound train barreling down on me. The folks on the other bank gave me a well-deserved tongue lashing for my carelessness.

I never told my mother or my aunts what had almost happened to me, and it never occurred to me to tell them. I lived in a house filled with problems and problem people. They had enough to deal with without worrying about me. I learned very early in life to take care of myself, and looking back now, I realize God certainly was with me every step of the way. But for His staying hand, I don't know where I would be today. Trust Him, dear friend. He will lead you, and He will guide you. It matters not your circumstances.

100 THERE'S A LADY IN OUR CHURCH CHOIR WHOM I LOVE to hear sing. Arriving early to church one Sunday morning, I'd heard her practicing "In His Time" before services, and I remembered the first time I heard her sing that song. We had just begun a ladies' ministry at our church and had kicked it off with a dinner at which she sang that particular piece of gospel music. At that time I'd just received the news that our younger daughter was pregnant, news that should have brought glee and joy to my heart. But it didn't. Six years prior to this, our daughter had been diagnosed with a chronic illness, one that could be severely affected by pregnancy and the demand that particular condition places on the body. My troubled heart fell victim to fear and apprehension.

And then this lady stood before us and sang the words: "In His time, in His time. He makes all things beautiful in His time. Lord, please show me every day as You're teaching me Your way that You do just what You say in Your time." The second verse goes on to tell us, "Lord, to You my life I bring, may the prayer and praise I sing be to You a lovely thing, in Your time."

These words comforted me for the next seven months, months that my fears and tremblings threatened to engulf and possess. But it was the message in these words that carried me through our daughter's delivery, and it is these words that sustain me throughout my daily walk with the Lord. All things are beautiful in God's time. God does exactly what He says He will do and He does it in His time.

101 That now seventeen-month-old little granddaughter of yesterday's vignette and I recently danced together. She and our daughter were visiting, and the child and I were watching a kids' program on TV. This little girl has rhythm, and she loves to sway in time to almost any music she hears. I clasped her hands and danced with her to the music of "I'm Gonna Sit Right Down and Write Myself a Letter." We swayed and we made circles and we laughed and we acted silly just like kids and their grandmas have done for eons. And then I looked into her baby-blue eyes, caught her in one of her charming smiles, and promised myself that I would sit right down and write the Lord a letter, thanking Him for her and for taking our daughter through to a safe delivery. I followed through on my promise after they left, but I didn't write a letter. Instead I sang, "In His time, in His time. God makes all things beautiful in His time. Lord, please show me every day as you're teaching me Your way that You do just what You say, in Your time." And then I added, "May the prayer and praise I sing be to you a lovely thing, in Your time."

102 Unfortunately, not too many of us are well acquainted with long-suffering. We want instant everything, from news to fast foods to abbreviated versions of best-selling novels or Cliffs Notes. If you were to ask many of us when we want something or other done, far too many of us would respond, "Yesterday if possible." Our generation demands instant gratification.

Waiting on people and events and things to happen grows us and shapes us into what God wants us to be. Long-suffering ushers in patience, self-control, tolerance, forgiveness, gentleness, and mercifulness.

My husband's grandmother was a woman well acquainted with long-suffering, and she was a woman who had a tremendous impact on my life. Let us be grateful when events come into our lives that call for long-suffering, for in this way we know that God is willing and working in us of His good pleasure, and He is shaping us into the image of His dear Son.

103 OUTSIDE THE WINDOW OF MY HOME OFFICE ARE SOME azalea bushes that are almost thirty years old. Their limbs touch the underhanging of the roof, and they are inviting to birds, who frequent them from time to time. A male cardinal in all of his dazzling and dashing feathers often comes to sit on one of the bush's branches. When he does, he gives me the once-over. He cocks his head from side to side and stares at me. I smile at him and also give him the once-over. I often wonder what he's thinking and where he's been and what brings him to my azaleas to sit a spell. I figure he wouldn't keep coming here if he felt threatened.

He reminds me of my trips of prayer to the throne of God, where I also periodically fly. I sit with Him a spell and commune with Him. But He never has to wonder what I'm thinking or where I've been or what brings me to Him. And for this I am grateful. I will never know what Mr. Cardinal thinks of me or even if he thinks. I will never know where he goes when he leaves my bush or why he keeps returning to it. But I am grateful to him, for he reminds me of my trips to the throne of God, and that is enough for me.

104 THE RUN-OF-THE-MILL CHRISTIAN ATTITUDE TOWARD anger puzzles me. It's as if this emotion has a reputation of being bad, and certainly one that is not condoned by the vast majority of Christians I've known. Yet, all that is within me tells me that God Himself created man an emotional being. This means all of us have a vast array of emotional responses at our disposal, and certainly anger is one of these emotions. If all that God created is good, then how can anger not in and of itself be good also?

I think where we slip up is in not separating an emotion from our response to it. Anger is like any other emotion, in that it is there for a purpose—to be expressed. It is up to the individual to decide how to accomplish this. We need to search for ways to dissipate anger through means that don't hurt us or injure someone else. No one can convince me that when Jesus took a whip of small cords and drove those unsavory merchants from the temple and overthrew the tables of the money-changers and seats of those who sold doves, that fire did not flare from His eyes and His voice deepen when he shouted, "Take these things hence; make not my Father's house an house of merchandise" (John 2:16, KJV). "It is written, My house shall be called the house of prayer; but ye have made it a den of thieves" (Matt. 21:13, KJV).

Anger in and of itself is good. It is we who pollute it and make it into something God never intended it to be.

105 I HAVE A FONDNESS FOR AZALEAS, ESPECIALLY THE Hershey red ones. I anticipate their arrival each spring. The problem is, they don't linger very long. In the twinkling of an eye, they come, do their splendid thing, and then vanish. But what they bring with them is well worth the forty-eight, give or take several weeks, wait. Their brevity reminds me of my own. And for this, I am grateful. To know that I don't have forever to roam planet Earth is what propels me to get moving and suck from each moment what that moment brings with it. Each moment is precious. Each one gifts us if we have the presence of mind to know it and to grasp it and to live it.

106 WHEN I WAS IN SIXTH GRADE, I TRIED OUT FOR AND GOT the leading part in a play our class would perform. A good friend and chum also tried out for that part. I was more than overcome with joy at my good fortune, and to my embarrassment, I must report that at that time I expressed myself inappropriately. I flaunted my plum before all who could see, and in so doing, I injured my friend with my inappropriate expression of my feelings of delight and happiness.

Guard your responses to your emotions, my friend. Everything is good that God has given us. It is up to us to choose wisely and express ourselves in a Godly way, one by which no one is injured or hurt.

107 "AND THE CHIEF PRIESTS AND ALL THE COUNCIL sought for witness against Jesus to put him to death; and found none. For many bear false witness against

Already Ours, Every Day of the Year

him, but their witness agreed not together" (Mark 14:55–56, KJV).

Palm Sunday and Jesus' triumphal entry into Jerusalem had passed. Judas Iscariot's betrayal of Him was now a matter of history. Jesus, accused of blasphemy, now stood alone before the council and the high priest. No man stood with Him. No man was at His side. He faced what lay ahead for Him without the comfort of mankind.

Jesus knows what it feels like to be utterly forsaken, for no man has ever been more forsaken than He. Jesus knows what loneliness is. There is nothing you or I have ever felt that He has not felt more keenly and deeply before us. This is why we are safe and secure in taking everything to God at any time and in any place. God understands what it is we're feeling. He comprehends our anguish. Others might ignore our pain. God never does. All too frequently, it is God alone who comforts us, but only His comfort will do—only His comfort will satisfy. A child of God is never alone. God the Comforter forever walks at our side whispering into our ears His love for us.

108 LONG BEFORE HIS CRUCIFIXION, JESUS TOLD HIS disciples it was going to happen. Peter, the impulsive one, said, "Lord, I am ready to go with thee, both unto prison, and to death." At this time, Jesus told Peter that before the cock bellowed out three crows, Peter would not follow through on his promise but would deny Him. And sure enough, when Jesus was arrested and brought to the high priest's house, Peter tagged a distance behind the entourage, not getting close enough to be included in the goings on. As Peter sat by a fire warming his hands, a young girl said of him, "This man was also with him" (Luke 22:56, KJV). Peter immediately denied her accusation. Later, someone else saw Peter at the fire and said, "Thou art also of them," and once again Peter denied the claim. About an hour later, someone else insisted Peter was associated with Jesus saying, "Of a truth this fellow also was with him: for he is a Galilaean" (Luke 22:59, KJV). Peter's immediate response was, "Man, I know not what thou sayest . . ." (Luke 22:60, KJV). Even while he uttered these words, the cock crowed and Peter immediately remembered Jesus' previous words to him regarding this matter. Peter then "went out and wept bitterly" (Luke 22:62, KJV), and my heart weeps with him because I, too, at one time or another, have denied my Lord by my actions or my words or my thoughts. I am in the same boat with Peter—denying Jesus. But, just as after Jesus' death, burial, resurrection, and ascension into heaven, Peter became a giant in service to his Lord, so can I become a giant as I follow in the footsteps of that once impulsive, fiery disciple of Jesus.

109

A GULLYWASHER ROARED THROUGH OUR AREA LAST night, accentuated with booms of thunder and flashes of lightning. We needed the rain, not so much for its moisture but for its calming effect on this spring's pollen. I wondered about the effects of such a downpour on the azaleas outside my office window, the ones that were so good-looking yesterday. Sure enough, the morning sun revealed the rain's dampening blow to those splendid blossoms, or this was what I thought when first inspecting them. Looking closer, I realized the rain served only to quench the plants' thirst. The less rich-looking blossoms this morning were not a direct result of the thunderstorm last night. Nature was just taking its course, and its course just happened to coincide with the storm. No longer was each branch loaded down with what looked like nothing but robust blooms. Where previously the eye could see nothing but flowers, new green leaves had moved in at the tips of each branch, stealing some of the bloom's glory. At first my heart sank, for I wanted those gorgeous, full blooms back, the ones that were so magnificent and splendid looking, but I knew I'd have to wait another year before seeing them that way again. And then epiphany came. It doesn't matter how long we have something, regardless of what that something is—a person, a relationship, a place, a job, a career, a house, or whatever else there is that captures our attention and our hearts, even gorgeous azalea blooms. That's not the point. What does matter is what we do with the moments we have, for regardless of how long they seem or how long they actually are, all moments eventually pass away and there is no way to recapture them. Once they are gone, they are gone forever, but experiencing them in their fullest measure and letting ourselves linger on the sweet memory of them and the pleasure they brought us, this is what counts. Each moment holds its own treasure. It is ours only if we take it and gain from it what it has for us.

Already Ours, Every Day of the Year

110 LOVE NEVER FAILS. LOVE IS LONG-SUFFERING AND IT IS kind. Love isn't envious, and it isn't all puffed up and wrapped up in itself. Love isn't selfish, and it doesn't act in unseemly ways. Love is not easily provoked, and it isn't ready to suspect evil. Love doesn't rejoice in wrong, but takes much joy in truth. Love bears all things, and it believes all things, and it hopes all things, and it endures all things. Love never fails. (1 Cor. 13)

What is love? God is love. He is love, my friend. God is love, and it is He who enables us to love in the way He loves.

111 SPRING IS AROUND THE CORNER AND IN MY NECK OF THE woods this means little league baseball and softball. The aroma of kids' sweaty feet along with the scent of blooming flowers fills the air, and I can almost hear the shouts of encouragement from parents: "Way to go, Johnny. Hit it out of the ballpark, Susie." Teams assemble, schedules get posted, and practice begins. Parents begin to smell victory and to dream of a team that will make it to the state championship. Potential team players scurry about hoping to be selected to play on the team of their choice.

Life is a team effort also, but by and large, we are unaware of it. Teams are summoned, players are selected, practice begins, schedules are compiled, games are played, and still we remain unaware that life is a team sport. Too often, too many of us flit here and there doing our own thing, going it alone. We neglect the support teammates offer or the comfort they lend when comfort is that which can mend us and heal us.

Life is a team effort. Why would any of us want to go it alone when there's someone out there eager to have us sign up and play on his or her team?

112 OUR OLDER DAUGHTER SURPRISED US GOOD FRIDAY BY driving up to see us with her two small boys. She was bringing the kids to have their picture taken by one of our local photographers, who annually poses his subjects with live rabbits and baby sheep. My schedule was rather full and I had a day's worth of activities planned, but I put away my plans and accompanied our daughter and grandsons to the photographer's. And I'm so glad that I did.

I hadn't noticed how brilliantly blue the sky was until they arrived. I hadn't been outside and let the cool breeze blow through my hair and let it caress my skin, reveling in its softness. Yesterday, I never dreamed that today I would watch the glee of two small boys petting and stroking a rabbit's fur and trying to poke a carrot down not only the rabbit's throat but the baby sheep's as well. I didn't know yesterday that today I would watch the boys tag after their grandfather at his store, mimicking him, trying to assist him as he filled prescriptions and waited on customers. I didn't know today I would be trailing after the boys as they made their way down our driveway on their small tricycles, giggling as they tried to outrun each other. I didn't know I would help our daughter load the boys back into their car seats, one crying because he had to go home and the other hugging a pillow because he was sleepy and wanted to get the van rolling so he could doze off. I didn't know I would look each boy in the eye today, tell them that I loved them, and hear the same words in reply.

Yesterday I didn't know today would be so pleasant, such a splendid Good Friday. The best things in life seem to come when we least expect them, but if we don't relinquish schedules and plans, those best things will be gone forever and we'll never be able to retrieve them.

113

THE PINK AZALEAS IN FULL BLOOM OUTSIDE MY OFFICE window are breathtaking this year. They are dazzling, causing me to want to walk among them and finger their blooms. As I surveyed their stateliness, all decked out in their royal splendor, I made my way to my office door to head in their direction, but not before I caught a glimpse of several huge bumblebees flirting with the blossoms. Whatever was I thinking, I told myself. Those bees were on a mission and would certainly consider me an intruder in their affairs. I couldn't approach the azaleas, not during daylight hours with the sun drenching them in its rays. If I wanted to walk among the plants, then I'd have to do when it rained or after dusk. Neither prospect enticed me.

The azaleas not only left me with a gift of beauty this season but also whispered a life lesson: There is a time and a place for everything, and no matter how small and insignificant a thing is, such as a bumblebee, we must respect it. If we don't, we're going to get stung.

114 TODAY I RECEIVED AN EASTER CARD FROM MY CHILDhood friend, the one I've written about several times already. Her father is now deceased and her mother lives with her and her husband. I immediately went to the phone and called my friend, for I had forgotten to send her a card. We chatted for awhile, and I told her to tell her mother hello for me. She then told me she could do better than this because her mother had just walked into the room. Soon I heard that familiar voice, thinking to myself that the person on the other end of the line didn't sound like she was eighty-four years old. Then a flood of memories washed over me, and for a moment I was once again a twelve-year-old child sitting in my friend's family kitchen eating dinner at their table, and I blurted out, "Have you made any spice crumb cake lately?"

She told she didn't do much baking anymore, but when I came for a visit, she'd bake a spice crumb cake for me. I tear as I write this because even today, even now, her kindness and generosity and ability to love one who was not her own touches me to the core of my being. And I thank God that he sent my childhood friend my way and for the happy memories of that time in my life and for these surrogate parents who did for me what my mother was unable to do.

115 ONE DAY TWO MEN WALKED ALONG A ROAD AND THE topic of their conversation centered around a recent world-shattering event. Soon, another man joined them, and he asked the men what they were talking about and why they seemed so sad. One of the men turned to the stranger and said, "Don't you know what's happened?"

The stranger replied, "What?" The men enlightened the stranger concerning the recent happenings, and then the stranger talked to the men about prophecies that he knew regarding the world-shattering event. Soon the two men arrived at their destination, but the stranger walked on, apparently continuing to his own journey's end. The two men then invited the stranger to come and eat with them. During their meal, the stranger took bread from the table and blessed it, and then handed the bread to the men to eat. At that moment, the men recognized the stranger, and when they did, the stranger vanished from their sight.

"And they said one to another, Did not our heart burn within us, while he talked with us, while he talked with us by the way and while he opened to us the scriptures?" (Luke 24:32, KJV).

How many times have we been so preoccupied with the troubles at hand that we don't recognize our Lord when He is in our midst talking with us, encouraging us, and explaining a situation to us? In this regard, we are like the two men who walked the road to Emmaus on that first Easter Sunday. It is difficult to hear God's still and small voice within us when we're clamoring about like chickens with their heads cut off, searching for an answer to what ails us when the answer has been with us all along.

116 SELDOM DO I SEE OUR OLDER GRANDDAUGHTER THAT she doesn't greet me with outstretched arms, indicating a desire for me to pick her up and pay attention to her. She wraps her arms around my neck and gives me a big hug. Nothing touches my heart as much as the knowledge that this child is happy to see me and enjoys my company.

And then I think about my Heavenly Father and His arms outstretched to me. They are ever there, beckoning me to approach Him and commune with Him. Just as I revel in the attention my granddaughter bestows on me, so too does our Heavenly Parent take pleasure in our company. Visit with Him today, my friend. He longs to pass the time with you.

117 MY GRANDSONS TELL ME, "I LOVE YOU," ESPECIALLY when I voice the sentiment first. This is usually the last thing we say to each other as we part company until another visit. Just as these words are like beautiful music to my ears, so too are the same words precious to our Lord as we utter them to Him.

It matters little how many times we tell Him. He never tires of hearing the words, just as parents and grandparents never tire of hearing them. It might be a good thing to say each time we end our prayer time with Him, "I love you, Lord. Thank you, Father. Amen."

Already Ours, Every Day of the Year

118 TODAY I LOOK OUT OF MY OFFICE WINDOW AND SEE azalea blooms in transition. No longer are the flowers at the height of their glory. No longer do they sway with the wind, inviting bumblebees to suck their nectar. Even when the sun shoots its rays their way, resting on the blooms, they look somewhat lackluster, somewhat off, not quite up to par. They are almost a has-been, a fly-by-night spectacle. And yet, as their petals grace the ground beneath their limbs, one cannot help but take note of the richness of the color of the green leaves left behind in their wake—leaves that will sustain the plant until next spring when the buds once again appear, break forth, and dazzle onlookers.

There is a time for everything under the sun. Let us pray that we don't become so captivated with a season, so taken up in a moment, that we fail to rejoice in what comes after the moment has evaporated, for what comes next is always the best, because it is all we have, and what we presently have is really all we ever need.

119 EVEN THOUGH THE AZALEAS IN FRONT OF MY OFFICE window are now fading, bidding onlookers adieu until new life appears next spring, bumblebees still hover around them, lighting on the blossoms. The bees have work to do, and the azalea blooms still have enough life to assist the bees in that work.

No matter how old we get, no matter how many wrinkles we acquire or how white our hair becomes or how much of it we lose, as long as there is life in us, we are able to help those who come after us—the younger generation, the ones who are in great need of the wisdom that only the elderly can provide.

Fading azalea blooms and aging people have a lot in common. As we grow older may we learn the lesson of the azaleas: As long as there is life in us, it doesn't matter how faded or old or ragged we look, as long as we reach out to others and give them what is in us to give.

120 IT IS QUIET OUTSIDE—UNEASILY SO. ONLY OCCASIONALLY do the grass and trees sway with the breath of the wind. The sky is overcast and there are no visible signs of the sun. Our dogs hug the earth; it seems they sense the stillness surrounding them and anticipate an event, probably one not of their liking. It is that time of the year, the time of waiting and watching the skies for the development of a tornado, for I live in that area of the country called Tornado Alley.

I know all the precautions one needs to take during an alert, for I've heard them often enough on the radio or television. I've even been sitting in my downtown office and become startled at the blaring of the fire station's alarm system alerting people to take cover. I've been in my car racing the weather for home, hoping the dark and twisted clouds above me were not in the midst of forming a funnel, one that could swoop down and whisk me away.

Yet through it all, I know God is in control and He is there watching over me and those around me, and I trust Him, whatever comes my way. He is my shield and defender and nothing wicked this way comes unless God allows it, and that is enough for me. God's grace has been and always will be sufficient.

121

OUR FIFTEEN-MONTH-OLD GRANDDAUGHTER HAS WHAT I call a musical jam box. My daughter tells me it plays sixty or so songs, and all one has to do to get one of the musical pieces going is push a button or a knob or a key. The first time I babysat the child, she was six months old. To entertain her, I often punched a number on her box, and soon found myself going back to the same selection over and over again. I don't know the name of the piece, but it's snappy with a beat that encourages movement. I'd dance around and clap my hands to the music. She seemed to love it, so I did it often. In my mind, I dubbed it our song.

Now each time I visit her, eventually she gets her jam box out, and we exchange knowing looks when we either select or accidentally push that particular button and the music begins. She associates the music with me and my love for her. Just so, when we hear certain gospel songs, ones that carry deep meaning for us, we link it to our Heavenly Parent and His love for us, and in so doing we are soothed and comforted.

122

WHILE WALKING THE DECK OF A CRUISE SHIP, I encountered a stiff head wind, one that threatened to topple me over, and one that caused me to struggle to make headway. Finally making it to the bow of the ship and rounding the corner of it to continue my journey, I sighed. I had the length of three football fields of tail wind ahead of me before wrestling a head wind once again. I had it made for awhile in my morning walk, or so I thought. It wasn't until I sparred with the force propelling me forward, however, that I understood my work was still cut out for me. I didn't have to duck my head and pit myself against a stream of air determined to keep me from moving forward, but I did have to remain alert, watch my footing, and maintain my balance. The tail wind was easier, but it wasn't without its own brand of elbow grease.

Regardless of whether we're experiencing trials and troubles or peace and tranquillity, we will have to grapple with maintaining our balance with whatever it is that life presents us. Trials and troubles are more draining, but peace and tranquillity are not without cost either. Had I taken my tailwind for granted, simply being grateful I was away from the head wind, I could have tumbled over and rolled down the deck, rather than walk down it.

"Therefore let us not sleep, as do others; but let us watch and be sober" (1 Thess. 5:6, KJV).

123 I RETURNED TO COMPLETE MY COLLEGE DEGREE WHEN our last child graduated college. My intent at that time was nothing more than to finish the work I had begun many years before, work I had planned to complete before I had children. It never happened that way, of course. Going back to college in one's fifties is no small feat. It meant reactivating many unused brain cells and competing with students in their twenties and thirties. When I began, I didn't know if I was up to the task or not. It didn't take long for me to come to the conclusion a mere bachelor's degree wouldn't suffice, for I wanted more than that. So, as soon as I had the bachelor's in hand, I embarked on a master's program.

Our home life changed at this time, and it changed drastically. I spent hours on end studying, not able to participate in many of my usual activities. I watched little television, and I seldom went to the movies. I read nothing other than textbooks and required readings for my classes. We no longer sat down to table to scrumptious meals, and we didn't take vacations. No sooner had I completed a semester with tests on top of tests than another one began. I had to deny myself many of the hustle and bustle activities of everyday life. My life became one of dedication to my mission—preparing myself to become a counselor.

Anything worth having will cost us, and it will cost us dearly. Jesus said, "If any man will come after me, let him deny himself, and take up his cross daily, and follow me. For whosoever will save his life shall lose it; but whosoever will lose his life for my sake, the same shall save it" (Luke 9:23–24, KJV).

Just as my master's degree cost me, so too does our walk with the Lord. He is willing and working in us of his good pleasure, and He will complete the work He has begun in us. Are we, His little children, willingly going with our Heavenly Father to a tub of water so that He can remove the mud from the puddle we've been playing in, or does He have to drag us there kicking and screaming along the way, not wanting to take a bath and be cleaned up?

It will cost to belong to Him, but it is so well worth it.

124

A CHILD TOLD ME YESTERDAY THAT SHE RUSHED INTO the hallway of her school building like all of her other classmates and huddled with them, waiting. She really wasn't sure what she was waiting for, but she figured it couldn't be something good. She was terrified. And yet she held on. Her friends surrounded her, and her teachers were close by. They were all in this thing together. She was not alone.

Blessed indeed is that person whose friends encase them in a circle of love and support during a time of crisis. Solomon said it so well: "A friend loveth at all times . . ." (Prov. 17:17, KJV), and "there is a friend that sticketh closer than a brother" (Prov. 18:24, KJV).

What kind of friends are we? Stick-to-'em or stick-it-to-them? "A man that hath friends must shew himself friendly" (Prov. 18:24, KJV).

125

"AS WE HAVE THEREFORE OPPORTUNITY, LET US DO good unto all men, especially unto them who are of the household of faith" (Gal. 6:10, KJV).

What an admonition—not just do good to all men, but as we have opportunity, do good to all men. As we all know, opportunity continually

Already Ours, Every Day of the Year

knocks at our doors. No sooner has one opportunity gone by than another one appears. And to top it off, we are to do good especially to those of the household of faith, which for us mostly boils down to members of our own flock in our own churches. People in our church become like a surrogate family to us, and all of us know the bickering and fussing that goes on in most families.

Opportunities are forever before us. Our church family surrounds us, as do the masses of mankind. Rather than waiting for the right moment to present itself, perhaps it might serve us better if we sought those events out. Smile. Encourage others. Be kind. Be patient. Be gentle. Be forgiving. Do good. We don't need this Scripture explained to us. We already know what it means. Our problem is not one of knowing but of doing.

126 DID YOU KNOW LUDWIG VAN BEETHOVEN WAS DEAF when he wrote his *Ninth Symphony*, the one from which we sing, "Joyful, joyful, we adore thee?" How could someone who couldn't hear pen such music? How did he manage to get down on paper what was in his head and know what he had put down sounded like what he had heard in his mind? If anyone were ever handicapped, Beethoven certainly was, and yet he didn't let his deafness become a stumbling block. He continued composing.

Just so, do we keep on keeping on when something of this magnitude comes into our lives? Or do we fold it up, put it up, and forget it? No one has a free ride. All of us pay a price to get where we want to go and be where we want to be. Keep on going, my friend. You will get there.

127 AS I LOOKED OUT MY OFFICE WINDOW TODAY, I SPIED A lizard inching its way up one of the limbs of the azalea bushes. Had I not been paying close attention, I would have missed seeing it altogether because its skin was the same color as the limb on which it crawled. As it made its way toward some azalea leaves, its color changed to green, making it almost impossible for me to tell it from one of the leaves. I wanted the lizard to move some more so I could watch it change colors again, but I lost where it was when I took my eyes off it for a second to grab my letter opener to tap the window, and cause the lizard to move away from the sound. When I looked for the lizard again, I couldn't find it anywhere, but I knew it was there, unless it had fallen off the bush. What a clever little creature it is to elude onlookers by camouflaging itself. God made it this way.

Though God didn't make humans this way, we often try to emulate lizards in this regard. In our eagerness to blend in with those around us, to be like everyone else, we camouflage ourselves, not showing our true colors, fearing if we do we won't be accepted or understood. We are not lizards. If God wanted us to be able to conceal ourselves, then He would have provided a way for us to do so. Had God not wanted us to be original, then we would be carbon copies of each other.

128

For the last two days, a lone vulture has hovered around a dead squirrel at the edge of our yard, only hopping away from its prey long enough to dodge a passing vehicle. It then returns to pick the squirrel's bones. No buzzards circle overhead. The vulture remains alone. It only takes one of their species to clean the flesh off the bones of any fallen animal. And it only takes one of the human species to rip apart the soul and the spirit of another wounded human, one who has fallen in some way or other. Humans are not vultures. There is no need for us to emulate buzzard behavior. God created us with an ability to love and to feel and show compassion to those in need of it.

129

The psalmist declares, "Thou art my hiding place and my shield: I hope in thy word" (Ps. 119:114, kjv). God is our hiding place. He is our shield. When the storms of life assail us, threatening to take us under, or when the darts and arrows of hatred, meanness, and unfairness head our way, let us take refuge in God and let us know the darts and arrows might strike and injure us but they won't take us out. If our Lord allows hatred, meanness or unfairness to come our way, then He will take us by the hand and lead us into His green pastures of understanding, compassion, and love—His shield for us—our hope in Him through His word.

Already Ours, Every Day of the Year

130 Today while driving home for lunch, I passed by three different intersections where I've had fender benders. These accidents occurred during a particular time frame in my life, when our children were in their growing-up years. Only one mishap would I consider to have been my fault. Nevertheless, they happened, and I must confess to you I've been involved in three traffic accidents. I don't even like writing this down because looking at something like this point blank causes even me to wonder at my driving skills. It's somewhat embarrassing.

But do you know what? It matters little what others think of us, the judgments they pass on us. What is important is how God sees us and our relationship with Him. If we're in a right relationship with God, and are at peace with Him, then what others think and say about us is immaterial.

131 *Touched By an Angel* is a popular television show, and it's one of my favorites. Often, during a telecast, I silently long to see an angel and talk with one. And then I laugh at my own foolishness. Were I to encounter an angel I actually could see, I would have to be told in very firm language the same words with which angels usually prefaced their human encounters in the Bible: "Fear not! Fear not! Fear not!" In my readings from God's Word, I don't recall an angel saying this more than one time, but I would have to hear this command more than once or I'd fall over in a dead faint.

I'm sure I've encountered angels I could see, and I'm just as sure they completed the mission God gave them without my knowing they were His messengers. The room in which I sit is filled with these invisible heavenly beings, and each of us has a particular one that watches over us. It sort of reminds me of getting babysitters for my children as they were growing up. When I wasn't directly watching after them, someone else was. Your guardian angel is taking care of you at this very moment.

132 For most of my growing up years, I was a latchkey kid, and I often dreaded going home to an empty apartment or room. I now realize my mother must have moved us as often as she did in order to have someone nearby to watch after me when she wasn't available. Mother was seldom available. She was too busy putting food on the table and keeping a roof over our heads, and when she wasn't doing this, she busied herself finishing off the contents of a bottle of whiskey. I now know my mother did the best for me that she knew how to do, but I also understand the deprivation of my childhood. Far greater than all this, I comprehend the words of the psalmist when he declares, "It is good for me that I have been afflicted; that I might learn thy statutes" (Ps. 119:71, KJV). It is because of my rearing, not in spite of it, that I can sing, "Thou hast dealt well with thy servant, O Lord, according unto thy word" (Ps. 119:65, KJV), and proclaim, "The law of thy mouth is better unto me than thousands of gold and silver" (Ps. 119:72, KJV).

"They that sow in tears shall reap in joy," (Ps. 126:5, KJV) and "weeping may endure for a night, but joy cometh in the morning" (Ps. 30:5, KJV).

133 SELDOM DO I READ THE STORY OF HANNAH THAT I don't weep. I weep for a woman who knew at the time of the birth of her child she would not keep that child past his time of weaning. I don't know how long this was in those days, but I figure it couldn't have been too much past a fifth birthday. I weep for the woman who knew she only had her son for a brief period of time. I weep for the woman whose heart was so pure she was able at that time to pray one of the most beautiful prayers I've ever read. I weep for a woman whose heart literally poured out goodness on all who came in contact with her. And I weep for all mothers, especially today's mothers, who have an uphill climb just to get today's children, to a somewhat safe environment unpolluted by the very meanest in our society. And I ask God to bless all mothers, to cause them to know how fortunate they are that God has blessed them with children and to give them the strength to do what God has commissioned them to do—mother their children. May God bless you, my friend, in your holy task of rearing your children.

134 BAILEY, OUR CHOW, IS NOW AN OLD DOG. HER SIGHT IS failing and her hearing is not as keen as it once was. Her puppy, Sammy Bear, is strong and robust, and even though he is well past puppyhood, he still likes to romp and growl and

tease her. Sometimes I think he goes a little too far in his wrestling matches with her and I scold him for it. Bailey knows she is top dog with me, for I usually save some of the meat I eat each evening and call her inside to lap up the scraps. It's gotten to be a ritual, and I often find her looking at me through the kitchen window almost verbalizing the words, "Is it time yet?" meaning am I ready for her to come inside for her treat.

Last night my husband grilled a steak for our dinner and, since we had only one steak, we had only one bone and I wanted Bailey to have that bone to gnaw on. We gave Sammy Bear meat drippings and some leftover steak. Of course he lapped it up in no time flat, which meant he had time to stalk Bailey as she gnawed on her bone. Sammy Bear is young and outweighs Bailey by forty pounds, and I knew if he took a notion to take the bone away from her, he could. So my husband and I remained outside while Bailey chomped on the bone with Sammy Bear circling her all the while, waiting for the perfect moment to snatch away her treasure.

Regardless of whether another dog outweighed her or not, Bailey could have held her own several years ago. This is no longer true. She is now an old dog, and as I look at her, I blink away tears and tell myself, "She wasn't always like this." She has been a faithful friend to me, loyal and true. I will miss her when she bids us adieu, but I will remember the time I gave her a bone and she gnawed it enough to satisfy a craving in her but had enough love and grace to walk away from the bone, leaving what was left of it for her puppy, something I'm quite sure he wouldn't have done for her. A parent's love is like this.

135 God made me. He created me in His image. He fashioned me and because He made me and fashioned me in the way that He did, I do not fault my mother for the way in which she raised me, because in the making of me and fashioning of me, God infused my heart with understanding—understanding of the woman who did the best she could with what she had, a woman who continually made unwise choices for herself.

My last prayers for my mother before her death were that she would find a measure of peace for herself here on earth. I don't know if she did or not, but I know that she now rests with the Prince of Peace and for this I am eternally grateful. She was my mother, and I loved her, and I will honor her in my heart on this Mother's Day, the anniversary of her birth.

136 Absolutely nothing is more precious than the smile of a child or the coo and babble of an infant or the feel of a teenager's hand in our own. The psalmist declares, "Lo, children are an heritage of the Lord: and the fruit of the womb is his reward" (Ps. 127:3, KJV). My thoughts on a Mother's Day lie not so much with mothers as with the children of those mothers, the ones who light up a mother's eyes and warm a mother's heart. "Happy is the man that hath his quiver full of them; they shall not be ashamed, but they shall speak with the enemies in the gate" (Ps. 127:5, KJV).

It is the mother's child who makes the mother a mother. It is the mother's child, once grown, who stands between the world and the mother and who stands firm because of a love between the mother and the child. "As arrows are in the hand of a mighty man; so are children of the youth" (Ps. 127:4 KJV).

Of all the gifts God gives to women, one of the greatest is the gift of motherhood.

137 My childhood friend and I used to dig traps for the iceman. We knew the path he took to get to the back of our house where he delivered a chunk of that cold stuff to her icebox upstairs and mine downstairs. We took great care in disguising the holes, crisscrossing sticks and piling grass and leaves on top of them. The iceman never fell into one of them, and looking back on it, I'm glad he didn't.

There are many traps for us as we travel along life's highway. Some we fall into, and some we escape. Let us thank God today that He walks along beside us every step of the way, and if and when we fall, He is there to pick us up and to make us new once again.

138 When my childhood friend was ten and I was twelve, we were star-struck. We saw every movie we could and bought every movie magazine that came out each month and carefully cut our favorite pictures from them. We wrote movie stars for photographs and got signed ones returned to us. They became my prized possession. When I was in eighth grade, Mother and I moved away from that happy place downstairs from where my best friend lived. We were back in a house filled with problems and problem people. No one valued my movie star collection, and somehow it vanished. I've often thought what a treasure I'd have if those signed photographs were still in my possession, and then I realize I have something far more precious than that within my heart.

Through the turmoil of my growing up years, God provided a surrogate family for me. I didn't get to stay with them long, but the time I was there was long enough. Just as one never takes medication for longer than it's prescribed, so too does one not prolong a season of life. One just moves on to the next step and revels in that which God supplies.

139 WHENEVER I THINK OF MY MOTHER, I THINK OF HER AS being sad. I don't remember her laughing very much. I never saw her in a fit of giggling, and looking back on it, I don't suppose there was very much for her to chuckle about. Her existence centered around providing the best she could for her children. She even sent one of them away in order to be able to provide something of substance for the other one.

My mother and I never talked in depth. We settled for surface stuff like the weather or what to buy at the grocery store. Perhaps if my father had endured life's harsh circumstances with her, our lives would have been different. I don't know. I only know my mother was a very sad woman all the days that I knew her.

As deprived as my childhood was, as sad as my mother seemed to be, as unwise as her choices for us were, one thing is certain: my mother loved me the only way she knew how to love me. She gave of herself what she was able to give. One can't expect another to give what they do not have. Whichever way, my mother loved me the only way she knew how, and that is enough for me.

140 THE BUMBLEBEES HAVE FINALLY ABANDONED THEIR work around the decaying azalea blooms. They came, they saw, they conquered, and now they're gone. They have been replaced by a lone butterfly who all but shouted at me to pay attention to it when it made its debut. Its graceful, yellow, black-trimmed wings slowly flitted through the air as it made its way in and out of the azalea limbs, occasionally resting on one of the withering blooms. There is no hurry in its work; there is no rush to do more than it already is doing—gracing the deteriorating blooms with its own unique beauty. It is as if in its dance, the butterfly is singing the national anthem, a sacred hymn and a fond goodbye all rolled up into one. If I listen carefully enough, I can even hear taps, and I hum along with that imaginary trumpet sound and bid farewell to blossoms that brought such joy and delight to my heart this season. I know that I will see them again next spring.

It's much the same when we bid a loved one farewell. We revel in the joy and delight they brought into our lives, but when they go home to be with God, we hear the mournful sound of a trumpet playing taps, whether silently or aloud, and through our tears, if we look hard enough, we can see the butterfly dancing and we know spring will come again when we are reunited with our loved one in heaven. On that day, we will bloom as we've never bloomed before.

141

I RECENTLY WATCHED A RERUN OF AN EPISODE OF *The Waltons*. The simplicity of that day and time once again grabbed hold of me and transported me to another day and another time, a time when people didn't believe they had to lock their doors and knew it was safe to walk down streets without fear of being accosted. Of course, whatever was going on in that family somehow got solved within the hour's time frame, and viewers left the Waltons until the next episode. In and of itself, this view is unrealistic, but the houses, the clothes, the cars, the language, and the people are reminiscent of another time, a quieter time, yet a poorer time in our history.

Our children have grown up with far more than we ever imagined possible. And yet I'm not sure they're the better for it. We never wanted them to suffer deprivation, or to do without. Yet, growing up in a house without hot water and cooking on a woodburning stove and gathering coal or wood to burn in a fireplace and sitting down to a meal of black-eyed peas and cornbread is better than some things our children must endure. Illegal drugs, crime and violence, serial murders, unprovoked killings, bombs and threats of mass killings, pressure to conform and to succeed, a demanding business world, and many other unsavory things nip at their heels. My heart bleeds at the deprivation of this generation.

Already Ours, Every Day of the Year

Let us pray today that as God calls this generation to Himself, they will come, and in coming, they will find peace and rest.

142 LAST NIGHT I WATCHED A PROGRAM ABOUT ST. JUDE'S in Memphis, Tennessee. This is the hospital founded by Danny Thomas that serves the children of the world who have many forms of cancer. As Marlo Thomas presented episode after episode about the illnesses and treatments of these children, I kept saying to myself, "I wish children didn't have to suffer," and I thought about Jesus when He said, "Suffer the little children to come unto me, and forbid them not: for of such is the kingdom of God. Verily I say unto you, Whosoever shall not receive the kingdom of God as a little child, he shall not enter therein" (Mark 10:14–15, KJV).

Today, let us pray for these children, asking God to grant strength not only for them but for their parents and families as well. Let us thank God for a man with a vision and the courage to see that vision through. Let us thank Him for those who have dedicated their professional lives to these children's care and treatment, and let us thank Him that as he gathers them in His arms, great peace and a stillness of heart will be granted to them.

143 YESTERDAY, A YOUNG WOMAN SAT IN FRONT OF ME AT church. I hadn't seen her in some time, and so I chatted with her and caught up on all the doings in her life. When it came time for the choir to enter the sanctuary, her grandmother, who is a member of that singing group, made her way toward her place in the loft, and as she did she almost knocked over one of the plants that line the entry into it. The young woman's shoulders shook, and I knew she was snickering. I latched on to the thought that as this family gathered for lunch after church, the incident would be talked about and laughed at and would provide a moment of humor for them, one that likely would come up time and again as the years roll by, perhaps turning into a private joke for the family.

We are blessed, indeed, that God has set us in families, those with whom we share the intimate details of our lives, and those who love us in spite of all our faults.

144 I have an elephant plant in my office, and it requires daily watering. Coming back from a recent ten-day vacation, I found a wilted blob of greenery hugging the floor. In my eagerness to get away, I had forgotten to make plans for someone to take care of it in my absence. I felt horrible. I immediately watered the plant and began apologizing to it for my carelessness, hoping it would somehow revive. I had little hope of this happening. The plant looked too far gone. By the end of the day, its leaves had eased somewhat from the floor, and by the next day were no longer touching it. By the end of the week, the plant was as good as new.

If a plant can endure and survive such deprivation and harshness, so can we. We might be drained and wilted to the point of being so low we can go no lower, but when love comes (and it will, my friend, it will), we will be revived, we will endure, and we will go on. My plant didn't give up, and it survived. Don't give up. Hang in there. There is light at the end of the tunnel.

145 Many years ago, some friends and I planned a luncheon for a bride-to-be at a hotel some driving distance away from us. All of us had been to previous functions here, and we looked forward to returning for a good time in celebration. You can imagine our chagrin when upon arriving at the establishment to check on last-minute details, we discovered someone had made a mistake, and our party had been preempted by another group. What were we to do? We expected twenty-four guests for a meal, and a place to seat them for it, and we had neither. We scrambled about, finally finding a restaurant who, at the last minute, would take us on. Someone had to remain at the hotel to divert our guests, while the rest of us scurried about trying to redeem a horrible mistake.

God is ever there watching over us and taking care of us. Had our group not been united in Him and bonded to Him, what could have been a social disaster would not have turned into the charming party it did. There are no coincidences or mistakes with God. He knows where we're going before we even begin to plan the trip, and He's there with us every step of the way, helping us, encouraging us and guiding us. Walk with Him, my friend. Walk with Him.

Already Ours, Every Day of the Year

146 After our Lord God finished His work at the end of each day of creation, the Bible records these words: "It was good."

These are words to cling to, especially when life becomes complicated, and there seems to be no end to the harshness of it. God takes everything that happens to us and works it together for our good as we love Him and are called according to His purpose (Rom. 8:28). How can we not say at the end of every day, "It is good." It matters not what a day might bring, but that God walks along beside us during it. Our day will always be good because God is there with us, and He is there for us. It might take some time for us to adjust to a day's happenings and some doing to understand those happenings, but we will survive and come to the see the day as being a good one because God is in it. He is there for us.

147 Today, the world in which we live is a very busy place. We go to jobs, we cart our children here and there, we cook meals, clean the house, do the wash, and mow the lawns, and we commit to many activities away from the home. We are pressed for time, and there is little of it left over for friendship. Our friends are as busy as we are.

"Two are better than one; because they have a good reward for their labour. For if they fall, the one will lift up his fellow: but woe to him that is alone when he falleth; for he hath not another to help him up" (Eccles. 4:9–10, KJV). No man can be warm alone, and no man can withstand the onslaught of meanness from others alone. "A threefold cord is not quickly broken" (Eccles. 4:12, KJV).

Beware of self-absorption. We are not horses with blinders on. We need others, and they need us. "A friend loveth at all time" (Prov. 17:7, KJV), and in so doing makes time for others. There's more to life and the living of it than work and chores and activities. Call your friend today, talk with her, and rebuild your bond with her.

148 When our three children were growing up, there were occasions when I wondered if the time would come when I didn't have three heads of hair to wash and groom. I also pondered messy fingerprints on the refrigerator door, thinking they would forever be there, and I would never escape the task of removing them. Spilled milk oozing through the cracks of the leaves of the dining table also seemed never-ending. Those days are gone and almost forgotten. Now I long to wash a child's head of hair and wipe his fingerprints from the refrigerator door and clean up his spilled milk. But I can't. Children don't live here anymore. When a moment is gone, it is gone. There's no bringing it back.

Teach us, Lord, to number our days so that we might become wise in the living of them.

149 An old song says, "You always hurt the one you love, the one you shouldn't hurt at all." How true. Why do we do this? Why do some of us bare it all, tell it all, and let it all hang out in those relationships that are dearest to our hearts? Many psychologists say open relationships are intimate relationships. Perhaps. But graciousness is graciousness, kindness is kindness, fairness is fairness, and good manners are good manners. Impoliteness does not necessarily signal intimacy. Intimacy is love, the kind of love spoken of by the apostle Paul. Love is kind, forever and ever kind. It isn't a bulldozer. Love bears all things, believes all things, hopes all thing, and endures all things. That, my friend, is the essence of intimacy. Whatever else of the earth's goods we have or the knowledge we possess, if we don't have love, we don't have anything.

150 It's become apparent to my husband and me that we need more room in our house. When all our children are home with their little ones, what was for us before their arrival a rambling house becomes a wee bit tight. Our grown kids need space, and so do our grandchildren. So, we've embarked on turning what was a storeroom in the garage into a bedroom and computer room. Circumstances in our lives changed, and we needed to update our living quarters.

It's the same way in our relationship with our Lord. Seasons come and go, and each one calls for a shifting here and there or an adjustment here or there, and we discover we need to move onward with the flow of life's events—to update our relationship with our Lord, to arrange it so there is room for all God sends our way. For many of us, change is difficult, but it

Already Ours, Every Day of the Year

isn't impossible. In fact, it can be downright adventuresome. Just as we update and rearrange our environments and lives from time to time, so too must we do the same for our spiritual growth and walk with the Lord.

151 A NUMBER OF YEARS AGO, WE OWNED A SMALL HOUSE on Caddo Lake. One evening we decided to load the three kids and ourselves in our fishing boat and motor to a lodge on the other side of the lake to eat a fish dinner. It was fun. We could have driven to the lodge, but it would have taken us three times as long to get there if we had. As we dined, unknown to us storm clouds had assembled in the sky, obliterating its blue color altogether. What a shock to see our small fishing craft churning by the dock in choppy waters as we made our way toward it to begin our trip home. The girls hugged the bottom of the boat, refusing to look at the predicament we were in. Our son feigned bravery, but he looked worried. My husband clenched his jaw and set off homeward, saying absolutely nothing. As we plowed through the choppy water, I prayed not to see lightning or to hear thunder. Boy, how I prayed. I wanted us all back at the cabin safe and sound.

It was then I took note of the channel marker we had just passed. It was marker number five. Number five runs in front of our cabin. Five would take us home. Five is the biblical number that represents God's grace. How grateful I am that whoever laid out the markings for this lake deemed the marker leading to our cabin number five. God's grace would lead us home. It always had. It always would. No matter how choppy the waters or bumpy the sailing, God will always lead us home.

152 MEDICAL FINDINGS INDICATE NEWBORN BABIES ARE nearsighted in that they are unable to see and distinguish objects more than eighteen inches from their faces. As babies mature, their eyesight improves, and they are able to recognize their parents and other objects at a distance. As time goes on, their sight finally equals that of adults.

The apostle Paul said that when he was a child, he spoke like a child, and he felt like a child, and he reasoned like a child, but when he became a man, he put away childish things. When any of us first come to the Lord and experience His saving grace, we come as little children with limited vision, a limited ability to understand spiritual matters in a mature way. As we grow in Him and His Word grows in us, we see more and more and better and better His plan for us and His will for our lives. "For now we see through a glass darkly; but then face to face: now I know in part; but then shall I know even as also I am known" (1 Cor. 14:12, KJV). This is the road to growth and to love.

153 "AND BE YE KIND ONE TO ANOTHER, TENDERHEARTED, forgiving one another, even as God for Christ's sake hath forgiven you" (Eph. 4:32, KJV).
Of the many qualities that can be attributed to today's society, kindness isn't necessarily one of them. There was a time in America when we went out of the way for others, did things for them without expecting something in return. Unfortunately, this sort of behavior is becoming an exception rather than the rule. Road rage, drive-by shootings, work-related fatal retaliations, and the like fill the headlines of our newspapers and the stories of our television journalists. Too often, we fear lending a helping hand to someone in need for fear of getting ourselves entangled in a mess or worse. How often do we read of passersby not lending assistance to those being assaulted or accosted. And yet, in spite of all this, I experience kindness and helpfulness on a regular basis. I cannot count the times when young men have approached me at self-service gas stations and offered to pump gasoline for me. Or the times when motorists have motioned for me to proceed ahead of them in traffic, or people have offered me their place in a bank or grocery store line. People still open doors for me.

Regardless of what we read in newspapers and magazines or hear on the radio and see on television, kind people do exist, and they are there for us. Let us be there for them too. What we hand out and give to others comes back to us in kind.

154 "I'LL NEVER FORGIVE YOU FOR THAT." EVER HEARD these words or uttered them yourself? Somewhere along the line, we all have. We're all guilty of unforgiveness. Too often, it becomes something we cling to, hang onto like a dog to a bone. Why do we do this?

Already Ours, Every Day of the Year

We're human, and it's human nature to become angry, hold grudges against others, and withhold forgiveness. But when we come into a saving relationship with our Lord, He touches that human part of us, that which some religions call our old sin nature, and time after time makes it possible for us to be able to move above our humanness and grant others that which God so freely gives us—forgiveness.

Every child of God has the ability to forgive. This doesn't mean it's easy or comes without tremendous effort and cost. Nevertheless, we do have the ability to forgive. What so many of us lack is the willingness to do it.

155 DEPRESSION IS FRIGHTENING. IT ASSAULTS A BEING, often robbing him of his will to live, to go on in spite of what lies ahead. Yet, when reading from God's Word, inspired writings penned by many of the prophets of old, it becomes apparent that some of these men, if not out and out depressed, had melancholy temperaments. Yet, where would we be without the words they left behind for us?

"Sorrow is better than laughter; for by sadness of the countenance the heart is made better" (Eccles. 7:3, KJV). Sadness, sorrow, depression, and melancholy eventually make our hearts better, able to discern rightly, and to live more productive lives. Never despair of depression if and when it comes. Seek out a counselor or pastor to walk along beside you for awhile, and then come to the other side of the darkness in you, renewed in spirit with a newfound ability to help others along the path you have trod.

156 I'VE BEEN A MEMBER OF THE CHURCH I ATTEND FOR THE past thirty-four years. During that time, I've seen several pastors, educational directors, music and youth ministers, and staff members come and go. I've witnessed deaths and births in our congregation as well as celebrated in joy and commiserated with sadness. We've experienced good times, and we've had bad times. We've built buildings, and we've gathered in people. There have been times of plenty, and there and been times of want. Through it all, though, one thing remains constant: we are God's people, and He who has called us according to His purpose is willing and working in us of His good pleasure to shape us into the image of Christ. God's spirit remains with our church because we are a people who seek His face and strive to do His will. We are not perfect, and we never will be perfect, but we belong to God, and He belongs to us. "But they that wait upon the Lord shall renew their strength; they shall mount up with wings as eagles; they shall run, and not be weary; and they shall walk, and not faint" (Isa. 40:31, KJV). And that's what counts.

157

When I came to Texas more than forty years ago, no one from home checked up on me to see if I had arrived safely or not. I have no explanation for this other than long-distance telephone calls were a luxury, and something in which my family didn't engage. I'd never been west of the Mississippi River before; in fact, I'd been no further west than central Alabama. I had no idea what the college I was going to looked like, much less what the town it was in was like. No one with a familiar face lived within seven hundred miles of me. I was alone, but I didn't stay this way for very long.

God gave me another surrogate family; in fact, He sent two of them my way. The first was a middle-aged couple who were the leaders of a Sunday evening Bible study at the church I attended. They took me in, gave me a home away from home, and treated me as if I belonged to them. The second family became mine by law—they were the McCutchan clan. God couldn't have blessed me more than by sending these people into my life. The McCutchans took me in as their daughter-in-law and became for me the family I always wanted but never had. They touched my life and uplifted me as no one else has. I hold them in my heart forever and praise God for leading me their way and giving me their son, who has walked along beside me for the past forty-two years.

"I will go before thee, and make the crooked places straight: I will break in pieces the gates of brass, and cut in sunder the bars of iron. And I will give thee the treasures of darkness, and hidden riches of secret places, that thou mayest know that I, the Lord, which call thee by thy name, am the God of Israel" (Isa. 45:2–3, KJV).

How precious are the treasures of darkness.

Already Ours, Every Day of the Year

158 So you see, my friend, "weeping may endure for a night, but joy cometh in the morning" (Ps. 30:5, KJV). Our Lord God "turned for me my mourning into dancing, He took away my sackcloth and crowned me with gladness" (Ps. 30:11).

"To the end that my glory may sing praise to thee, and not be silent. O Lord my God, I will give thanks unto thee for ever" (Ps. 30:12, KJV). Whatever is in your life at this time, my friend, don't despair. Joy will come after your tears are wiped away, and joyfulness will replace mourning. It is the Lord God who makes our mountains stand strong and who walks along beside us every step of the way, hearing our pleas and healing us from whatever it is that has put us so low. Sing a song of thanksgiving unto the Lord, my friend. "The Lord will give strength unto his people; the Lord will bless his people with peace" (Ps. 29:11, KJV).

159 There's a traffic light in town that, during certain hours of a school day, causes a major backup of southbound traffic. It can become an almost impossible task for a southbound vehicle to make a left-hand turn at that intersection without causing a pileup of cars that extends past the traffic light north of it. Yesterday I had already sat through two changings of the light waiting for cars ahead of me to turn left. Nearby, a woman sat in a parked car waiting to ease into traffic. When the light finally changed again and only one car in my lane had made it through it and I had the opportunity to move forward, I debated what to do. Should I let her in, causing the cars behind me to wait longer, or should I proceed forward with the flow of traffic. I didn't know which choice would be the best one for everyone concerned. Finally, I motioned for the woman to cut in front of me so she could get in line to await her turn to cross the intersection.

I don't know if I made the most courteous choice. The mission of those behind me was delayed, and I wondered at my right to make this decision for them. Following this woman through the intersection, however, my dilemma and debating with myself ceased. I finally recognized her, and she is someone I've known for a long time. At the present time, her husband is desperately ill, and I'm quite sure she needed to get where she was going as quickly as possible. But, you might say, how do you know those people behind you didn't have urgencies of their own? I don't. Of only one thing am I sure: I belong to the Lord, and I am responsible to Him for my actions. I had to make a quick decision, and in the making of it one thought kept coming to mind. "Choose you this day whom ye will serve . . . As for me and my house, we will serve the Lord" (Josh. 24:15, KJV). To serve my Master, I must continually be in touch with Him so that I will know what my Master wants.

160 I CAME TO TEXAS BECAUSE OF A COLLEGE SCHOLARSHIP. I got room and board, tuition and books, plus fifty dollars a month in exchange for services rendered to the college. Fifty dollars isn't a lot of money in today's economy, and it wasn't a whole lot back them. It took most of it to buy such things as toothpaste, deodorant, soaps for washing me and my clothes and other odds and ends. There only was enough to buy an occasional piece of clothing, and perhaps go to the movies once. Before I spent any of my paycheck, however, I took five dollars out and gave it to my church as a tithe.

One day a group of students was going to the movies, and they asked me to go along. I had no money, so I shrugged, stuffed my hands into the pocket of my coat jacket and declined their invitation. I fingered a piece of paper in my pocket, and on the way back to my room I took it out to see what it was. It was a five dollar bill. I was stunned. Where did it come from? How did it get there? I've never known. Of one thing I am certain: I hadn't put it there. I kept what little change I had in a locked closet.

God knows about our weariness, and He understands our need to recreate ourselves. I needed recreation, and God provided a way for me to get it. In fact, I had enough money to go to more than one movie. We never have a need, spoken or unspoken, that our Lord doesn't meet.

161 BAILEY, OUR CHOW, HAS NEVER LOOKED THE WAY SHE now does. Her coat is fuller than I've ever seen it, and it's smooth, not all tangled and knotted up as it usually is. She's gotten old, and her eyes have taken on that quality associated with aging. Her hearing is not as acute as it once was, and except for an

Already Ours, Every Day of the Year

occasional romp with her now-grown puppy, she mostly lays around the yard sleeping. Sometimes I find myself staring at her breathing as she lays on the ground to make sure she's still doing it. I dread the time when I walk into the yard and discover she is no longer living. I've begun taking pictures of her so that I can have something to remember her by after she dies, and it is as if she knows this and is cooperating with me by looking as good as she does.

I think she knows she's nearing the end of her life because I often find her staring at me as if she wants to tell me something. How I wish I knew what that something is. I will grieve when she leaves, and I will remember her, thanking God that our younger daughter brought her to us and gave her to us when she could no longer keep her in her apartment. Bailey's been a good friend. I will miss her when she leaves. Thank you, Lord, for giving me a dog to love, someone who's been a loyal friend.

162 THE FIRST BIBLE VERSE I EVER MEMORIZED WAS Philippians 4:13: "I can do all things through Christ which strengtheneth me." The second one is found five verses before the first one. "Finally, brethren, whatsoever things are true, whatsoever things are honest, whatsoever things are just, whatsoever things are pure, whatsoever things are lovely, whatsoever things are of good report; if there be any virtue, and if there be any praise, think on these things" (Phil. 4: 8, KJV). I learned both verses the only time in my childhood I ever attended Vacation Bible School. A classmate who lived across the street from me insisted I go to this school with her, and I'm so glad she did.

I've carried these Bible verses in my heart ever since, and I often think on them and the girl who looked at me and decided I needed some spiritual training in my life. ". . . and a little child shall lead them" (Isa. 11:6, KJV). We are blessed indeed that our Lord takes the smallest things in life and the smallest creatures of it to accomplish His purpose.

163 IF WE HAVE NOTHING AND WE HAVE JESUS, THEN WE have everything. If we have everything and we don't have Jesus, then we have nothing. As I was growing up in Georgia, no one had to tell me my family had nothing. I already knew it. My family didn't have worldly goods, and they didn't have Jesus either, at least not in the sense I now know Him. My only spiritual recollection of those days was of a grandmother who, every Sunday morning, played old-time gospel music on the radio. My four-months-older-than-me aunt and I used to dance around to the beat of the music, and Grandma never reprimanded us for it, or told us not to do it. I think I know why she didn't. For whatever reasons, Grandma didn't attend church, but she loved me enough to expose me to Christian music, and she loved me enough to let me experience the music in my own way. She had the presence of mind not to be dogmatic in that which she was able to give in the way of spiritual training. And I'm grateful for it. I've long known my family had nothing as I was growing up, but I've also long suspected they had the love of God in their hearts, and that they gave me everything they had.

164 I HAVE A FRIEND WHO IS A SINGLE MOM RAISING (AND quite well, I must add) two children. Her son is ten years old, and getting up and getting ready for school is quite a chore for him, and something he'd rather not do. My friend has agonized over this, and this morning decided rather than get him back up again after he climbed back into bed, she'd just leave him sleeping where he was, put a note where he could find it and then go on to work. He called her soon after she got to work to ask if she were coming home to pick him up to take him to school. As soon as she could, she left what she was doing, went home, and took her son to school. He was tardy, and he knew he was the one who would have to explain to the office person why he was late.

My friend agonized over the decision she made to teach her son a valuable lesson. As she related the story to me, I could tell she was anxious and wondering if she'd done the right thing. He told her later, "I learned a lesson, and I won't be doing that again," and I could hear her sigh of relief when she reported to me the results of her discipline.

God disciplines us like this, too. He leaves us be and lets us suffer the consequences of our actions so that we, too, might be able to say, "I won't be doing that again."

Already Ours, Every Day of the Year

165 WHILE DRIVING HOME FROM WORK THE OTHER DAY, there was a car in front of me whose driver couldn't decide which of the two lanes of westbound traffic he wanted to be in. I became frustrated with him and mumbled, "Well, commit one way or the other."

I wondered then at the indecisiveness in my own life and its effect on those around me. And I pondered further God's thoughts at my inability to commit everything in my life to Him. I traveled on down the road, thankful for the man who had just taught me a valuable lesson, and with a resolve to be more consistent in my walk with the Lord.

166 A NUMBER OF YEARS AGO, I RECEIVED A GOLD CROSS AS A gift. It was delicate with intricate etchings, and it was lovely. I rejoiced in having it, but seldom wore it, fearing I wouldn't be able to be true to its teachings. I didn't want to let people down and wag their heads from side to side as I had on hearing of the flagrant misbehavior of several prominent Christian television personalities. Their actions had greatly disappointed me and disillusioned me, and I didn't want to be guilty of doing this to someone else. Wearing the cross would proclaim to all who saw it that I am a Christian.

And then, a thought occurred: I don't have to wear a religious symbol to let others know what I am. Actions speak louder than words and symbols. Regardless of whether I wear a cross or not, I belong to God, and He belongs to me, and I am responsible for what I say and what I do. Someone, somewhere, and at some time is watching me, and also watching you, to see how we act and to hear what we say. May we be faithful to that to which He has called us.

167 YESTERDAY AN INTESTINAL BUG FELLED ME, AND I HAD to leave work and go home and seek rest in bed. I felt wretched. I hugged the covers and didn't know my husband had come home to check up on me until I opened my eyes and saw him standing by the bed. He brought me a swallow of Coke, urged me to drink it, and then instructed me to stay in bed until he got home in the evening. For the rest of the afternoon, I continued to sleep.

When he arrived home after completing his work day, he prepared chicken noodle soup, dry toast, and more Coke for me. Later on he brought me a peeled apple. This morning, he cooked an egg, fixed half a grapefruit and some dry toast and, once again, brought it to me to eat in bed. Only a slight dizziness remained of yesterday's illness.

All this from a man who promised over forty-two years ago to love and honor me, and to cherish me until we parted at death. And then I think of all God's promises in His Word. If a human being can honor a vow, then how much more does He who is Holy honor that which He promises us. How great is God's faithfulness, and how blessed we are to be united in love to Him.

168

While lying in my sick bed yesterday, I thought of another time many years ago when I was ill with the same kind of intestinal bug. Our children were young then, and as most mothers know, it isn't an easy matter to stay in bed for an extended time with three children running around wanting first one thing and then another. Our older daughter poked her head in my bedroom door and informed me she was making lunch for me. I said, "Okay," and rolled over. About an hour later, she reappeared at the door, carrying a tray. On it was a napkin and a giant chocolate chip cookie neatly placed on a dinner plate, and it was as big as the plate. I later learned she had used almost half her cookie dough to bake this for me. The last thing I wanted, the last thing I needed, was a giant chocolate chip cookie. But, I ate it anyway, and it stayed where I put it.

I could have told her that her offering was not quite right, or that I couldn't eat it right then, but I didn't, because she had gone to great lengths to help me, to let me know she loved me and wanted to take care of me. I was willing to suffer any consequences of eating something like this on such a queasy stomach.

Often we push aside the offerings our children bring us, and in so doing squelch that very thing within them we so desperately want them to learn: giving of themselves to those they love. Take whatever gift your child brings to you, my friend. It may not be perfect or in the best taste, but rest assured it comes from a heart of love.

Already Ours, Every Day of the Year

169 AS OUR CHILDREN WERE GROWING UP, THEY OFTEN came home from school and heard me say, "Don't touch that pie. So-and-so died today, and I'm taking it to their house." Usually, as soon as I could afterwards, I baked our family the same treat. One evening, while rushing around to get ready for a covered dish church supper, I managed to corral the two older children, telling them the huge banana pudding on the counter was to take to our party and not to dive into it. I hadn't had time to get this message to our youngest child, however, and I walked into the kitchen just in time to see a heaping spoonful of that dessert hit her plate. She had dipped smack-dab out of the middle of the pudding. Immediately, she looked at me, saw the expression on my face, and said, "Whoops. Uh- oh."

I lost it. I'm really ashamed to admit that.

My husband and I stayed home from the covered dish supper, and looking back on this now, I'm greatly disappointed I chose that path. Had I had my wits about me and a presence of mind, I would have taken the banana pudding and gone to the dinner anyway, and explained (if asked) the missing center portion of it. But I didn't do that. Instead, I took something from the bottom of the pile of a priority list and literally shoved it to the top, granting it prominence, a position it didn't deserve. I should not have reacted the way I did, and I should have gone to the dinner. But as a wise professor of mine used to say, "It isn't nice to should on yourself."

Remember this, my friend. It isn't nice to should on yourself. And it's downright emotionally unhealthy to take insignificant things and grant them a priority they don't deserve.

170 MANY YEARS AGO WHEN I WAS AT BACCALAUREATE services commemorating my graduation from ninth grade, I was seated by a classmate whom I'd known since beginning junior high school. On signal, our class stood and led in singing, "Onward Christian Soldiers." I knew the words to the first stanza of this song, but I couldn't remember the other verses. Soon my friend put her hand on top of mine, which was resting on the back of the pew in front of us. She did this, I supposed, to comfort, support, and encourage me, for she was one of the students in my class whom I knew attended church services regularly. At that time, my family didn't attend church and neither did I, though I did know some of this particular church song.

Now each time I hear or join in singing this old church hymn, I am reminded of my classmate, who was motherless and whose father was raising her by himself, a young lady who wanted to reassure a friend whom she believed was embarrassed. And the words in one of those forgotten verses rings out loud and clear: "Like a mighty army moves the church of God. Brothers, we are treading where the saints have trod. We are not divided; all one body we, One in hope and doctrine, one in charity."

We, the church, are one body, one in hope and doctrine, one in charity—God's army, treading the soil of those who've gone before us. I've never forgotten her kind gesture, one born out of love for a friend.

171 I FIRST MET MY HUSBAND'S GRANDMOTHER WHEN SHE was seventy-five years old. Her skin was wrinkled and her hair was a salt and pepper color. I thought she was old then, and now looking at the fading azalea blooms on the plants in front of my office window, I wonder at the wisdom of that thought. The azalea's pink blooms are now drooping and wilting. They have grown old and almost have seen their last hurrah, and yet, studying them, I think of my husband's grandmother. Like these decaying blooms at their height, she brought much joy and happiness to the lives she touched, and she did so just by being who she was—a radiant lady, a gracious lady, and a lady filled with God's love and with a desire to serve God all the days of her life.

Never again will I see an azalea in full bloom that I won't think of her and her legacy to those of us fortunate enough to have known her and have our lives enriched because we did.

172 ONE DAY, WHILE STANDING AT THE KITCHEN WINDOW, I spied our son's rear propped up in the air with his face hugging the ground so closely he was almost to the point of having to breathe in some of the backyard's dirt. He remained in this position for quite some time, and I wondered

Already Ours, Every Day of the Year

what on earth he was doing. Finally he came back into the house.

"Let me tell you about ants," he announced. He proceeded to give me a blow-by-blow description of what he had learned through his observations.

This is how we come to know God's Word, what He says in it—that which makes a path for us through the darkness and guides us to light. Just as our son studied an anthill to learn all he could about ants, so, too, do we study God's Word to learn more about God, His ways, and His will for our lives.

173 There's a beautiful natural lake not too far from our home. As a boy, my husband often fished that lake with his father and came to know all its lovely nooks and crannies. Shortly after our marriage he introduced me to Caddo Lake, and I fell in love with her, too. A number of years ago, we were nestled in one of her fascinating inlets, and I took a notion to take leave of my fishing and just drink in what nature had put before my eyes. It was late in the afternoon. As I looked across the water, I gasped at the loveliness before my eyes. The sun caressed the water in such a way that millions of sun diamonds winked at me, inviting me to share her wealth. And I did—for as long as it lasted.

Our Lord continually invites us into His wealth, to open our eyes that we might see what is really there and how much He has freely given us. Sometimes we, too, might have to quit what we're doing in order to see what is there. My friend, the sight is magnificent. It's more than well worth the effort.

174 Several years ago, when our older daughter and son-in-law were on vacation in San Francisco, she took a picture of a lone tree perched on a rocky cliff overlooking the Pacific Ocean. She enlarged the snapshot, had it framed, and gave it to me to hang in my office. I often wonder about that tree, and many who visit my office comment on it. Do they, as I sometimes do, see a lone tree, one isolated from kindred spirits? Or is the tree standing fast against the elements of the weather, determined to withstand whatever might come along to rip it from its roots and send it crashing into the sea below?

Are you standing alone, or are you standing fast? Whichever way you view yourself, it is imperative you understand that whatever your stance, if you belong to the Lord, you are in Him, and that's what matters.

175 I HAVE ANOTHER PRINT HANGING ON THE WALL IN MY office. It is of a multicolored path running through a thicket of trees. A rainbow of leaves cling to the ground and hug the trail. When I ask those who stare at it what they see, numerous answers come, but mostly people see themselves either isolated and alone on the path or on their way to an important event or an exotic and exciting destination.

Regardless of how we view our environments or circumstances, God is with us. He will never leave us or forsake us. We might not always have a sense of His presence in us, but nevertheless, He is always with us. We are never alone.

176 I CLEANED OUT MY DESK AT WORK TODAY AND CAME across something I had scrawled on the back of a legal pad: "To do well that which we choose. To choose well that which we do." I couldn't remember when I'd jotted these words down, or what was going on in my life at the time. But I do know what I meant by what I had scribbled down.

We can and do make many choices in life. Some of our choices are good, and some of them aren't. Some choices turn out well, and some don't. Regardless of how long we dawdle and remain in indecision, eventually we will have to choose one path or the other. Once a choice is made, it is up to us to make the best out of that choice, and to do the best we can with it. It's sort of like the chicken and the egg. Which comes first? I don't know, but this I do know: To do well that which I choose, and to choose well that which I do.

177 THE PSALMIST SINGS, "THE LORD IS THY KEEPER: THE Lord is thy shade upon thy right hand" (Ps. 121:5, KJV). Our Lord God, who never sleeps, the One who never goes on vacation, the One who is ever present in the hearts and lives of His children, is our keeper. As our keeper, God protects us by day and by night, and He takes note of our comings and our goings. God is forever present with us.

This doesn't mean unfortunate or even evil things won't come our way. It doesn't mean we will never suffer or bear hardships, and it doesn't mean we will never cry or feel despair. What it does mean is God is our keeper and as such is ever mindful of where we are and what is going on in our lives. He is with us during the good times, and He is with us during the bad times. Whatever comes our way, God is always with us. We have to do nothing more than lift our "eyes unto the hills, from whence cometh my help" (Ps. 121:1, KJV). Any meaningful help that comes the way of God's child comes from God. God will keep us in His way, for we are His children and He is our keeper.

178 ONCE AGAIN, I MISPLACED AN ITEM. THIS TIME WHAT came missing wasn't insignificant, like a scarf or a belt. It was my telephone and address book. I had taken it to the office to copy some information from it onto my Rolodex file. Weeks later when I went looking for the book, it wasn't in its usual resting place at home. At first I panicked because the book has more than addresses and telephone numbers in it. From time to time I've tossed some very personal information in there, things I wouldn't particularly want to share with the public at large. Having exhausted every nook and corner of the house, I began to suspect it could have rolled off the car seat as I brought it home and wedged between the seat and door and accidentally dropped from the car when I opened the door. I gulped and fervently prayed this hadn't happened.

Finally, I quit searching for the book and making more of the incident than it called for. I resigned myself to having lost the book. I decided to let the whole matter rest with the Lord and just take the next step as it came. It was then I spied the book lying on top of the VCR in our bedroom. My lesson came swiftly: *Don't sweat the small stuff . . . and it's all small stuff,* the title of a book by Richard Carlson, Ph.D. God is in control. He always has been, and He always will be. Now, if that is not a blessing, then I don't know what is.

179 ON THE FIRST WORD-PROCESSING PROGRAM I BOUGHT for my computer, there's a box at the top left of the screen that lets the user select what kind of spacing she wants for the work she's doing. This is not the case with another program I bought. I don't like reading directions, and so I usually end up fooling around on the computer long enough to get it to do what I want it to do. Since there's no box to select spacing on the second program, I began clicking here and there and wracking my brain to figure out how to get double-spacing to magically appear on my screen. Surely, the task couldn't be as difficult as I was making it. Weeks later, after going through quite a complicated route to get this job done, I accidentally figured out all I had to do to get double-spacing is click on format and then select spacing. Very simple.

Epiphany time once again: How many times have I taken a very simple matter and complicated it because I failed to read God's directions and follow through with them until the right path plopped before me and the right answer all but exploded in my face?

180 LAST EVENING I WANDERED THROUGH ONE OF THOSE megabookstores, looking for the book I had quoted in day 178. I needed information from it in order to give Dr. Carlson credit. After I completed my mission, I began thumbing through some of the best-sellers and, to my chagrin, found two books very similar to the one I'm writing. My heart fell, and with it my self-esteem. These two books are best-sellers, for goodness' sake. What on earth was I thinking? I allowed myself to become intimidated. And then, I thought of other times I've done this: when I've shown up either overdressed or underdressed for a function, when I've been in a group of people from parts of the country other than the South and I've drawled my words, when I've done a presentation and I know others on the program have outdone me, when I've opened my mouth and stuck my foot into it, and when . . . well, I really could go on and on, but I think you get my drift.

Did you notice the word *allowed* above? Self-esteem comes from within. If we look outside ourselves for it, we won't find it. It is neatly tucked deep inside us, and it is put there by God. He approves of us. We are pleasing in His sight. He loves us unconditionally. It doesn't matter to Him how we're dressed, or how we talk, or in what language we talk, or the errors we make, or the blunders we commit. All that is important to Him is His love for us and His approval of us. "If God be for us, who can be against us" (Rom. 8:31, KJV)?

I did find two excellent best-sellers similar to the book I'm writing, but please note, I'm still writing. If I can bypass negative influences from outside myself that might cause my confidence and self-esteem to plummet, so can you.

181 I WEAR SOFT CONTACT LENSES, AND DUE TO MY presbyopia, I wear monovision lenses, meaning one eye is fitted for distance and the other for close work. Sometimes I struggle with inserting my left lens. That's my close vision eye, and perhaps because I'm right-handed, now and again I have difficulty inserting it. Several times the lens has folded over on itself as I'm trying to get it into my eye, and I have to take it out and take another stab at it. Sometimes the lens slips up into my eyeball, hiding itself and snuggling down beneath my eyelid. When this happens, I have a difficult time retrieving it, and sometimes I can't tell whether I've even gotten the lens out or not. Soft contact lenses, for you who don't wear them, can be elusive little boogers once they're not on your finger or on your eyeball. They can become shifty little objects when dropped, almost impossible to see or retrieve.

This kind of scenario happened yesterday. The lens doubled on itself and went straightway to the top of my eyeball, out of sight. A familiar scratchiness occurred each time I blinked. I couldn't see the lens no matter how far I stretched my eyelid and looked for it, so I decided to take another lens and insert it in the eye, hoping the original lens would attach itself to the new one. Nothing happened, and I began to panic.

"Lord, please help me get this lens out," I prayed as I blinked and teared.

Still nothing happened, and I became concerned, wondering what on earth I'd do if I couldn't retrieve it. It was Sunday, and my optometrist certainly wasn't at work, and I'd feel rather foolish getting him down to his office for something like this. So I took a deep breath and prayed for its retrieval once again. Still nothing happened.

I calmed down, but my prayer intensified. I was desperate.

"Lord, please, please, please, help me get this lens out of my eye."

Somehow, I instinctually knew whatever the outcome of this, it would be all right. I was wasting energy worrying and fretting about the matter. Immediately, I decided to move the second lens around toward the top of my eyeball, and when I did, I instinctually blinked and both lenses rested on my bottom eyelid. Needless to say, I was relieved, and I was much wiser, for two reasons. First, too often I'm impatient with this chore and rush in the doing of it. Second, God is aware of whatever is happening to me, and He is in control. He has never failed me yet, and He never will. Trusting Him is at the core of our relationship, and it is immensely important. In fact, it is critical. Trust. Faith. My relationship with God goes nowhere without them.

182

A NUMBER OF YEARS AGO, I ATTENDED A WEEKLONG writing conference where the guest speaker was Newberry Award winner, Madeleine L'Engle. At that time, I remember thinking I had made contact with the most brilliant mind I'd ever encountered. Not only is this gracious lady intelligent, talented, gifted, accomplished, and quick-witted, she is also deeply spiritual.

At that time I was very much into writing techniques and the writing process. As God would have it, I passed her in the hallway one day, stopped her, and chatted briefly with her about this topic. After I had elaborated on many of my picked-up notions of the no-no's of writing for children, this woman, who had listened intently to my words, locked eyes with me and simply said, "Write for yourself. Forget about what others say about writing for an audience. Write for yourself."

And since then, I've done that very thing. I write for myself, and this means when I can't continue writing a sentence until the exact words I'm searching for come, I stop and search for the word, knowing that it is okay for me to do this because this is the way I am, and this is the way I write. I've put aside what experts say about doing this kind of thing. I just write for myself, and in so doing have gained more insight into living life itself. As you "write" your own life story, do it for yourself. Forget the audience out there watching you. Chart your course. Find your way. God is with you in all your endeavors.

Already Ours, Every Day of the Year

183 AND SPEAKING OF CELEBRITIES, IN 1998 OPRAH Winfrey was in Amarillo, Texas, defending her right to tell television viewers she'd eaten her last burger. Imagine. She was being sued by the cattle industry for voicing her opinion about beef. What is our world coming to? A horrible beef-consumption-related disease attacks England and could get into our country, Oprah had a program about it, and whammo, the cattle industry sued her for a corresponding financial dive in the beef industry. One does wonder if the suit was really about loss of revenue because of mad cow disease, Oprah's remark, or about all of us in general. Unfortunately, we live in a society where too many eyes are focused on prominent and affluent personalities, or anything or anyone else with sums of monies, waiting, it seems, for an opportunity to grab some of their assets for ourselves. What does this say about us?

I remember Jesus saying, "But seek ye first the kingdom of God, and his righteousness; and all these thing shall be added unto you" (Matt. 6:33, KJV). These words are preceded with comments regarding murder, adultery, divorce, oaths, retaliation, love, almsgiving, prayer, and fasting, and they come after His teachings in the beatitudes. Jesus continued on with words regarding judging, asking, seeking and knocking, the golden rule, two ways of life, and the true way into the Kingdom. He ended with a parable about two builders. Remember them? He said the wise man who heard His words and obeyed them was like the man who built his house on a rock. When the rain and the floods came and the wind blew, the house reminded standing. And those who heard His words and didn't do them were likened to the man who built his house on the sand, and when the rain and floods came and the winds blew, his house fell. "And it came to pass, when Jesus had ended these sayings, the people were astonished at his doctrine: for he taught them as one having authority, and not as the scribes" (Matt. 7:28–29, KJV).

Let us look within our own hearts and spirits and ferret out that within us that urges us to go after what we believe we can get from another, or what we believe they owe us. My heart goes out to the cattle industry for their loss, but anyone who is in business, whatever that business might be, knows at any given moment, anything can happen that will cause a nose dive or a downward spiral. But, does such an event cause a house to fall? Not if the house is built on rock.

184 I REALLY THOUGHT LONG AND HARD ABOUT MY WRITINGS for day 183 and wondered at the wisdom of my saying what I had. My first thought was having the cattle industry furious at me, and my second one was of being a Texan and living in a portion of cattle country. I debated whether to delete the thoughts of day 183, and instead substitute another theme. As you can see, day 183 remains as written. I must be true to that which I believe, and that which comes to my mind from God.

Let us take heart when we see dark clouds looming on the horizon and wonder if a storm is brewing and coming our way. Others have blazed the path before us and are there on the other side of it encouraging us not to be afraid to walk where God leads us.

185 EVEN THOUGH WE LIVE ON A FEW ACRES OF LAND, WE fenced in our backyard to keep our dogs from running onto the highway and getting hurt or bothering our neighbors. I often find the dogs perched on their hind legs, eyeballing the woods behind our house as if something out there is calling them, wooing them to come and be a part of whatever is there.

Would that we as God's children felt a compulsion to answer such a call within us, that indescribable something that compels, urges us to follow Him totally, to be where He is, to be a part of that which belongs to Him. Whatever our dogs might be doing at any given moment, I know before long their heads will turn toward the woods, and I can see that longing in their eyes, a longing to answer that which is instinctual. We, as God's children, have similar instincts, except it is not a call of the wild, but a call to commune with and serve the One who issued the call.

186 THE APOSTLE PAUL URGED THE CHURCH AT Thessalonica to excel in their newfound faith. He encouraged them to love one another and to be thankful. He prodded them regarding prayer, saying, "Pray without ceasing. In everything give thanks: for this is the will of God in Christ Jesus concerning you" (1 Thess. 5:17–18, KJV). I've often pondered those first three words, however. "Pray without ceasing." What did he mean? How does a person go about praying nonstop? I've heard sermons on this topic and Sunday school lessons about it, but I've not clearly understood what the words really mean. Am I to be continually on my knees, prostrate before the Lord, talking with Him?

In writing this book, I've gotten an answer. Between working each day, sleeping each night, doing household chores, and writing as I've never written before, I've not had the time I once had to pore over God's words in the Bible, or even have lengthy conversations with Him. But, in putting down my thoughts regarding God being everywhere and in everything and very much involved with and interested in our lives, and His richest blessings already being ours, I've come to my greatest epiphany: Seeing God in everything and knowing His richest blessings are already mine is praying without ceasing. I see God everywhere I look. I see Him in everything that happens. I see Him in other people and what they say and what they do. I see Him in the wind and the rain and the snow. I see Him in the grass, and I see Him in a leaf. I see Him in animals. I see Him in germs and warfare. I see Him in hospitals and in hotels. I see Him in times of danger, and I see Him in times of want. I see Him in times of peace. I see Him everywhere. Not a moment passes that I don't see Him and feel His presence in everything that happens to me. I think this is what Paul was talking about. Pray without ceasing, my friend. "Faithful is he that calleth you, who also will do it" (1 Thess. 5:24).

187

LAST NIGHT I ATTENDED A DINNER WHERE THE KEYNOTE speaker was someone I had known years ago. There were eight of us ladies sitting at the table, and one of them was the speaker and another, her sister. The speaker leaned over to her sister, made eye contact with me, and said, "Betty, tell my sister what your favorite movie of all time is?"

I was somewhat startled, but I responded, *Sound of Music*.

This was also her sister's favorite movie, and the woman gushed, "I know almost every line by heart."

She and I talked briefly about our favorite scenes, and then I looked at the keynote speaker and said, "How did you remember that about me? It was so long ago."

She didn't respond verbally—she just smiled. Not only had she remembered what movie, but she also recalled my favorite scene from the movie. I was more than impressed. I was immensely flattered. And, for once, I was speechless.

We never know the impression we make on others or the things about us they deem noteworthy. This in and of itself would be reason enough to walk and talk carefully, being more mindful of the things we do and say, should they be remembered or thought about by others, and bring joy to them and us and not sorrow or despair.

The speaker never answered my question, but I left that event with a fresh understanding of my responsibility toward others. Nothing I say or do is inconsequential. Someone, somewhere is taking note of me. If I am to be remembered, then my prayer is that the memory is a good, worthy, and positive one.

188 As I talked with a lady yesterday, she spoke of the house she grew up in, saying she would like to be able to go back inside it, especially to see her bedroom. I too would like to revisit my favorite growing-up dwelling place, but I can't do that. It no longer exists. It was torn down years ago to make room for other structures on a college campus. It only remains in my mind.

The other day, I accidentally came across a picture of Grandma standing on the porch of that house. There she was, right hand propped on her hip, a broad smile on her face, her sackcloth dress covered with a dark sweater. It was a close-up shot, showing only her and the banister she stood behind. How I wanted to reach out to her, take her hand, and stroll through our house together. And then an epiphany occurred: I don't need to revisit that place or see it as it was. What came from that house is neatly tucked away in my heart, and all I need do to touch base with those days and reclaim them is remember Grandma—a woman who stood between the world and me. She loved me and she nurtured me, and it came from a heart saturated with compassion and duty. Love is never destroyed unless we let go of it. Grandma has never let go of me, and I will never let go of her. We can always revisit Plum Street together. We just won't do it in the flesh.

189 I've always seemed to have a fascination with things under construction, especially tall buildings or business establishments. I've taken great pleasure in

Already Ours, Every Day of the Year

driving by such places in progress and gloating over a day's accomplishment. One would have thought I had some sort of vested interest in the work going on, the way I've smacked my lips and gloried in the least headway.

I can only imagine God's great delight as He stands aside and savors His work in us. He too is in the process of building, and what He is fashioning is a far greater work than an earthly structure made of wood, brick, or stone. It's more precious than diamonds, rubies, silver, or gold. It is the work He began in each of His children, and unlike earthly structures, it is a work continually in progress, but it isn't complete until we see our Lord face to face.

"For it is God which worketh in you both to will and to do of his good pleasure" (Phil. 2:13, KJV). "Being confident of this very thing, that he which hath begun a good work in you will perform it until the day of Jesus Christ" (Phil. 1:6, KJV).

Whatever comes our way, be it good, bad, or indifferent, we are the Lord's, and it is He who is willing and working in us of His good pleasure to bring us into the very image of His Son. I've now taken a keener interest in His work in me, and just as I glory in earthly constructions, I also revel in spiritual ones, the one in you and the one in me.

190

YESTERDAY I MADE THE ROUNDS OF SEVERAL FURNITURE stores, hunting for a computer armoire. I knew exactly what I wanted, for I had seen it in an office supply house some months ago. On the way to complete this mission, I prayed, asking God to grant me wisdom in my task. Of course I wanted the best financial deal I could get, and so I decided I would buy from the dealer who would offer me the best price. Only one store had the armoire in stock, but the price quoted on it was the highest one offered by the various dealers. There wasn't, however, a vast difference between all the offers. But I had made my mind up, and I had already decided what I wanted to pay and what I was willing to pay. All the bids were above what I wanted, but not that much above. And then, revelation came. I had asked God for wisdom, and then I had run away from that encounter with Him to set about doing my own thing, doing it my way. What I had wanted was for God to agree with me, to help me find what it was I wanted in the way that I wanted it, not necessarily to gain wisdom from Him.

I could have spent additional time and gasoline money traveling around my area to get a better price, but I doubt I would have found it because I now know my figure was an unreasonable one. And if I had gotten what I originally wanted, what would I have proven? I was right, and I could get my way. I had not asked God for that. I had asked for wisdom, and this is what He gave me. All I had to do was agree with Him and accept His gift. He had led me to what I wanted. I just didn't get it exactly the way I thought I would.

191 A FRIEND AND I WERE TALKING THE OTHER DAY ABOUT the aging process. She related a story of seeing an old man slowly making his way down the street. His shoulders were stooped, and his walk unsteady. She then went on to say that her grandmother, who had taught music in her younger days and was an accomplished artist in arias and concertos and the like, was in a nursing home. One day as a group of people there gathered together to listen to some gospel music, rather fast-paced music at that, her grandmother clapped in time to the music, surprising onlookers. My friend said, "Didn't those people know my grandmother hadn't always been like she is now, but once was a vibrant young woman much involved in music and capable of performing it?" She also said of the man she had seen walking down the street, "Don't people understand he wasn't always like that? He once had a steady gait, and he stood upright."

Far too many of us are guilty of passing judgments, especially on older people, people who once were quite capable of the tasks presented them, people young and vibrant and full of life. Inside, these people are still the same as they were in their younger days—only their exteriors are changed, and perhaps some of their mental functioning is somewhat diminished. Don't we know that they weren't always like this? For all practical purposes, they are the same people. And they deserve our respect and attention. Take time today to listen to an "ancient" one, one who has seen another time, and who can enrich our lives because of it, if we give them the chance.

192 NOT LONG AGO, I WAS SCHEDULED TO HAVE A MINOR part on the program at a church banquet for women. All I had to do was offer the closing prayer. There would be no formal preparation for this task as prayer is something that springs from the heart, words uttered to God in praise, petition, and thanksgiving. At least this is my interpretation of it. Yet, even spontaneous public praying is not without a certain measure of planning or preparedness. We are to "be instant in season, out of season" (1 Tim. 4:2, KJV). What we are is what comes from our lips, and what comes from our lips is what we are.

A day before the program, disturbing event after event engulfed me. My spirit became disquieted, and I began to fear opening my mouth, not knowing what might come forth from it when I did. I was out of sorts and in no mood to attend such a meeting, much less pray at the end of it. I began to formulate a prayer so that I would have something to say when the time came the next evening to say it. But my words sounded contrived, planned, and not in the least bit warm and spontaneous and praiseworthy. By the time of the banquet, I had allowed myself to become something of a basket case, just wanting to be done with my assignment and leave. But when time came for me to close the evening's events with prayer, peace came. Throughout the dinner and program I'd prayed for a quietness of spirit and words to say—words from my heart. Those who had prepared the meal and decorated the hall, the keynote speaker, the music and others on the program had touched my heart and spirit in such a way that quietness came, and with it the ability to see God's hand in the recent happenings in my life and put those events in proper perspective. It is I who hoisted those happenings into a place of priority in my life. It is I who allowed fretfulness to come and reign over me. We have more control over our reactions to situations than we think we do. We just have to let God's Spirit within us take over and guide us to where He wants us to be.

193 ONE OF THE MEN SERVING AT TABLE THE NIGHT OF THIS banquet almost whisked my dinner plate away before I was finished with it. When he realized what he had almost done, he was embarrassed, but unknown to him, this added to a quietness of spirit that was beginning to wash over me. Grandma used to do this to me. In her eagerness to complete the meal, which meant having the dishes washed, dried and put away, she ran circles around the table, waiting for our forks to rest on our plates so she could snatch, wash, dry, and store as quickly as possible. She was a woman with a mission, and she wanted her job over and done with. We used to joke about holding on to our plates between bites so Grandma couldn't yank them right out from under our noses.

The man waiting tables at the banquet and I had more in common that he knew. He had a job to do, and so did I. His was to wait tables. Mine was to end the meeting with prayer. Grandma also had a goal. It was to be done with her never-ending task of cleaning up after others. Had Grandma not been this way, and the actions of the man waiting tables hadn't brought her to mind, I don't think I could have reached the calm waters I was able to at that time. There are no coincidences with God. Nothing is happenstance. Every event in our lives becomes a piece of the puzzle to it. No time do I think of Grandma that a great sense of peace doesn't engulf me. I'm thankful my grandmother was a plate snatcher, and that this man was the diligent waiter he was, and in so being brought pleasant memories to a troubled mind.

194

I'VE NEVER KNOWN A CHRISTIAN LIKE MY HUSBAND'S grandmother. She not only talked the talk, but she walked the walk as well. She once told me if she couldn't say something good about someone, then she didn't say anything at all. There were times when I heard her say nothing at all.

Perhaps this is a good lesson for us too. It would serve us all well to remain silent and cease the wagging of our tongues when that which we have to say is uncomplimentary or hurtful to another.

195

THE APOSTLE PAUL SAYS CHRISTIANS GLORY IN tribulations (Rom. 5:3). Did you notice he used the plural form of the word *tribulation*? Just say the word over to yourself softly. Tribulation. It doesn't even roll off the tongue very easily, does it? Tribulation means hardship, trouble, distress, heartache, pain and suffering, agony, torture, bad times, adversity, disaster, and even affliction. Glory in these things? Notice Paul didn't say we should. He said we did.

Tribulations usher in patience, a steadfastness in our lives. And it is by patience we gain experience, and it is experience that steers us toward hope. The saddest creatures on the face of the earth are hopeless people—people who have tossed in the towel and given up. Hopeless. Now say this word aloud very slowly. Doesn't it ring a chord of sadness within? Tribulation. Hope. We cannot have one without the other. It is by the first that we gain the last. So when tribulations come, and they will, hang on, my friend, because if tribulations come, can hope be far behind?

196 HAVE YOU EVER JUST SAT ON A PORCH IN THE SUMMER evening doing nothing but just listening to what is out there? Crickets, a distant train whistle, a babbling brook, the laughter of a child, a passing car, the rumble of thunder, or the buzzing of a bug. What lovely sounds, sounds that a busy day can quickly squash. Is this not the way it is with God's small voice? His voice is easier to hear when we leave off our busyness and eagerly listen for it.

Sometime during this day, quit whatever it is you're doing so that you might hear that sweet, loving voice. It'll do more for you than a million coffee breaks or a million bucks. He longs to talk to you and to me.

197 DID YOU KNOW THE WORST THINGS IN OUR LIVES often turn out to be the best things in our lives? One of the worst things that ever happened to me was my mother's marriage to the man who for awhile became my stepfather. We didn't like each other. He constantly found fault with me, and as result, I had as little contact with him as possible.

But had my mother not married him, we never would never have moved to that part of town where I met my best childhood friend. As I've said earlier in these writings, I don't know what would have become of me had it not been for these people. My friend took me to church with her, and it was that church that became responsible for my eventual move to Texas. Had I not come to Texas I never would have met my husband, and had I not met my husband, we never would have had the three beautiful children we now do. My life would have been totally different, and not of the radiant quality it now is. Taking care of my mother, who was well able to care for herself, would have become the focus of my life.

So, the worst things that can happen to us often turn out to be the best things that can happen to us. Such tribulations usher in patience and steadfastness, which guide us toward the experiences that eventually steer us toward hope. The days of my stepfather seemed like hopeless days for me. But hope rings from the housetops today and sings from the hills. There are no coincidences with God.

198 ONE SATURDAY AFTERNOON I BECAME VERY NOSTALGIC. I went out into the backyard, sat down on a stoop and surveyed our children's tree house. Even though our children are grown and no longer living with us, I longed to see them romping about having a good time. To hear their squealing voices would have been heaven on earth. Our chow dog (incidentally a hand-me-down from one of our children) nestled beside me on the ground. She did nothing but intently look at me as I began tearing and finally crying. I glanced her way and said, "Well, if that's all the sympathy you can offer, then I'm going inside." Once there, I set about doing first one thing and then another, and my recollections and moping faded.

Every evening for the next two weeks when I arrived home from work, Bailey silently greeted me at the gate, her stance and look inviting me to come to her so that she could lick my hand. If you know anything about chows, you know they can be rather standoffish when they take a notion to be (and more often than not, they take a notion), so her behavior was somewhat puzzling. Then I remembered our encounter that Saturday afternoon. She had understood my heavy heart, and she was concerned about me. She wanted me to know this, and she did it the only way she knew how to do it—welcoming me home in a different way, one that conveyed her sympathy. My sorrow was important to her. She wanted to make sure I was all right.

The Bible tells us that our tears are precious in God's sight, that He collects them. Bailey's behavior served to remind me of this and to let me know that God was there with me that Saturday afternoon, and He not only heard and saw my tears, but they were precious in His sight. Isn't a dog's love wonderful? And aren't we blessed indeed that God gave such loving creatures to us for our joy and comfort?

Already Ours, Every Day of the Year

199 I RECENTLY ASKED A YOUNG COUPLE HOW MUCH THEY laughed together. They looked puzzled and didn't know how to respond to my question. I surmised they didn't engage in this kind of behavior frequently. And yet laughter is often the best medicine for what ails us. Some of the most precious moments in my marriage have been the times when my husband and I have gotten a good case of the giggles. When these occasions occur, it reminds me of scenarios I've seen on the bloopers television shows. One of us mixes up our words, tries to correct what we've done, makes what we've already said worse than it already is, with both of us ending up in a fit of laughter, unable to make any kind of intelligent sounds at all. I love these moments for in them we come to know each other even better than we already do.

There is a time to laugh (Eccles. 3:4). Snatch the season of laughter when it comes and ride the waves of it. Laughter is good for what ails you. Another season will come all too soon.

200 WHEN ALL THREE OF OUR CHILDREN WERE BABIES, each one went through a time of fretting. Nothing we did or said seemed to ease their fussiness, and all we could do was soothe as best we could and wait the crankiness out. We had been told from time to time all babies do this kind of thing, and so we prepared ourselves for it. But no one briefed me regarding my own fretfulness, the times when I've allowed myself to stew and fume about first one thing and then another, seeking solace and finding none, and in the process making myself and everyone around me miserable. I mistakenly thought no one had laid the groundwork on this issue, but Someone did. I just wasn't listening or paying attention. In one psalm alone, God commands us three times not to fret (Ps. 37). King Solomon wrote, "The foolishness of man perverteth his way: and his heart fretteth against the Lord" (Prov. 19:3, KJV), and "Better is the poor that walketh in his integrity, than he that is perverse in his lips, and is a fool" (Prov. 19:1, KJV). Better to walk in integrity, trustworthiness, faithfulness, honor, decency, and with backbone than to flounder around in worry and anxiety. It is when we chart a course away from the straight path the Lord lays at our feet that we begin to encounter that very thing within us that causes us to lose sleep over even trivial matters. Our foolishness brings on our whinings and complainings. Solomon goes on to write that our foolishness is what keeps us away from God's path. Better to walk the path He lays out for us than to stray from it and set ourselves up for fretting against Him and working ourselves into a lather.

201 A VERY SPIRITUAL YOUNG LADY RELATED THIS STORY TO me. About everything that could go wrong in her life was going wrong. She was having problems in her marriage, her small children were giving her fits, and she had a demanding job, one that required extra work hours. She was at her wit's end, not knowing which way to turn or what to do. She confided her troubles to her best friend, who seemed interested in what was going on with her and eager to listen to her tales of sorrow. When the young lady got to the end of her woes, her friend looked her squarely in the eye and said, "'This is the day which the Lord hath made; we will rejoice and be glad in it' (Ps. 118:24, KJV). You just need to learn how to rejoice. That's what your problem is." Needless to say, the young woman left the encounter with an albatross of guilt tied around her neck, another burden adding more weight to an already bewildered heart.

Our Lord God makes all of our days. Every one of them. Some are worth getting out of bed for, and some aren't. As my grandmother used to say, "Into every life, some rain must fall." Every day won't be a sunny day. Every day won't be a beautiful day. This is the way life is. But God is always there, watching over and taking care of us—on the good days as well as the bad days. My young friend understood this. What she needed and what she wanted was empathy, someone to whom she could talk who would not only hear her words, but also sense the feelings behind those words. The last thing she needed was judgment.

Sometimes in our eagerness to help another, we offer a solution, usually a simplistic one, not realizing we don't have to solve a problem at all. All that is required is to listen emphatically, letting the speaker know we are with them and behind them. Isn't this rejoicing? I don't know about you, but when another hears my words and the feelings behind those words, I awake even the dead hollering my joy.

Already Ours, Every Day of the Year

202 My basic nature is that of a worrier. It's a characteristic that's plagued me ever since I can remember. Shortly after the arrival of our first child, the worrying escalated into brief bouts of anxiety—times when I became extremely restless and fretful and frightened for reasons I usually wasn't able to figure out. My heebie-jeebies were for the most part short-lived and soon forgotten once they passed—that is until another occurrence reared its ugly head, threatening to take me into a dark tunnel I thought I might not be able to escape. Fortunately these events eventually landed me in the pages of God's Word, searching for help.

As I read and reread the Scripture in Philippians 4:6 that instructs us not to worry about things, I'd scream to myself, "Quit worrying!" It wasn't until I stumbled across the first eight verses of Psalm 37, however, that God's plan to quell my apprehensions struck me like a bolt of lightning. In those verses, I counted twelve imperatives with one of those twelve listed three times. I latched on to God's instructions, and to this day pull out His road map whenever a worrying spirit threatens to engulf me.

When fretfulness and worry rear their ugly heads, I immediately repeat to myself: "Don't fret about this situation. Don't be envious of those causing it or those escaping it. Trust God with the situation and what is in your heart and head. Do good, regardless of how you feel. Delight in the Lord, for it is He who has saved you. Commit your way to the Lord for there is no better commitment on the face of the earth. Rest in the Lord, for that's the only place of peace. Wait patiently for Him to act for He's never failed you yet. Don't fret because there is no need to worry about something God is already in the process of straightening out. Cease from anger because unrelenting anger will poison your spirit. Forsake wrath. Vengeance belongs to God. Don't fret. Don't fret. Don't fret."

Letting my mind and spirit dwell on these things ushers in an immediate episode of thanksgiving to God—a loving, gracious, and kind heavenly Parent who is ever at my side watching over me and taking care of me. Peace comes and it reigns. Depending on the severity of the cause of my entreaties to God, His road map might have to be employed multiple times with periods of peace interspersing the times when fretting gains a temporary upper hand. I don't chide myself when this happens, but just accept it as an indication that what is going on is of a serious nature, and as such, my heart and mind need a concentrated focus on God, His work in me, and His power displayed by that work in me.

Regardless of our personalities or how we cope with life, all of us will come to times when worrying and fretfulness threaten to overtake us. Don't be afraid. Our most gracious and kind and loving heavenly Father has made a way of escape for us.

203 From time to time, feelings of deep peace seem to overshadow my spirit. Nothing is like it. Yet it seems when such feelings come, inevitably a crisis follows in their wake. It is as if the Lord is somehow preparing me for an onslaught of anything but peace, harmony, happiness, and contentment. God seems to be getting me ready to be able to deal with whatever ill winds are sweeping my way.

The euphoria produced by such terrific feelings is incomparable, but when they descend on me, I sometimes quiver and shake, knowing a dam's going to break and the floodgates of hell are going to come crashing down over my head. At such times I remind myself that the Way, the Truth, and the Life are with me as "Mercy and truth are met together, righteousness and peace have kissed each other" (Ps. 85:10, KJV). I might not visibly witness righteousness and peace kissing each other, but they are. My vision is temporarily clouded, and I remind myself if I remained in a constant state of contentment with an absence of conflict, then I would never come to know "God is for me" (Ps. 56:9b, KJV). I wouldn't be able to proclaim, "In God have I put my trust: I will not be afraid what man can do unto me" (Ps. 56:11, KJV).

God delivers us from all our troubles. He keeps our feet steady beneath us. And we can proclaim with David, "In God will I praise his word: in the Lord will I praise his word" (Ps. 56:10, KJV). When I'm frightened, I will trust God and I will praise Him. I will not allow myself to be afraid of what human flesh can do to me or bring my way.

In the meantime, when God visits me with that delectable feeling of perfect peace, I can revel in it, knowing that whatever comes my way afterward, He is walking with me in it and will lead me through it. When the onslaught is over and done with, I will hold in my hands a precious

Already Ours, Every Day of the Year

jewel, one wrought by God's work in me. Mercy and truth have met together and righteousness and peace have kissed each other, and I am a better person because of it.

204 YESTERDAY AS I DROVE TO THE POST OFFICE TO MAIL some letters in their drive-through dropoff box, a lady was in the car in front of me. Her gray-haired head barely cleared the top of the seat's headrest. For reasons I'm not quite sure of, I thought perhaps she might be a widow. She was having a difficult time getting her car in the exact spot to be able to pass her mail through the car window. Cars began piling up behind me, and looking in my rearview mirror I caught glimpses of impatient faces. I knew the woman would be unable to reach the mail slot without getting out of her vehicle, and I wondered if I should get out of my own, approach her car and mail her letters for her. I decided not to do this.

I was sure this lady had been in this position before, and I was just as sure whenever this happened motorists behind her became impatient waiting for her to transact her business before getting to their own. I wanted to grant this woman autonomy, and I also wanted those behind me to be patient with her. I could do the first, but I could do nothing about the second except stand between her and the other drivers. And this is what I did. My prayer for her strength to cope with life's realities stood between her and those behind me. For a moment, I became her defender. Of course no one but the Lord knew this, but it didn't matter to me, for in my mind I had taken this lady to the Lord and talked with Him about her. After we both had mailed our letters and she turned left and I turned right, I whispered to myself, "She hasn't always been like this, and all of us need to understand that." Perhaps the wind caught my words and carried them to the other drivers. I'd like to think it did.

205 LAST WEEK I HAD HOPED TO GET A LOT OF WRITING done, but it didn't happen. My phone seemed to ring off its hook with people on the other end of the line needing my attention. I could have cut most of them short, put my nose to the grindstone, and proceeded with my original plan. But I didn't, not for two of the calls that ended up taking a lot of my time.

Over the years I've trained myself to listen not only to what another says, but to what he or she doesn't say as well. Most of the time, I can sense a person's genuine urgency. I think something of this nature happens to all of us if we tune into it. At least I pray it happens to all of us.

My plans didn't go as I had hoped they would, but I wasn't really sidetracked. Jesus said, "Inasmuch as ye have done it unto one of the least of these my brethren, ye have done it unto me" (Matt. 25:40, KJV).

206 THE FOURTEENTH CHAPTER OF THE GOSPEL OF JOHN IS one of my favorite chapters in the Bible. I think the reason I gravitate toward the words written there is because of the humanness of Thomas and Philip and Judas—not the Judas who betrayed Jesus. Jesus had just finished telling the disciples not to let themselves become troubled over coming events, and that He was going to prepare a place for them and come back for them at a future time, and when He did he would take them with Him so that where He was, they could be too. He told them they already knew the way to get to Him.

The disciple we call doubting Thomas lived up to his name as he exclaimed, "Lord, we know not whither thou goest; and how can we know the way" (John 14:6, KJV). Jesus explained the way to them, and then Philip piped up and said, "Lord, shew us the Father, and it sufficeth us" (John 14:8, KJV). Jesus' response contains some of God's most beautiful promises. Then Judas said, "Lord, how is it that thou wilt manifest thyself unto us, and not unto the world?" (John 14:22, KJV). With patience, Jesus expounded on love, telling them about the Comforter, the Holy Spirit, coming to them and residing in them.

And then He said, "Peace I leave with you, my peace I give unto you: not as the world giveth, give I unto you. Let not your heart be troubled, neither let it be afraid" (John 14:27, KJV). How these words must have soothed the hearts of these men, men not unlike you and me, men prone to doubting, disbelief, and questioning. If the disciples who later became apostles could question the Lord, then it seems reasonable to assume it's all right for us to question Him too. And when we do it, we'll get the same answer as did they, "Peace I leave with you, my peace I give unto you; not as the world giveth, give I unto you. Let not your heart be troubled, neither let it be afraid." Take your questions to the Lord, my friend, and receive His peace. He readily gives it to you. It is yours.

Already Ours, Every Day of the Year

207 When our two oldest children were preschoolers, it seemed a toy became desirable to one of them only if the other had possession of it. Needless to say, many outbursts of anger occurred. I decided to end their squabbling by setting the oven timer for several minutes while the child in possession of a toy played with it. When the timer sounded, that child had to relinquish the toy so the other child could take a turn. I'd then reset the timer, and on and on, until both children lost interest in the toy.

One summer day, while the children were playing in the backyard, I busied myself baking in the kitchen. The oven alarm sounded, indicating time to take the cake out to cool. Suddenly, our son burst through the back door yelling, "Mommie. Mommie. What's it my time to do now?" I had trained him to respond to a signal. A treat followed a specific sound.

Would that we as God's children were as responsive to His signals. They are everywhere, and they come in many different shapes, forms, and fashions. It could be in the rustling of the wind or a person's comment or a sunset or an opportunity to move to a new job or location or an inner gnawing, urging us to respond. The trouble is, we're often too busy wrestling with the tasks at hand to sense what God has put there for us. Let us pray we'll become more sensitive to God's signals, listening for them, for they are there and waiting for us to respond.

208 Grandma was a worrier. Granted, she had enough of life's troubles to keep herself in turmoil. Did you notice I said "keep herself?" Worrying is a choice. Grandma had an option, and apparently she chose to stew and fret rather than trust and obey. Apparently she was unaware of the apostle Paul's instructions to believers at the church in Philippi regarding this matter. I wish she had known because she could have saved herself countless moments of anxiety.

God tells us not to worry about anything (Phil. 4:6), and He tells us how to do it. We are to take everything to Him in prayer, expressing our deep needs to Him. And as we do this, we fill our hearts with thanksgiving for all He has done for us. We simply have a gabfest with God, filling our hearts with gratitude for gifts already given, and laying out before Him the fears and tremblings which cause us such unrest.

It truly is this simple. We might have to return to Him again in prayer the moment we complete our original one, and before we're done with it, we might have to have a very lengthy conversation with our Lord. As you know, we have a tendency to be this way, but peace will come, and that peace will keep our hearts and minds through Christ Jesus. God promises us this. Others may fail us and renege on their word, but God never does. How I wish Grandma had known this.

209 AS THE CHOIR ENTERED THEIR LOFT AT CHURCH yesterday, once again the artificial ficus tree near the entry into the loft got in the way. This time, it went plummeting to the floor. The member who brushed it couldn't catch it, but another member did. He tried to right it, but the plant would have none of it, and the choir member ended up taking it out of the sanctuary altogether. Of course, most of the congregation focused their attention on these happenings, snickering at this turn of events. It got our attention, and set us in an upbeat mood for what followed, words revolving around "this treasure in earthen vessels" (2 Cor. 4:7, KJV).

Who would have thought an artificial tree falling to the ground would have set the stage for such profound thoughts as being troubled but not distressed, perplexed but not greatly puzzled at a turn of events, persecuted but not forsaken and cast down? God speaks to us in many ways, and each time He does so, He sets the stage for what He is about to reveal to us. Our problem becomes being so tied to the temporal world, those things which we can see and hear and smell and taste and touch, that we don't tune in to our spiritual worlds, that realm readily available to us, but which we seldom allow ourselves to fully experience.

To me, that church ficus tree represented all of us. It doesn't take much to knock us over, sometimes nothing more than a slight nudge. But we're human, not inanimate objects. We're flesh and blood beings who have the treasure of the Holy Spirit residing in our spirits, and, as such, we are able to withstand that which comes our way. And God plans it like this so that His power can shine in us, and we will know it is not our work in us that produces fruit, but God's work in us. How intricate is His work in His children! Open our eyes, Lord, that we might see Your mighty works in us.

Already Ours, Every Day of the Year

210 NOT TOO MUCH PLEASES ME MORE THAN TO HAVE ONE of our grown children engage me in conversation. During these times, we might discuss our individual lives and hopes and dreams for the future, or reminisce about the past. It matters little what we talk about. What matters is we talk.

I think it's the same way with God too. When any one of His children seeks Him out to converse with Him, I'm sure it delights His heart as much as it does the human parent whose child has done likewise. Talk to your heavenly Parent. He's just waiting for you to approach Him. He longs to have a chat with you.

211 WHEN I WAS A CHILD, THERE WAS A SAYING FLOATING around—one that from time to time I took up and chanted. It went like this: "Nobody loves me. Everybody hates me. I think I'll eat worms." Of course I never went out and snatched up a passel of worms and had them for dinner, and I don't suppose anyone else has either. Nevertheless, there have been times when I believed no one cared what happened to me. I suspect inherent in all of us are transient feelings of aloneness and isolation, with our trying to reach out for someone who isn't there for us. Loneliness is a wretched feeling. It is unbearable and seemingly more than flesh and blood can bear.

For the child of God, there is no such thing as aloneness. God, whose Spirit indwells us, is forever there. He is at our sides, walking with us. He is ahead of us, guiding us by His hand. He is behind us, urging us onward. He is above us, pulling us to heavenly heights, and He is below us to catch us should we lose our footing and slip and fall.

In his heart King David knew this, but nevertheless he said, "I looked on my right hand, and beheld, but there was no man that would know me: refuge failed me; no man cared for my soul" (Ps. 142:4, KJV). David erroneously believed nobody cared what happened to him. David succumbed to feelings of hopelessness and helplessness.

On one occasion, Martha—the outspoken sister of Mary—complained to Jesus that He didn't seem to care that Mary had left all the work of preparing and serving a meal up to her while Mary did nothing but sit at Jesus' feet, listening to Him talk. Martha believed nobody cared about her. Even Jesus' disciples, those men who physically walked with Him here on earth and audibly heard His words, accused Jesus of not caring what happened to them. They shook the sleeping Jesus awake where he lay in the back of a boat in a raging and stormy sea. "Don't you care that we're going to die?" they screamed. They incorrectly believed that Jesus had abandoned them.

It is human to believe, to feel that nobody cares what happens to us. We've all done it from time to time. It doesn't seem to matter that we know the very hairs of our heads are numbered. We seem to have a tendency to forget God notes when even a sparrow falls to the ground. We are worth far more to God than many sparrows.

God cares about us and what happens to us. He cares so much that He allowed His Son to die for us. Nobody else has come even near doing as much for you or for me. Somebody cares about you and that Somebody is God.

212 Across the street from my office is a quaint white house that is surrounded by a white picket fence. It is a perfect view of what, as a child, I envisioned I would have some day. I would live in a perfect house with a perfect fence with a perfect family doing perfect things. Not so. Life is never perfect. How many of us don't know that yet? How many of us mistakenly set our standards at perfection?

It took a big chunk out of my adulthood to realize perfection doesn't exist—not on planet Earth, at least. The only perfect person to grace this world was Jesus Christ. How important is perfection to you? That little white picket fence needs a board missing. I can't take it out, but I can imagine it out. And if I can do that, then I can take that imaginary measuring stick that I used to gauge things and chuck it in the nearest pond. Did yours just go in the pond too?

213 At lunch time today, I stopped by the grocery store to buy some bread so that I could make myself a sandwich when I got home. I was in a hurry, so I quickly made my purchase and then dashed back out to get into my car. Nearing it, I became frustrated because my electronic door opener didn't work. I kept clicking and clicking, but the familiar clunking sound that signaled an unlocked door didn't happen. I looked inside the car, wondering what on earth was going on. And then I heard a thumping sound on the window of the car next to me. A lady sat in the passenger's seat in the car next to the one I was trying to gain entry into. She smiled sweetly and pointed to her right. My car was on the other side of the one in which she sat. The car I wanted to get into was the same make and model and the same color as my car. I felt silly as I stopped by her window and asked, "How did you know?"

"I saw you when you parked and went inside the store," she replied.

Her thoughtfulness served only to remind me of God's watch over His children. He's there when we sleep, He's there when we're awake. He's there at work or play. God is forever there, and He always knows where we are.

214 BEETHOVEN COMPOSED ONLY ONE VIOLIN CONCERTO. Some critics believe it is the finest work of its kind. Beethoven had stormy relationships with his friends and family, and he never married. He became disappointed by a nephew to whom he was guardian, and it is said of him he was belligerent and quickly took offense at imagined slights. He came from a poor family, and his father drank excessively. He probably began losing his hearing in his late twenties, and could hear almost nothing by his late forties.

Yet, all one has to do to see into the depths of this man is listen to his violin concerto, especially the second movement. I don't know the spiritual condition of Beethoven as he walked planet Earth. All I know is what I hear, and what I hear is a spiritual experience for me. God can and does take everything of man and brings it together for our good.

215 YESTERDAY AS I SHOPPED FOR A PARKING SPACE AT church, I became amused as I passed a familiar sign on the street beside the church: "Thou Shalt Not Park Here." I thought the sign clever and the words amusing. And then I prayed a silent prayer: "Lord, your Word is a lamp unto my feet and a light unto my path. When and if I don't remember what You have told me, then it's okay with me if You erect a sign to remind me." Then I cut loose giggling, for in my mind's eye I envisioned what the world would look like if God literally granted my prayer. No one would be able to get down a street because the streets would be littered with millions of signs. "Thou shalts" and "thou shalt nots" would be everywhere. But, God did hear my prayer, and I meant what I had said. It always sets well with me when God puts his tender loving hands on my heart, pulls me back, or urges me forth, instructing me and guiding me when I have forgotten what He's told me.

216 Our pastor's sermons usually contain three significant points, and knowing this, I listen for them and try to write them down in my head. In one of his sermons, he says, "You reap what you sow, you reap more than you sow, and you reap later than you sow." Paul tells us, "And let us not be weary in well doing, for in due season we shall reap, if we faint not" (Gal. 6:9, KJV).

It's been my experience in life that I do reap what I've sown, and more often than not I reap much more than I've sown and much later. Since I sometimes become weary in doing what I know God wants me to do, I frequently need to hear someone tell me, "Don't give up. Keep on keeping on." This is my message to you, my friend. Keep on keeping on. God is there for you, and He is leading you. Trust him. You will reap what you've sown, so don't become discouraged in well doing.

217 This morning as I drove to work I passed two women out for their morning walk. I've seen them many times before and in different seasons of the year. They're young, they dress appropriately for the weather, and they seem to enjoy walking. Their arms are bent at right angles, and they vigorously swing them in step to their feet. They're obviously into physical fitness. Keeping the body fit and trim seems to be the rage today, not only for the young but for all ages. And I guess it's about time.

But it's also time we focused on keeping our minds and thoughts, morals and scruples in shape too. We have become somewhat of an unfit society in this regard. "For as he thinketh in his heart, so is he . . ." (Prov. 23:7, KJV). We are what we think. Some of us spend inordinate amounts of time figuring out how to get the best deal for ourselves

Already Ours, Every Day of the Year

regardless of what we have to do to get it, and often we don't consider ethics or morals when we get down to wheeling and dealing. Some of us don't even know what ethics and morals are. Too many of us have forsaken honor. Our consciences have become dull. Far too many of us throw caution to the winds and just let it fall where it falls.

Fitness centers and gurus have programs and plans to get us in physical shape. God has a program and a plan to get us into spiritual shape, too, one which leads to uprightness, honesty, high-mindedness, principled living, and all that is fitting for one who calls herself a child of the King. All we have to do is avail ourselves of His plan. He makes it simple for us, the work is hard, but no one becomes spiritually fit without effort. No pain, no gain.

218 I WAS TALKING WITH A FRIEND RECENTLY, AND SHE asked my advice about a problem. I looked her straight in the eye and told her what I thought. With somewhat of a dazed expression on her face, she said of my proposal, "Yes, but . . ." and went on to give her objections to the plan. Again, she asked me what to do, and I formulated another answer. And, you guessed it, her response was, "Yes, but . . ." and she rejected the second solution I offered, stating one reason or another as to why the plan wouldn't work. We did about four rounds of these scenarios. Finally, I reached for a sheet of paper, picked up my pen, and scribbled on it. When she again stated her problem and asked for possible solutions, I held up the piece of paper so she could see what was written on it. It said, "Yes, but. . . ." At first, she looked stunned, but then she burst out laughing, saying, "I'm shooting myself in the foot, aren't I?"

"I don't know. What do you think?" I replied.

I wonder if this is not what we often do to the Lord. Do we go to Him with a problem, get a clear indication of the answer to our question, and then "Yes, but" Him to death as my friend was doing me?

219 MY OLD COMBINATION DIGITAL ANSWERING MACHINE and phone finally bit the dust. I had to buy a new one. The new one was superior to the old one except, as far as I could tell by reading the manual, it didn't allow me to block out a caller's statement. I find it distracting to hear a message in progress.

I finally decided to return the recorder/phone and replace it with one that could do what I wanted. And then I began fooling around with the volume controls. And do you know what? Turning the volume down to zero equals no sound as a message is being recorded. Nothing was said in the manual about this, and I had read it thoroughly.

Sometimes, we just have to experiment to find the answers we're looking for. As my grandma used to say, "There's more than one way to skin a cat."

220 Quite a few years ago a friend and I decided to take flying lessons. I haven't the foggiest notion why we did this other than I wanted to impress my aerospace engineering son with my personal knowledge of aerodynamics. Neither my friend nor I have a sense of direction, and for either of us to fly a plane would have been nothing less than a minor miracle indeed. We trudged on to the bitter end—of ground school, that is. She never soloed and neither did I. I don't know about her, but I knew from the very beginning of our jaunt that I would never ever be alone in the cockpit of any kind of airplane.

So what did I accomplish? A lot. I learned something new. I gained confidence in my ability to understand what I thought was not understandable. I experienced the loveliness of flying in a small aircraft and looking down on the world below, and I spent endless hours giggling with my friend as we sat side by side in class, exchanging quizzical looks with each other as our instructor explained a new facet of aerodynamics.

But the greatest lesson I learned was not to turn away from any experience or new idea life offers. Regardless of whether what comes along is good, bad, or indifferent, flying lessons taught me to embrace what is there, for I know what is there is not there by accident. There's something to be learned from every experience in life if we simply embrace it and go where it takes us. God's Holy Spirit walks along beside us every step of the way. We have nothing to fear but fear itself.

221 Some kids just seem to spring from the womb cooperative, jovial, easy, and a delight to be around. Others are anything but, and we often call them difficult.

Already Ours, Every Day of the Year

In order to keep our sanity, we sometimes find ourselves wanting either to pawn them off on a family member or a friend for a spell, or, if they don't belong to us, to avoid them as much as possible.

God's children are the same way. Some of us are easy, and some of us aren't. Some of us push our Heavenly Father to the maximum, almost daring Him to intervene in our lives or to prevent us from participating in behaviors detrimental to us. It matters little to the Lord, however, what kind of child we are. He loves us whether we're easy or difficult. That's one of the major differences between God and us. His love is unconditional. By and large, ours is not.

222

A COUPLE OF WEEKS AGO, I VISITED OUR DAUGHTER IN Dallas. Her eighteen-month-old daughter is enrolled in a developmental gymnastics class, and I had the privilege of watching five toddlers run through their paces. I was amazed at their attention span and their eagerness to copy what their instructor modeled for them. At the end of each child's performance, the child would throw both arms skyward and sing-song, "Ta-dah."

It didn't occur to me until I returned home and flipped on the switch to my computer that it proclaimed the same message: "Ta-dah." Needless to say, each time I hear this signal, delightful thoughts of five little girls tumbling around and scampering about to balance themselves on whatever is beneath them fill my head with glee and bring me a light chuckle. And now, each time I accomplish a task, especially one of which I didn't think I was capable, I sing to myself, "Ta-dah." And I remember the words of the prophet "and a little child shall lead them" (Isa. 11:6, KJV).

223

A SCHOOL CHUM CALLED ME RECENTLY TO CHAT. Before ending our conversation, she scolded me for not keeping in better touch with her and insisted we meet for a luncheon date in the near future. I agreed, but as the time approached for our get-together, I found one excuse after another not to do it. Presently, my days overflow with activity after activity, and I just didn't think I had the time to do this. And then epiphany came.

I really didn't have time not to go to lunch with her. If I were too busy to keep in touch with an old friend, then I was too busy and I needed to curtail and prioritize the hustle and bustle of my days. We did have lunch, and I am the better for it. I needed the giggles and light-heartedness that permeates this friendship. Be watchful of busyness. Take time to ask yourself what all the hustle and bustle in your life is about. It may be time to prioritize and rearrange life's events.

224 I OFTEN GET TO CHURCH EARLY BECAUSE I ENJOY sitting there and meditating. One Sunday, our pianist of thirty-two years entered the sanctuary, sat down at the piano, and played several bars of music over and over again. This surprised me because she is a superb musician, and it never occurred to me she would have any trouble with any part of a musical composition. And epiphany came.

Complacency and overconfidence hinders any work or performance. I reminded myself that if she, first-rate musician that she is, agonized over several bars of music, then there is a need for all of us to emulate her in this regard. I left services that morning with a renewed commitment to any task at hand, reminding myself of my grandmother's words: "Anything worth doing is worth doing well."

225 THAT SAME SUNDAY MORNING, TWO MEN STOOD IN front of the podium chatting. I watched them as they laughed with one another and from time to time slapped each other's shoulders. It was obvious they enjoyed each other's company and the topic of their conversation. And then I thanked God for friendship and what joy friends bring into our lives. Reach out to a friend today and let him know your love for him.

226 SUSAN ASHTON RECORDED A SONG ENTITLED "Beyond Justice to Mercy." The words of the song convey the message that two friends have become alienated through some sort of disagreement, and one of them wants reconciliation while apparently the other does not. One of the parties agrees that they don't "see eye to eye and have let angry words flare and bitter words fly" and pleads for them to go beyond justice to mercy, saying she's chosen a path of love to get to mercy and mend the broken relationship. In the song, we're not told the outcome of the plea, but are left with the hope these two warring people will straighten out their misunderstandings and renew their friendship. Ashton sings toward the end of the song: "Though the distance seems so far, the love that used to hold our hearts wants to take us beyond justice to mercy."

Countless examples regarding unforgiveness are laid out for us in the Bible, and we witness as many in life. Yet far too many of us refuse to go the distance to reunite with another we believe has wronged us in some way, to elect to experience the love that carries us beyond justice to mercy. Perhaps it is time we pondered the wisdom of the message of this song: "It doesn't matter who's to blame." We need to move to "the place of compassion where hearts were pure and free." "A friend loveth at all times . . ." (Prov. 17:17, KJV).

227 OUR YOUNGER DAUGHTER AND I RECENTLY ATTENDED a seminar to gain continuing education credits for our licenses. We had to be at the appointed designation by eight that morning, and we had to fight rush hour traffic to get there. Her babysitter was late in arriving at her house, and this meant we would have to scramble to get to our destination on time. It soon became apparent to us that we wouldn't make it on time. Our daughter knows my feelings regarding being late for any event. I don't like it and I avoid it at all costs. She glanced my way, apparently to check my reactions to the goings-on, repeating over and over again, "I'm sorry, I didn't mean to make us late."

"It's okay," I assured her. "Quit worrying. It's a done deal."

She gave me a look that I thought said, "Is this my mother?"

I smiled, feeling quite smug. It was indeed a done deal, but it had taken me years to realize it. All my rushing around and my insistence that I was late if I wasn't early for an event was a thing of the past. I am learning not to sweat the small stuff, and it's all small stuff. What good does it do to ruminate and agonize over something that can't be undone?

228 MY HUSBAND MADE AN APPOINTMENT FOR US TO SEE our accountant, who lives quite a distance from us, one evening after hours. When we completed our business, I left the accountant's office without my purse. Fortunately I realized this before getting on the freeway for home. Unfortunately, our accountant left and locked his office when we left, and I knew he lived about ten miles out of town and perhaps wasn't even going home afterward. I could have begun to stew about my carelessness and the trouble it caused, but I didn't. As I dialed the accountant's home telephone number, I told myself, "It's a done deal. Don't sweat the small stuff, and this, my dear, is small stuff." As it turned out, the accountant's wife took my message and sent him back to town to retrieve my purse.

All's well that ends well.

229 THERE WAS A TIME IN THE STATE OF TEXAS THAT SOME of our highway signs folded down on themselves so that when what they warned of was imminent, a highway crew could ride around and unfold the signs displaying their message. Nowadays these signs are not folded over on themselves. They remain opened year round. So it is with some humor while driving down the highway on a hot summer day, I read aloud, "Ice On Bridge."

"Yeah. Right," I say, "and the island of Manhattan's for sale too." I wonder what is the point of such a sign anyway? If it's up all year, then it's basically up to individual drivers to decide weather conditions for themselves.

And then I thank God because His signs for us are forever open and visible for anyone who will look and see. I thank Him for His clear and direct words in what He says to us and what He asks of us, and I thank Him for walking along beside us so that we are never in the dark or unclear about what to do at any given moment. A state's resources may be limited, but God's never are.

230 TEXAS ALSO HAS TRAFFIC SIGNS THAT ADMONISH, Slower Traffic Keep Right. By and large, Texans know what the signs mean: if you don't go with the flow, then move over and let the flow pass.

I often wonder if such signs were posted in churches, the congregations would move forward more effectively. I've never known a congregation yet where all its members were in synch and moved at the same pace. I've seen churches split over issues where two groups squared against each other, both proclaiming the right of way.

There are times when I'm in the slower lane of Texas traffic, and there are other times when I'm in the fast lane. It all depends on where I'm going. Would that we in our churches adopted the same rule: if you don't go with the flow, then move over and let the flow pass. Everybody will get to their destination.

231 Recently I approached a construction area on the interstate. It was dusk and difficult to see well. A red sports utility vehicle whizzed pass me on my right and cut in front of me in order to beat me into the left lane where traffic had been diverted. At first the driver's actions annoyed me. I wanted to give him a tongue-lashing for his irresponsible and dangerous actions. And then I realized a truth. We were the only vehicles heading west on the highway. His taillights enabled me more clearly to distinguish the highway markings of the construction work ahead. All I now had to do was follow his lead. I no longer thought him an inconsiderate driver but one sent by God to guide me along the way. How we choose to look at a matter is important.

232 Recently while driving along the highway, I passed a lady in the front yard of a rural home. She bent over to retrieve something or other on the ground, and as she did so the posterior end of her body loomed skyward. It was an uncomplimentary pose and one I'm quite sure would have been embarrassing to her had she realized what she looked like. Immediately I glanced the other way, granting her a privacy she didn't even know she needed.

A moment of insight occurred for me: how many times have I engaged in embarrassing behaviors and not been aware of it? How many times have I been observed doing something I wouldn't have done had I known onlookers were present? We never know who is watching us or listening to us. We don't know who looks to us for guidance. We forever model behaviors for the world to emulate.

It doesn't matter if we're conscious of it or not. Everyone is an example to someone.

233 CHILDREN ARE PRECIOUS CREATURES. THEY ARE indeed gifts from God. Few of us don't like being around them. Watching them at play is a pleasure, for it brings to mind that which once belonged to us and dwelt in us and caused us to see everything as new and fascinating and fun. Time can snatch these things from us if we let it. Circumstances can make us cynical and bitter if we let them. We can never return to childhood, but we can allow ourselves to be silly and funny and forever curious.

Find a child today. Let yourself explore his or her world with him or her. Laugh. Be silly. Ask dumb questions. This is what children do, and this is what makes them so precious to us.

234 I'VE OFTEN HEARD THE EXPRESSION "POINT OF NO return" but never really understood it until I flew across the Pacific Ocean. There is a spot on the ocean that marks the point where going back to a previous land destination is as far as proceeding on to the land destination ahead. Being in that spot was an odd feeling for me because I knew I had nowhere to go but forward. And then I understood that all points in life are points of no return. At any given moment, all any of us can do is go forward.

Once a moment is gone, it is gone. I need to live each moment to its fullest and extract from it all there is in it. It will never return again, and the only reasonable thing to do is experience it fully and then move on to the next moment.

235 A CAPPELLA SINGING FASCINATES ME AND CAPTURES MY attention. Voices united in harmony soothe my spirit and warm my heart. "It is like the precious ointment upon the head, that ran down upon the beard, even Aaron's beard: that went down to the skirts of his garments" (Ps. 133:2, KJV). Like so, "how good and how pleasant it is for brethren to dwell together in unity!" (Ps. 133:1, KJV). Unity of voice—singing different parts, yes, but singing in unity.

Already Ours, Every Day of the Year

236 I CANNOT COUNT THE TIMES IN LIFE WHEN ADVERSITY has come knocking at my door and a Bible verse or a portion of one of them has popped into my head, bringing with it encouragement, help and comfort. Even in my youth when I didn't know many Bible verses at all, the one that I did know sustained me: "I can do all things through Christ which strengtheneth me" (Phil. 4:13, KJV). I memorized those ten words the only time I ever went to Vacation Bible School, and those ten words kept me and stood between me and the world until I began to collect and hide God's word in my heart.

237 QUITE FREQUENTLY I ARRIVE AT CHURCH BEFORE others, sit in the sanctuary, and read from Scripture or study the stained glass windows and meditate. During this time, the two men in charge of our sound system busy themselves with checking the microphones, often whispering into them, "Testing. One, two, three. Test. Test." One Sunday, the younger of the two men was on the podium and going through his routine of testing the microphones. I looked up at him and said in jest, "When you're in church you're supposed to say, 'Hallelujah,' not 'Test.'" He grinned and whispered, "Hallelujah" into the microphone.

Recently, I sat in my pew before the congregation gathered, and once again the young man went into his routine at the main microphone. Then he reached over to touch another microphone on stage, which I supposed to be for the soloist scheduled for the morning services. He quickly jerked his hand from the mike, looked to his partner in the balcony and exclaimed, "It shocked me."

I glanced his way and quipped, "That's because you didn't say 'Hallelujah.'"

He seemed somewhat embarrassed, but he snickered, briefly glanced my way, and then left the podium. That night during evening services, we sang the song, "I Will Celebrate," which has a verse of nothing but hallelujahs, and also the chorus, "Hallelujah." Afterward, our pastor explained that hallelujah means "praise ye Yah(weh)" or "praise ye the Lord." I don't think I will ever hear the words, "Testing. One, two, three. Test, test," without thinking "Hallelujah, praise ye the Lord." And in my heart I thank this young man for this magnificent gift.

238 GONE ARE THE DAYS WHEN PRIVACY REIGNED. TODAY, out of necessity, video cameras are everywhere, tracking, it seems, our every move. They record bank transactions, fast food purchases, and gasoline fill-ups, and they monitor us throughout department stores and even track our vehicles through street intersections. Some record us at our work places, and through them we can keep track of our children at their day care centers and as they ride their buses to school. If we're stopped for a traffic violation, the camera is on, taking it all in. Even private moments are sometimes captured by people who don't know us and whom we don't know, people who videotape any and everything that crosses their paths. Some of us have made our television debut on such programs as *Candid Camera* or the evening news. The camera is on us and it is rolling, and yet many of us don't act like we know it.

"Be careful how you act; these are difficult days. Do not be foolish; be wise: make the most of every opportunity you have for doing good" (Eph. 5:17–18, RSV). The apostle Paul proclaimed this admonition over two thousand years ago, and yet we remain foolish, not taking every opportunity we have for doing good—we, who are not only watched but recorded, it seems, every step of our way. Perhaps this is what Paul meant when he wrote, "Redeeming the time . . ." (Eph. 5:16a, KJV). And perhaps this is what Moses had in mind when he said, "So teach us to number our days, that we may apply our hearts unto wisdom" (Ps. 90:12, KJV).

239 MY HUSBAND AND I THOUGHT OUR THREE ADULT children were settled in homes of their choices and in towns of their choices, but now, it seems, two of them might have to move due to job changes. All three now live within a three-hour drive of us, and we'd like to keep it this way, but life is not always so easy. Life isn't always the way we want it to be or how we want it to be. Life changes, and as it does, loss often follows in its wake.

My first reaction to the news was to fall to my knees and implore the Lord to keep our children living exactly where they are, but my second reaction was to ask God to lead them to make wise choices and, as He did so, to give them the good sense and presence of mind to follow His directives.

Already Ours, Every Day of the Year

And then that adventuresome part of me found its way to the top of my consciousness, and I reveled in thoughts of visiting new and exciting places as my husband and I beat paths to the children's new doorsteps. Life is an adventure, but sometimes we mess up God's enterprises for us by trying to twist His arm, imploring Him to give us something other than the magnificent gift He already has for us and instead replace it with a trinket or two. For a child of God, life is forever served on a silver platter, one void of Godly trinkets. It is we, His children, who don't see the silver because too often our eyes are clouded with faithlessness, doubt and fear, and a desire to experience life on our own terms.

240 It's tough to lose a leader, especially if you're the one who is replacing the leader. After the death of Moses, God elected Joshua to take Moses' place. God instructed Joshua to cross the Jordan River and to take the land there. God told Joshua that every place on which the sole of his foot walked was land given to the Israelites by Him, and it was up to Joshua to take the land for them. After marking off the boundaries of the Promised Land for Joshua, God told him no man would be able to stand before him, and as He had walked with Moses, so too would He walk with Joshua. And then God said, "I will not fail thee, nor forsake thee. Be strong and of a good courage: for unto this people shalt thou divide for an inheritance the land, which I sware unto their fathers to give them. Have not I commanded thee? Be strong and of a good courage; be not afraid, neither be thou dismayed: for the Lord thy God is with thee whithersoever thou goest" (Josh. 1:5b–6, 9, KJV).

Joshua then instructed the people to cross the Jordan River, and then addressed the Reubenites, the Gadites, and half the tribe of Manasseh in particular, telling them they along with their wives, children, and cattle would remain on this side of Jordan, and their men would help the other nine-and-one-half tribes take their own land on the other side of Jordan. Their response was, "All that thou commandest us we will do, and whithersoever thou sendest us, we will go" (Josh. 1:16, KJV). They ended their discourse with Joshua emphasizing God's previous words to Joshua: "only be strong and of a good courage" (Josh. 1:18b, KJV).

God told Joshua to be courageous and to be strong. The men in two-and-one-half tribes of Israel repeated God's command to Joshua. It doesn't matter whether we're chosen to lead or we're chosen to follow. All of us need strength and courage. As God did not fail Joshua or the Israelites or forsake them, He will not fail us or forsake us either. Go with God, and he will go with you. Don't be afraid and don't be dismayed.

241 THE OPEN BIBLE TELLS US THAT UNDER THE LEADERSHIP of Joshua, God's people engaged in three major military campaigns that involved more than thirty enemy armies. The Open Bible goes on to tell us that the people learned that "victory comes through faith in God and obedience to His word, rather than through military might or numerical superiority." It is faith in God and obedience to His word and His commands that take any of us to victory. It doesn't matter the battle we are in or the people who oppose us. It doesn't matter how long we struggle and fight. It doesn't matter how many people strike out against us. What does matter is faith in God and obedience to His word. If our swords drop to the ground and the enemy threatens to engulf us, faith in God and obedience to His word will rescue us—every time. God never fails. It is we who fail ourselves through our own lack of faith and our disobedience to God.

242 BEFORE CROSSING THE JORDAN RIVER, JOSHUA SENT two men to secretly spy on the people who lived on the other side of Jordan. Once there, the men went to a harlot's house, a woman by the name of Rahab. She took the spies in and protected them from the king of Jericho, who had been told the men were at her house. Rahab hid the spies among stalks of flax on her roof and then lied to the king, telling him the men had come and gone. The reputation of the Israelites had spread far and wide, for Rahab told the spies she knew that the Lord had given their land to them and that she, along with many others, feared them because they'd heard how the Lord had dried up the water as they crossed the Red Sea. She went on to tell the men that she'd also heard what the Israelites had done to the two kings of the Amorites, and because of everything her people had heard, their hearts melted and they were without courage. Rahab then made the men promise when the Israelites invaded their land that they would show kindness to her father's house and not kill her father or mother or brothers or sisters. The men agreed to her bargain.

Why did the spies choose a harlot's house for refuge? Why Rahab's house? It could have been because her house was on the town wall and escape from it would have been easier if the men had been seen or chased. But I rather think it was because Rahab was a harlot. Of all the places in Jericho the men could have sought refuge, a prostitute's house would have been one of the safest ones. After all, men who visited this house probably weren't too eager to discuss it or the goings-on there with friends and neighbors.

And this particular prostitute was savvy. Apparently she'd figured out who the spies were and had taken seriously the stories she'd been told about the Israelites. Thank goodness these two spies weren't judgmental creatures. Praise God, they looked past Rahab's reputation and into her heart, a heart willing to take a chance on the truth she'd heard about God's people, a heart willing to go out on a limb for two foreigners.

This Bible story urges me to search my own heart regarding judgments I might make on others. May I, Lord, as did these two spies, look at what is on the inside of another rather than focusing on what I think the outside represents.

243 WE SOMETIMES WONDER IF GOD IS WITH US, LEADING us every step of the way. Seemingly insurmountable barriers and obstacles snarl our paths, and one after another circumstances threaten us with defeat, but God is with us making the crooked places straight and taking pebbles from beneath our feet so that we might trudge ahead with strength and courage, just as did His people when He led them out of Egypt and into His Promised Land. When we belong to God, we are never alone and we are never defenseless.

244 THE TIME CAME FOR THE ISRAELITES TO MOVE NOT only into the land God had promised them, but to move away from dependence on manna, the bread God provided for them in their wilderness wanderings. They moved away from manna from heaven to the fruit of the land of Canaan. They were to stay put in the land in which God put them. They no longer needed miracle food. The land God gave them would now sustain their lives. It really didn't matter whether God rained the food from heaven or provided it from the ground, it was sufficient for the day. God's grace is always sufficient—for yesterday, today, and tomorrow. His grace is sufficient for any day of any year.

245 Shortly after celebrating Passover while encamped in Gilgal, Joshua was by Jericho, and he looked up and spied a man with a drawn sword in his hand. He asked the man, "Art thou for us, or for our adversaries?" (Josh. 5:13, KJV).

The man replied, "Nay; but as captain of the host of the Lord am I now come."

Joshua fell on his face to the ground worshipping and said, "What saith my lord unto his servant?"

The captain of the Lord's host said, "Loose thy shoe from off thy foot; for the place whereon thou standest is holy" (Josh. 5:15, KJV).

Joshua obeyed. These verses of Scripture always remind me of the gospel song about standing on holy ground, the one with angels all around. And I am awed when I read these words, and I wonder how many times I have stood on holy ground and was unaware of it. I pray God will open my eyes so that I can see the majestic acts He performs on my behalf, but I know that I can only snatch a glimmer of God's holiness, because His essence is awe-inspiring and overwhelming and for me to see more than I already see at any given moment would be too much for me to see or to know.

246 I could read about Joshua's victory at Jericho time and again without ever tiring of it. My anticipation of the event reaches a fever pitch when I read, "And it came to pass on the seventh day, that they rose early about the dawning of the day, and compassed the city after the same manner seven times: only on that day they compassed the city seven times.

Already Ours, Every Day of the Year

And it came to pass at the seventh time, when the priests blew with the trumpets, Joshua said unto the people, 'Shout; for the Lord hath given you the city.' So the people shouted when the priests blew with the trumpets: and it came to pass, when the people heard the sound of the trumpet, and the people shouted with a great shout, that the wall fell down flat, so that the people went up into the city, every man straight before him, and they took the city. So the Lord was with Joshua; and his fame was noised throughout all the country" (Josh. 6:15–16, 20, 27, KJV).

Yes, God was with Joshua, a man of strength and courage. And the walls of Jericho came tumbling down just like the walls that imprison us will come tumbling down as we lean on God, trust His word, and follow Him where He leads us.

247

Do you remember Zacharias? He was a priest and his wife was named Elisabeth. They were a Godly couple who lived at the time of Jesus' birth. They had no children, for Elisabeth was barren, and both Zacharias and Elisabeth were well past the age for bearing children and had no hope for having them.

One day while serving in the temple of the Lord, an angel appeared to Zacharias, and when Zacharias fell prostrate on the floor from fear, the angel said, "Fear not, Zacharias: for thy prayer is heard; and thy wife Elisabeth shall bear thee a son, and thou shalt call his name John. And thou shalt have joy and gladness; and many shall rejoice at his birth. For he shall be great in the sight of the Lord, and shall drink neither wine nor strong drink; and he shall be filled with the Holy Ghost, even from his mother's womb. And many of the children of Israel shall he turn to the Lord their God. And he shall go before him in the spirit and power of Elias to turn the hearts of the fathers to the children, and disobedient to the wisdom of the just; to make ready a people prepared for the Lord" (Luke 1:11–17, KJV).

One would have thought this old priest would have danced for joy at such tremendous news, but Zacharias said to the angel, "Whereby shall I know this? for I am an old man, and my wife well stricken in years" (Luke 1:18, KJV).

Imagine being the recipient of such a glorious message, but in essence, Zacharias's reply to the angel was not unlike words that might come from my own mouth or perhaps even yours: "Prove it."

Search our hearts for skepticism, O Lord. Cleanse us from disbelief. Create in us a new heart and a new mind, one willing to trust and obey You and to follow wherever You lead.

248 I RECENTLY GOT A LETTER FROM AN AUNT, ONE OF MY mother's sisters. She is only nine years older than I, but I've always thought of her as being much older because she's always acted older. As I was growing up, I remember her being a terrific storyteller weaving fascinating yarns—stories that kept me on the edge of my seat, ones filled with suspense and speculation about where they would end and how they would take up from where they had left off. I never tired of hearing them, and apparently she never tired of telling them.

Her letter brought this memory to mind because in it she wrote about her daughter and son-in-law's efforts to rescue a Guatemalan orphan girl through adoption. The couple were on a work-trip in Guatemala and visited an orphanage there and found the baby. The Guatemalan baby already had a name—the exact name of my only niece, whose middle name is my mother's name. I couldn't believe my aunt's words. Were she spinning another tale, it couldn't have been more fascinating and almost unbelievable.

My cousin and her husband went on a work mission to Guatemala and came back with papers for adopting a baby girl, a girl already bearing the exact name of my only niece, one named after my mother. Coincidence? I don't think so. I rather think that my cousin and her husband were led to this baby by God, and that this child is destined to become a part of our family. I'm so glad God led my cousin and her husband to this baby, and I'm so grateful my cousin decided to keep the baby's name as it now is, only changing her family name.

249 MY HUSBAND IS A FRUGAL PERSON. HE GREW UP hearing, "Waste not, want not." It is extremely difficult for him not to make use of every scrap of paper, every vestige of a drop of liquid remaining in any kind of a bottle, any remains of food on a plate, or anything that he figures still might have

Already Ours, Every Day of the Year

use to it. His frugality is often annoying—that is, until I also take note of and absorb his generosity. He is a man willing to work long hours to provide for his family, and he is a man who I know would actually lay down his life for me or for his children or grandchildren. He rains words of love and affection on those charged to his care, and he follows through with actions to suit his words.

Yes, my husband is frugal, but he is frugal in the truest sense of the word. He is self-denying and self-sacrificing and willing to use himself up for the benefit of those whom he loves.

250 I TALKED WITH MY AUNT ON THE TELEPHONE RECENTLY and we discussed events occurring in my childhood, stories I'd never heard before and ones that not only were enlightening but also puzzling. She related the tale of my parents living in a downtown hotel on Peachtree Street in Atlanta, Georgia, telling me I probably didn't remember this because I was only three or four years old. She related how on a Sunday morning she used to load up an old red wagon with the top part of a child's chair, a chair with missing legs, and head out from Grandma's house for downtown Atlanta to get me and my brother. Once at the hotel, she'd load my brother in the chair-wagon and place me in the wagon in front of him and then pull us both to the nearest church. She was only twelve or thirteen at the time. When church services were over, she'd haul us back to the hotel.

Her story prompted me to ask her why our family never attended church services. She never got around to answering my question, and I figured she didn't know, or she did know and didn't want to talk about it. And then I realized a truth: my family might not have attended worship services and instructed the children of the family in religious matters, but God intervened. He placed a desire in the heart of an adolescent girl to do what she could to provide what religious training she could to a niece and nephew, children only eight and nine years younger than herself. Even though I have no memory of this, the Lord and my aunt do. And I thank God for this aunt and her intercessory prayers, not only for me and my brother, but for all of her family members as well.

Betty McCutchan

251 AT THE OUTBREAK OF WORLD WAR II, I WAS BARELY ten years old. That year my uncle, who was an officer in the army, lived close to Grandma's house. His first child was born shortly after the war began, and I remember thinking how sad it was for the baby that she had to come into a world filled with such hatred and strife. I feared for all of us, but especially for this innocent baby, one who didn't get asked to be born into such a world. And I prayed for her safety. All that seemed to matter to me was her safety.

After recently talking with my aunt, I now understand why she went to such lengths to help my brother and me and why she spent so many years praying for her family. We are family and we are tied by a bond of blood. Some of us are weak and some of us are strong. It is up to those of us who can to reach down and pull those of us who can't upward, ever upward, helping them to be all it is that they can be. This is one of the reasons God placed us in families. Reach out to your family today. Lend a helping hand to the one who is not as strong as you are.

252 I LIKE LOOKING THROUGH OLD FAMILY PICTURES. I have some of my mother when she was a teenager, when fashions were quite different than they are today. Mother's hair was bobbed, and in many of the snapshots she wore frilly dresses that reached almost to the floor. In some of the pictures, she has a ladies' hat on her head, and I get the impression from the expression on her face that she is quite pleased with how she looks and how she's dressed.

And then I come across pictures of me as I was growing up. In some of them, I too carry a facial expression that clearly indicates I am pleased with myself. This is the way fashion is. It comes and it goes, and what is in at a particular time might seem rather peculiar, if not garish, at another time. But when a particular fashion is in, it's in, and most of the time we don't see it for what it really is until it's out.

Life is the same way. Situations come and go. When we're experiencing one set of circumstances, we believe at the time that they are the best circumstances we could possibly encounter. And then something new and

Already Ours, Every Day of the Year

better comes along, and we look back on the situation, realizing it really wasn't all that grand and glorious after all. And we move on, but as we do so we come to know that all things work together for our good as we are called by God according to His purpose (Rom. 8:28). Any place we are in at any given moment and any circumstance we experience at any given time is at our disposal for our use. Regardless of how we use it or look at it, God takes it and works it together for our good. Most of the time, we don't apprehend the meaning of a moment until it's no longer there. We seem to understand a moment more clearly, what it really is, and the impact it has had on our lives once the moment is gone and we can no longer reach it. Nevertheless, God takes it and works it together for our good. What blessed gifts He bestows on us.

253 Hardly a day goes by when we don't hear of or read about some tragedy. Tornadoes tear through an area, leaving destruction in their wakes. Floods devour houses and land. Airplanes crash. Fires destroy property. People take leave of their senses, thinking nothing of taking the lives of innocent people. Freak accidents happen. Gas leaks occur and tanks blow up. Terrorists threaten to destroy that which they cannot control. Event after event happens and is recorded for us and proclaimed to us. We can't escape the sufferings in the world.

But those of us who belong to Him know that "the sufferings of this present time are not worthy to be compared with the glory which shall be revealed in us" (Rom. 8:18, KJV) and that every creature suffers. But "if God be for us, who can be against us?" (Rom. 8:31, KJV). Nothing can separate us from the love of Christ. No troubles, no distresses, no persecutions, or famine or war. Not even death. Nothing can separate us from "the love of God, which is in Christ Jesus our Lord" (Rom. l8:39, KJV).

So let the winds blow and the fires come and the floods boil. When tragic events occur, we will not be afraid, for nothing can separate those of us who belong to God from His love. As children of God, we are heirs of Christ, and as His heirs we understand "the sufferings of this present time are not worthy to be compared with the glory which shall be revealed in us." What a wonderful message to hear. What a wonderful message to proclaim. What a fantastic position to be in.

254 MOST OF US LIVE BUSY LIVES. WE HAVE DUTIES AND responsibilities to ourselves and to our families. Activities fill our schedules. No sooner do we complete a chore than another one seems to surface, demanding our attention. American families flit helter-skelter about, seeking to cram twenty-eight or more hours of activity into the twenty-four allotted to us each day. There seems to be little or no time to invest in any activity other than what is absolutely essential. Too often friends and their needs get swept aside.

But what about the apostle Paul's admonition to us to "Rejoice with them that do rejoice, and weep with them that weep" (Rom. 12:15, KJV)? Who has time to do this? If we are too busy to hear a friend's good news or share a moment of their sorrow, then perhaps we're too busy. Paul also wrote, "And whether one member suffer, all the members suffer with it; or one member be honoured, all the members rejoice with it" (1 Cor. 12:26, KJV). We who belong to Christ are in the same boat together. We need each other. God put us in the church, the same entity he often refers to as the Body of Christ, because we need each other. We complement each other. We need to rejoice with others in their good news, and we need to stand by those who are in sorrow. Perhaps we could juggle our schedules more efficiently if we stepped back from them and asked ourselves where it is we're going. Perhaps if we grasped that if we were to get everything there is to get in life, and in the getting of it we neglect to love others, then in reality what we've gained is really nothing of value at all. Of all God's spiritual gifts, the greatest of them is love (1 Cor. 13:13).

255 RECENTLY, I HEARD THE ROAR OF WHAT I PERCEIVED to be a piece of heavy-duty highway equipment outside the window of my home. I groaned. One of those familiar orange working-on-the-road signs rested two hundred feet away at the end of my driveway. I remembered reading several years ago that by the turn of the century the state of Texas would be converting the two-lane highway that runs in front of my house into a four-lane highway. The turn of the century is almost here, and I'm definitely not ready for tar and mud and warning signs and uneven

Already Ours, Every Day of the Year

entrances into and out of my driveway. And I'm not ready to relinquish fifteen or more feet of my front yard. But my wishes are unimportant to our highway department. Plans have been formulated, and the time is approaching for them to be implemented.

Looking back on it, I now wish we had put our house further back from the road, and we could have had we known the road would be widened some day. In this regard, we just didn't plan well enough for the future. I am beginning to understand why I see those For Sale signs in front of houses where road work is in progress. Getting down such a road on any given work day is a chore, it's often messy, and the construction seems to last forever.

But roadwork, like everything else in life, eventually comes to an end. Former landscapes dim and recede from memory, and soon we forget what our environment used to look like. We accept what now is, and we move onward. This is not too unlike a grieving process. Grief ushers its way into our lives, suddenly, with a roar. We figure somewhere along the line, mourning will make a pitch for us and usually we don't think about it until loss rears its ugly head. By and large we don't plan for it. When loss comes, we trudge a path through the pain and anguish it brings, and finally, if we're diligent enough and determined enough to work through our pain, resolution makes a bid for our attention. Our environments are forever changed, and sometimes we forget how beautiful life was before sorrow headed our way. Just like roadwork seems to last forever, so too does our heavy heart when it hovers over us. Heaviness eventually gives way to lightness, our sadness comes to an end, and we go on. I don't look forward to what is about to happen on the road in front of my house, and I certainly don't look forward to a future loss requiring energy directed toward resolving that loss, but I no longer dread either state. This too shall pass. And I will move on in life, and I will do it with joy in my heart.

256 Last Sunday morning a teenager sang a solo presentation during church services. She sang, "Jesus Will Still be There." I'd never heard this particular melody before. She looked like she knew what she was talking about when she sang, "When it looks like you've lost it all,

Jesus will still be there." And then later on, a choir member sang a solo part in a choral prayer presentation, "Jesus, We're Depending on You." This lady really got into the musical message as she proclaimed, "Jesus, we're depending on You to see us through." The first soloist looked like she hadn't experienced enough of life to know that even when it looks like we've lost everything, Jesus is there for us. The second soloist was old enough to have walked a ways with the Lord, and she proclaimed that we can depend on Jesus regardless of what happens to us. Two generations, both announcing the same message. No matter what happens to us, Jesus is there for us. No matter what happens to us, we can depend on Jesus to see us through it. Wisdom comes in all kinds of packages—some small, some large, some new to the faith, some old to the faith, some who look like they're still wet behind the ears, and some who look no worse for the wear. God speaks to us through the young and not-so-young alike. And we are blessed by them all.

257 SUFFERING SURROUNDS US. IT IS EVERYWHERE. IT IS A part of being human. We accept it as being part of life, and yet as God's children we somehow expect God to deliver us from the universality of pain and suffering and the uphill climb. Sometimes we convince ourselves that once we belong to God, our roads will be smooth, straight, and plain. Rocks and crags will not encumber our daily lives, or so we believe. We reason that Christians should be spared needless anguish and pain, and as far as we are concerned, we don't need it.

If God removed the unpleasant circumstances in our lives that usher in sorrow and misery and woe, then we would be unable to grow into the image of Christ. God would hinder His own work in us. God is our heavenly Father and, as such, wills and works in our lives to bring us into the image of Jesus Christ. In God's work in us, however, he always prepares a way for us—a path of deliverance. God rescues us from all our troubles. Everyone of them.

No one goes without experiencing hard times. No one escapes suffering. Christians suffer just like the rest of mankind suffers, but God's children are never alone in their sufferings like the rest of

Already Ours, Every Day of the Year

mankind are. God is in our midst watching over us, taking care of us, and encouraging us. When the dark clouds of trouble appear on the horizon, we look upward to God who is always there for us. He takes us into His loving arms, wipes away our tears, and soothes our spirits. God loves us, and He watches over us because He cares about us.

"Many are the afflictions of the righteous: but the Lord delivereth him out of them all" (Ps. 34:19, KJV).

258 ONE OF THE THINGS I LIKE ABOUT BRANSON, Missouri, besides the shows, mountains, and sights in nature is talking with the people who work in the restaurants, motels, and theaters, as well as those on vacation. I usually engage these people in conversations, coming away from such encounters richer for it. Many of these people are retired and bring memories of their past lives and careers with them. Most of the workers are very good at their jobs, very dedicated to them. They're also kind and eager to please.

One such lady, not of retirement age, helped me find an excellent seat for one of Shoji Tabouche's shows. He's one of my favorite performers in Branson, and getting a good seat at one of his shows isn't always an easy task, especially if you haven't reserved a ticket before getting there. Eager to help me, she instructed me to sit down in the theater lobby and told me she would call me to the ticket area once a cancellation for the show's seating came in. I sat where I could see her, and from time to time noticed her looking my way, smiling and winking, urging me to hang in there. Finally, she motioned for me to come to her, and I did. My husband and I got wonderful seats. As she produced the tickets and I paid for them, we talked. I also talked with our usher, a lady in her senior years. And I talked with the people sitting on each side of us and behind us—all retired. The more I talked with these people, the richer I became. Each one left a part of himself or herself with me—a part of his or her wisdom.

People will respond to us and interact with us if we give them a chance to do so, especially the people in Branson, Missouri. The town has few traffic lights, but drivers from all over the United States yield to those wanting to gain entry into a line of traffic. I always leave there wanting to take the gentle spirit of Branson with me, but alas, this city is unique. I don't know what makes it so, other than so many retired people either live there or work there or visit there. Perhaps we mellow as we age, and as we do so, it rubs off on those who are younger. Each place we encounter in life has a spirit about it. Branson's spirit is refreshing, and in it I take hope in America regaining her spirit of neighborliness, kindness, and a willingness to help those who cross our paths.

259

From my earliest years, I remember having a difficult time parting from a house, a school, friends, or a place. My family moved often as I was growing up, and I spent hours longing for a previous residence. I also had to change schools often, and I yearned for each schoolhouse that no longer was a part of my life. I missed old school chums who didn't make the transition with me. I've only lived in five different cities or towns in my lifetime, but when I had to bid adieu to one of them in order to embrace another of them, I often felt my heart would break, and I visited my old haunts back in previous cities and towns as frequently as possible.

Looking back over the events of my life, I sort of figured out that my inability to roll with the punches in this regard probably had its origins in my father's sudden disappearance from my life. My parents divorced when I was four. I have only one memory of their life together and it is a faint one. I can count on my hands the number of times I saw my father after that and have fingers left over.

It's only been in recent years that I've been able to leave places and people without looking back and longing for what was and no longer is. It was when I finally understood that God is my heavenly father—the One who walks along beside me every step of the way, the One who loves me even when I'm unlovable, the One who accepts me the way I am, the One who is pleased with me even when I'm not pleased with myself, the One who died for me—that everything began to fall in place for me regarding this aspect of my life.

I no longer have problems with leaving old haunts or old friends from other places and old times. And this is an absolutely astounding and

Already Ours, Every Day of the Year

wonderful blessing as I hear that small, silent voice of God saying, "You are home, my child. No matter who leaves you, no matter where the roads in life take you, I am with you as I've always been with you. My peace I leave with you." And I cry with joy as I realize what this kind of peace feels like and that it has finally come for me.

260 THIS MORNING I REACHED FOR A BANANA TO PEEL AND slice for my cereal. It was a healthy looking banana, but when I peeled it, the bottom third of it was inedible. Apparently that part of the fruit had been injured because it was bruised so badly that I ended up having to throw that part of it away. No one would have guessed by looking at the banana that it wasn't whole and what it seemed to be. It took exposing the fruit to see the condition of the fruit. Its exterior revealed nothing of what was inside it. Even if I had known the banana had been treated roughly and was damaged, I would never have guessed a part of it was inedible.

Those around us don't know what's inside of us either—unless we tell them. Many times we don't bother to do this. Onlookers might know of our emotional or physical injuries, but from all outward appearances, we look okay to them. For reasons perhaps we don't even understand ourselves, we sometimes prefer to suffer in silence, and after having done so, become hurt or agitated or even angry that no one seems to care what is happening or has happened to us. Bad experiences through our openness with others might have taught us it's useless to let others know what's going on inside us. Few people haven't been let down by someone along this line, and many people suffer, giving no outward manifestation of it.

God's children aren't bananas. We're brothers and sisters in Christ. God places us in His church together, expecting us to exhort, uplift, encourage, help, heal, love, and take care of one another. When we've been hurt, it's beneficial to share our pain with someone. It's healing to talk and to know that someone is willing to listen to us without judging us or hitting us over the head with the Bible or ramming advice down our throats.

So what if we've gone this route before and been rejected or even worse—hurt more deeply? Keep searching for that someone with whom you can share your pain. Someone is there but likely won't fall into your lap unless you prepare a way or open a door. Someone will listen to you and extend a helping hand if you keep searching for someone to listen. If no one comes, remember God is ever present in you and is always there for you. Perhaps God might allow human help to bypass you and instead have His Spirit minister directly to you so that He can teach you how to minister to others when the time comes for you to be there for them.

261 In recent months my husband and I have taken a notion to motor to a nearby city to have dinner at the end of several of the week's workdays. It's not that we enjoy eating out, because we usually end up at the same restaurant, eating pretty much the same foods. It's the time spent with each other going there and coming back that intrigues us. We enjoy each other's company—just being together, whether we're talking or not. We could do the same thing at home, too, but we don't because too many chores or obligations or activities intrude, demanding our attention. It is these excursions where we can do nothing else but sit side by side, reveling in the essence of the other, that gives us this opportunity.

The same principle applies to our time alone with God. If we don't figure out a way that we can commune with Him without interruptions, then the demands of our busy schedules will rob us of much needed time in His company—together time that bonds us to Him and enables us to make it through a day.

We might not be able to hop into an automobile, set its cruise control, and head in a certain direction with our Lord, but we can withdraw from the ringing of a telephone, the hum of a running washing machine or dishwasher, distant sounds of a television set no one is watching, or the other distractions home brings our way. In our minds, we can withdraw to our own private place around the house or outside of it, wherever that happens to be, telling those who occupy that house with us that we are traveling with the Lord and we have much to discuss with Him and we'll get back with them once our visit is over. Nothing is like taking in the essence of someone we love, and nothing is like being in God's presence and communing with Him.

Already Ours, Every Day of the Year

262 OBEDIENCE TO GOD IS OF VITAL IMPORTANCE. IT always has been and it always will be. Yet, many of us act as if obeying and adhering to His principles is optional. And it is. This is the way it always has been and the way it always will be. In the book of Judges, we read about the failure of Judah, the failure of Benjamin, the failure of the tribes of Joseph, the failure of Zebulun, the failure of Asher, the failure of Nephtali, and the failure of Dan in obeying God. Yet, when they and when any of us make a decision to go our own way and do our own thing, not only do we suffer for it, but the generations that follow us also suffer.

As their heavenly Father, God commanded the Israelites to destroy the people who inhabited the Promised Land into which He was leading them. God knew the Israelites couldn't withstand the pagan ways of the Canaanites, and if they allowed these pagans to coexist with them in the land, they would succumb to their idolatry. Obedience was optional for them and it is optional for us, but disobedience comes with a hefty price tag and it is costly. The generation of those who left their wilderness wanderings to go in to possess the Promised Land finally died out without doing what God had told them to do—take the land and inhabit it, driving out the people who lived in it.

The tribe of Benjamin didn't drive out the Jebusites, the tribes of Joseph didn't drive out the inhabitants of Bethshean or Dor or Ibleam or Megiddo, and Ephraim didn't drive out the Canaanites and on and on. Down the line, each tribe disobeyed and then "there arose another generation after them, which knew not the Lord, yet the works which he had done for Israel. And the children of Israel did evil in the sight of the Lord, and served Baalim. And they forsook the Lord God of their fathers, which brought them out of the land of Egypt, and followed other gods, of the gods of the people that were round about them, and bowed themselves unto them, and provoked the Lord to anger. And they forsook the Lord, and served Baal and Ashtaroth" (Judg. 2:10–13, KJV).

Obeying God is of vital importance not only to us but to the generations that follow us. Adhering to God's principles is optional; it always has been and it always will be, but may we say and mean the words of Joshua, "choose you this day whom ye will serve; whether the gods which your fathers served that were on the other side of the flood, or the gods of the Amorites, in whose land ye dwell; but as for me and my house, we will serve the Lord" (Josh. 24:15, KJV).

263 WHILE EATING DINNER IN A RESTAURANT BETTER known for its breakfast fare, my husband and I watched as a young woman made her way from the bus station across the street and strolled toward the restaurant. She pushed a baby stroller in which a young child sat. Two boys flanked her, and everyone except the small child carried a diaper bag. It was dusk, and I surmised the woman was either between buses or en route to her destination with enough time at the bus stop for her to be able to feed herself and her children. Something about how the boys clung to her, making sure to leave little space between them and her sides, tugged at my heart strings. I couldn't help but wonder what circumstances had put her on the road alone with her three children. Was she making her way home in the wake of bad news or just to visit? Was she a widow or a divorcee? Where was she going? Would there be someone at the end of her destination to meet her? How could she manage all three children alone? And then my eyes fell on the small child in the stroller. She didn't seem to have a care in the world. Her mother was behind her, and her brothers were equally close by. There was nothing for her to fear, for those who loved her surrounded her.

After offering a brief prayer heavenward for this family, I thanked this woman for the lesson she brought my way: You do what you have to do, and you do it in the best way you can. You put one foot in front of the other, taking one step at a time until you arrive at your destination. And this, it seems, is when you become like that little child, knowing your heavenly Father is behind you, taking you every step of the way. Our brothers and our sisters in Christ are at our sides so that there is no need for us to fear. God bless that woman and her children. And God bless us as we make our own way to our own destinations.

264 THE PSALMIST TELLS US, "GOD IS A SUN AND SHIELD: the Lord will give grace and glory: no good thing will he withhold from them that walk uprightly"

Already Ours, Every Day of the Year

(Ps. 84:11, KJV). No matter what circumstance comes into our lives or who might go out of it, God is our shield and our sun as well. Not too much is more terrifying to me than to experience daytime skies that turn so dark during a thunderstorm that automatic streetlights come on in response to the surrounding darkness. It's eerie and so out of synch with what I suppose the daytime sky ought to look like. And yet, through the scariness of it, I know that God is my shield and He is the sun lighting my path so that I can find my way. It doesn't matter whether I can physically see his shield surrounding me or His sun beaming earthward in spite of dark clouds, He is there, watching over me and protecting me. And on top of all this, no good thing will He withhold from me as long as I walk with Him. He gives me grace, and He gives me glory. What more could I possibly want?

265 FEW WOMEN HAVE NOT HAD A TIME WHEN CIRCUMstances in their lives called for some sort of action on their part and they've felt inadequate to act. Some women have a tendency to believe they are without strength and resources—lacking the ingenuity to make do with what is there. And in so being we put aside or forget those brave women who have gone before us—the ones who at first glance seemed incapable of much of anything but became the heroines of the their day. One such woman was Jael, a woman lauded in the book of Judges. Deborah, a prophetess, judged Israel at this time for this was the era in Israel's history when God raised up men and women to lead the nation away from idolatry and back to His will of driving out the pagan nations from the Promised Land. Deborah enlisted Barak to go into battle to rid the land of pagans. He said to her, "If thou wilt go with me, then I will go; but if thou wilt not go with me, then I will not go" (Judg. 4:8, KJV).

Deborah said to Barak, "I will surely go with thee: notwithstanding the journey that thou takest shall not be for thine honour; for the Lord shall not sell Sisera into the hand of a woman" (Judg. 4:9, KJV). And Deborah went with Balak with his ten thousand men to Kedesh, where God delivered Sisera into Balak's hands. Sisera's nine hundred iron chariots could have inflicted great harm to the Israeli army, but God intervened and the Israelis routed the pagan chariots, with Sisera fleeing the battlefield and ending up in the tent of Jael, the wife of Heber, a Kenite "for there was peace between Jabin the King of Hazor and the house of Heber the Kenite" (Judg. 4:17, KJV).

Jael welcomed Sisera into her tent and told him not to be afraid. Sisera asked her to hide him, and he also asked for a drink of water. "And she opened a bottle of milk, and gave him drink, and covered him" (Judg. 4:19, KJV). He then asked her to go to the door of the tent, and if anybody came to ask about him, to tell them nothing. Sisera was tired and weary, and the milk made him sleepy. When he fell sound asleep, Jael took a nail from the tent and a hammer "and went softly unto him, and smote the nail into his temples, and fastened it into the ground: for he was fast asleep and weary. So he died" (Judg. 4:21, KJV). Then she went out to meet Barak and told him what she'd done.

If a woman has the physical strength to do something like this, something that seems so far-fetched for a woman to be able to accomplish, and the presence of mind to use that which is at her disposal, then women can and must rise to the circumstances that face them in their everyday lives. Strength and resources will come for any task God calls us to. It is said of Jael, "Blessed above women shall Jael the wife of Heber the Kenite be, blessed shall she be above women in the tent" (Judg. 5:24, KJV).

We no longer live in such a time, a time when a woman was called on to do such a deed, but no woman needs to sell herself short. We're not without strength and we're not without resources, for God is our refuge, a very present help in trouble.

266

My childhood friend's mother's used to bake spice crumb cake, and I remember it as being the most delicious dessert on the face of the earth. Not too many years ago, I got the recipe from my friend and tried to duplicate it, but I couldn't get the same taste. Try as I might, my cake fell far short of my childhood memories of it.

This friend and I also made ourselves mayonnaise and bologna sandwiches, which we stuffed with potato chips. I compiled this concoction for myself not long ago, and it too fell flat on its face, the sandwich not coming anywhere near my memory of it. As I pondered

Already Ours, Every Day of the Year

the reasons for the two so-called failures, an epiphany occurred.

That which so often is sweet to the taste and pleasant to the mind is bathed in love. The ingredient missing from the cake and the sandwich was my friend's and her mother's love, care, and concern for me. This is what held me together during that time of my childhood, and this is what made my desire to duplicate something from that era fall flat on its face. I am no longer a child searching for love. I'm an adult who has it in abundance. I no longer need spice cake or bologna sandwiches to know that I am loved and cared for. But I do thank these two for being there when I needed them, and the Lord for providing such wonderful people to succor a lonely child.

267 A YEAR AGO WE BOUGHT AN AUTOMATIC DEVICE FOR one of our outside water faucets. We figured our dogs could better be served with their liquid needs in this way. All they had to do was touch their tongues to the spout, licking it, and water would fall into their mouths. Neither dog bothered with the nozzle, however, and in fact seemed puzzled by it until we massaged our hands with ground beef and rubbed the spout with our hands. Bailey caught on first. She licked the greasy tube, seemed delighted with what happened, wagged her tail, and then turned my way with an expression that seemed to say, "Oh, I see. Thank you. That was nice of you."

God is our living water. He makes our path to it easy. Sometimes, like our dogs, we don't know what to do with that which He has supplied. Our Lord then finds a sure and simple way to lead us to where we can drink of this living water. And we, like Bailey, turn to him and say, "Oh, I see. Thank you, Lord. That was nice of You."

268 SOMETIMES WE TAKE FOR GRANTED THE NURTURE, succor, and tender loving care that so often comes our way from our fellow church members. And sometimes we decry any assistance or semblance of rescue from the very same source. Our outlook depends on what we've experienced as a member of any given church. Some people are easier to minister to than are others, and some people make it extremely hard, if not impossible, to nurture and support. But God set His children in church congregations, and one has to figure that God has done so for a reason.

Church congregations are like families. God set us in families too. Families are headed by parental figures with children and siblings, grandparents, aunts and uncles, and cousins, sometimes by the dozens. But not all families get along all the time. Family members are not always there for other needy or troubled members of the family, and fighting and quarreling sometimes erupt. Sometimes a family member has to go it alone with no semblance of help coming from any quarter. This is sad, and it is as equally sad when such occurs in the church body.

Pray for families today, whether those families are bound by blood or bound by the love of God and allegiance to His word, His principles, and His laws. Take heart. Both kinds of families are inhabited by people who are human, and, as human, prone to the frailties of humanity. Nothing brings more joy to the heart of a human being than to be in a well-functioning family, whether that family is one in which God places us at birth or one in which He places us at rebirth.

269 My husband and I got a late start on grandchildren. It took a while for them to come for us, and as such, it's unlikely we'll be around to do a lot of things I'd like to do with them, such things as shopping with a college student or young adult for a new spring outfit, taking one of them on a trip for just the two of us, or experiencing the grandchildren's joy as they bring their own children into the world. Nevertheless, we have four of these delightful creatures in our midst, and I do for them now that which I might not have opportunity to do later on, whether through my death or through a physical disability.

The grandkids are too young to go shopping with me, but their mothers aren't, and their mothers are smart enough to let me buy them frilly little girl stuff and dress-up guy stuff. The mothers cater to me and my tastes and whims in clothing, just as I know the grandkids would do if they were grown and I was on such an excursion with them; for does not any current generation understand that the generation before them believes the old is better? And I drink in every

Already Ours, Every Day of the Year

minute of it, ever thankful that God has sent these children our way, both the kids, their spouses, and now the children of their union. And I marvel at how blessed we are that God placed such wonderful creatures in our home.

Thank God today for your children and your grandchildren and for blessing your life with such love.

270 Never have I been in distress and called on God for help that He hasn't responded. People have failed me, and I have failed people, but God has never failed me. It doesn't matter what kind of trouble comes into my life, it doesn't matter what season of the year it is, it doesn't matter what time of the day or night it might be, it doesn't matter what part of the world I'm in, God has never failed to respond to my pleas for help. Never. And He's never failed you either. Great is God's faithfulness.

"In the day of my trouble I will call upon thee: for thou wilt answer me" (Ps. 86:6, KJV). What more could any of us want?

271 I've often wondered about a vow a long ago general made to God so that God would give him victory over the enemies of his nation. His name was Jephthah and he lived during the time of the judges of the Old Testament. He was the son of a harlot, and his half brothers kicked him out of the family telling him, "Thou shalt not inherit in our father's house; for thou art the son of a strange woman" (Judg. 11:2, KJV). Jephthah ran away to the land of Tob, but when the children of Ammon got ready to make war against Israel, the elders of Gilead sent for Jephthah to return and be their captain—to lead them in a war with the Ammonites. Jephthah came back to his people and he made a vow to God, telling the Lord if He would be with him in battle then Jephthah would sacrifice the first thing that came out of his house upon his return home.

"And Jephthah came to Mizpeh unto his house, and, behold his daughter came out to meet him with timbrels and with dances: and she was his only child; beside her he had neither son nor daughter. And it came to pass, when he saw her, that he rent his clothes, and said, Alas, my daughter! Thou hast brought me very low, and thou art one of them that trouble me: for I have opened my mouth unto the Lord, and I cannot go back" (Judg. 11:34–35, KJV).

Over the years, Bible scholars have debated Jephthah's vow and the outcome of it, and I really don't know what I believe about it, but this I do know: his daughter submitted to her father's wishes. She said, "My father, if thou hast opened thy mouth unto the Lord, do to me according to that which hath proceeded out of thy mouth; forasmuch as the Lord hath taken vengeance for thee of thine enemies, even of the children of Ammon" (Judg. 11:36, KJV). She went on to tell her father, "Let this thing be done for me: let me alone two months, that I may go up and down upon the mountains, and bewail my virginity, I and my fellows" (Judg. 11:37, KJV).

This young lady honored her father and, in so doing, honored her Lord and God. Either her father or her mother or both of them had instructed her well in her growing up years and reared her in the nurture and admonition of the Lord. Neither parent neglected her spiritual training. She went willingly to whatever future her father deemed for her.

I leave the ethical debates of this Bible story to the scholars because the story teaches me a great lesson: to honor my Lord and my God, to do that which He instructs me to do, to go willingly where He leads me. It teaches me that no matter the rash behavior of others or the consequences of it, I belong to God; whatever He tells me to do I will do. God has never failed me yet, and he never failed Jephthah's daughter. Whatever the outcome of her father's vow, it went well with her because God was with her, walking with her every step of the way. Wherever He leads me, I will go.

272

"Blessed are they that dwell in thy house: they will be still praising thee, Selah. Blessed is the man whose strength is in thee; in whose heart are the ways of them" (Ps. 84:4–5, KJV).

I, too, cry with the psalmist that as I dwell in God's house—bathe and saturate myself in His words—and as I exchange my strength for

His own strength, a day in His courts is better than a thousand anywhere else (Ps. 84:10a, KJV). The location of other places is immaterial, how glorious or rich or luxurious they might be is irrelevant, because just one day totally committed to communion with God is better than a thousand days anywhere else doing anything else. Yes, indeed, "I had rather be a doorkeeper in the house of My God" (Ps. 84:10, KJV) than to dwell anywhere else on the face of this earth or do anything else on the face of this earth.

273 KING DAVID OF THE BIBLE LOVED GOD. HE WANTED to build a tabernacle in which to place the ark of the covenant. David chose to do a good thing for God, but God did not choose David to do this task. Rather, God selected David's son, Solomon, to build His tabernacle. David could have resented God's plan. He could have ignored God's will, and God would have permitted him to do so. However, David chose God's way over and against his own way. This earthly king had enough presence of mind to acknowledge that God knew him better than he knew himself, and that was enough for David. May we join David as he said to his creator, "thou art great, O Lord God; for there is none like thee, neither is there any God beside thee" (2 Sam. 7:22, KJV).

God knows each of us better than we know ourselves. "For thou, Lord God, knowest thy servant" (2 Sam. 7:20, KJV).

274 IF A CHILD HASN'T BEEN ABUSED IN SOME WAY, THEN that child innocently trusts people and his or her environment. He trusts his parents to feed, clothe, and house him. He trusts his parents to protect him, and he trusts their love for him. He trusts them with the decisions they make on his behalf, knowing their decisions are good and in his best interests. Children expect parents to discipline them, not letting them get out of bounds. Innocent children are not anxious, and they awaken refreshed and eager for a day's activities. Innocent children expect nothing but good to happen to them, and they expect the world to be a friendly place as long as they obey their parents' rules and regulations. Children know they are safe as long as they obey their parents.

"Whosoever therefore shall humble himself as this little child, the same is the greatest in the kingdom of heaven" (Matt. 18:3–4, KJV). To be great in the kingdom of heaven is to be innocently trusting of our Lord. God will take care of us. God will provide for us. Earthly parents can protect just so much because their control over life's circumstances is limited. This is not so with God. His protection of His children is without limits or boundaries. God is always in control. Nothing can occur in our lives unless God allows it to be there. God is forever in control of the circumstances of our lives. He takes adversity and works it out for our good.

There is no need for us to fret and worry. God is our heavenly Father. He is in control of everything. As God's child, we are granted greatness in the kingdom of heaven. God's children trust their father. God's children know their Father loves them. God, our heavenly Father, takes care of each and every one of His children.

275 IN THE MOVIE *Paradise Road*, ENGLISH, IRISH, DUTCH, Australian, and American women living in Singapore during World War II are taken captive by the Japanese. They are marched to a prisoner-of-war camp in Sumatra where they endure harsh circumstances. One of the English captives is a missionary, while another one is well-versed in music, having been trained at the Royal Academy. The two ladies form a choral orchestra and teach the members of it to sing symphonies and other pieces of classical music. At first one of the captives opposes the formation of such a group, thinking the two ladies who propose it mean that members will learn to play musical instruments gotten through asking the Japanese for the instruments. She scoffs at the idea of their captors granting such a request.

No request from their captors for anything outside of themselves was needed. All the women had to do was use what God already had given them—their voices. They already had within themselves the resources they needed to help them in their sufferings and trials at the hands of Japanese soldiers. Some of the women survived their ordeal while others did not. All of their lives, however, were made somewhat less harsh and burdensome by their willingness to do what the two ladies had requested they do—use the gift of music to make their lives somewhat more bearable.

Already Ours, Every Day of the Year

As Maria said in the movie, *The Sound Of Music*, "Whenever God closes a door, He always opens a window." Become aware of the windows God opens in your life. They are always there.

276 MARGARET, THE ENGLISH MISSIONARY IN *Paradise Road*, reads a poem at the burial of one of the Oriental captives, a woman soaked in gasoline and torched to death. She says, "How silent is this place. The brilliant sunshine filters through the trees. The leaves are rustled by a gentle breeze. A wild and open place by shrubs pink-tipped, lobe-blossomed is all grown. A hush enfolds me, deep as I have known, unbroken save by distant insect strum. A jungle clearing. A track through which we bear our load to Him. It is our paradise road. How silent is this place. How sacred is this place."

Margaret is one of the few prisoners who comprehends from the beginning of her capture that she is now on the road to meet her God—paradise road. She bears no hatred for the cruelty and inhumanity of her captors. She feels nothing but pity for them. She witnesses one after another of their hateful acts, and yet she keeps on keeping on until she can go no further. At the time of her death, Adrienne, the English woman who trained at the Royal Academy, is at Margaret's side, and one of the ladies tells Adrienne that Margaret is asking for something. Adrienne bends down close to Margaret's ear and listens as Margaret whispers something. Adrienne, co-founder of their choral orchestra, repeats Psalm 23 for Margaret:

"The Lord is my shepherd: I shall not want. He maketh me to lie down in green pastures: he leadeth me beside the still waters. He restoreth my soul; he leadeth me in the paths of righteousness for his name's sake. Yea, though I walk through the valley of the shadow of death, I will fear no evil: for thou art with me; thy rod and thy staff they comfort me. Thou preparest a table before me in the presence of mine enemies: thou anointest my head with oil; my cup runneth over. Surely goodness and mercy shall follow me all the days of my life, and I will dwell in the house of the Lord for ever."

Margaret then opens her eyes wide and says, "This is what I wanted," and then closes her eyes and dies. Her paradise road was an unthinkable one—a road filled with torture, pain, anguish, and sorrow, but the joy of music and accomplishment, deep friendship, and camaraderie also occurred on that road. Regardless of what happens to us on our heavenward journey, the Lord is our shepherd on our way to Him. We will never want for anything because "no good thing will he withhold from them that walk uprightly" (Ps. 84:11, KJV). He restores us, He leads us, He walks with us—every step of the way. He comforts us, He bathes us in His love to the point of our cup running over with that love. God's goodness and mercy will follow us all the days of our lives, and at the end of them, we will live with God forever.

Margaret knew this from the beginning of her sorrowful journey down a road of horrors. Most of us will not travel such a road, but we all have our own paradise roads, our own tracks along which we bear our loads to Him, and these roads, too, are just as silent as they are sacred.

277 IN THE MOVIE, *Paradise Road*, MISSIONARY MARGARET stands over the coffins of two of her co-captives and says words over their graves: "Father, in captivity we would lift our prayer to thee. Keep us ever in thy love. Grant that daily we may prove those that place their trust in thee, more than conquerors they be. Give us patience to endure. Keep our hearts serene and pure. Grant us courage and charity, greater faith, humility, readiness to own thy will, be we free or captives still. Amen."

The two prisoners who had just died were a beautiful, young English woman and a once-wealthy elderly English woman. Both had been captives for four years, both had suffered cruelty at the hands of their captors, and both had learned to endure through God keeping their hearts serene and pure, granting them courage, giving them faith, and teaching them humility. At death it didn't matter that they were captives because God reached down and set them free.

As we travel toward our own paradise roads, may we know God is with us now and forevermore. If we have the love of God in our hearts, it doesn't matter what other things we don't have. All we ever need on our paradise road is God's love. Nothing else matters.

278 IN *Paradise Road*, ALL OF THE WOMEN CAPTORS OF THE Japanese soldiers learn something about themselves through harsh circumstances imposed on them by

Already Ours, Every Day of the Year

their captors, something that needs the touch of God for healing and spiritual growth. Many of the English women are snobs, thinking their class and station in life imply they are better than others. Some of the women are judgmental, thinking themselves better than those from other nations. Others are skeptics, believing answers come through intellect. Some are envious and jealous, thinking that others are stealing from them or taking food that belongs to them. Some are traitors, trading information on fellow captives to the Japanese for cigarettes or food or privileges. Some agree to live a better life in a distant house away from the camp, one that houses Japanese officers, so that they can eat well and have soap and hot water at their disposal, knowing they will serve the sensual appetites of their captors in return. All, however, are captives—prisoners of the Japanese. All are on their own personal paradise roads. Just as they learned their own personal lessons regarding pride and prejudice, fear and caving in to it, honesty and integrity, envy and jealousy, so do we as we travel our own roads toward our Heavenly Father. We are blessed, indeed, that the Lord is our shepherd. What a magnificent One we have watching over us, guiding us and teaching us and loving us enough to deliver us from our own sinful natures.

279 I OFTEN MARVEL AT GOD'S WORK IN ME SINCE I became a Christian. God's word as revealed in the Bible stirs me and comforts me as no other words can, and yet I was not reared on them. Classical music reaches to the depths of my soul and soothes me as no other music can, and yet I was never exposed to that kind of music as I grew up. No one ever instructed me on color, how to use it or how it can influence us, and yet any shade or hue of any color captivates me and intrigues me. Dogs terrified me as a child, and yet today I view them as compassionate, loving, friendly, and necessary creatures. Art appreciation eluded me as I was growing up, and yet today it plays a pivotal part in my life. The healthy foods and beverages I now enjoy were not a part of my formative years. All that I now am doesn't seem to have been a part of me as I was growing up, and yet it was, for God set about growing me into the image of His Son, and as He did so, I became more like Him and less like the person I was before my rebirth in Him. All that He implanted in me at my natural birth simply came alive and blossomed at the time of my rebirth.

All God's children can shout with the apostle Paul: "Being confident of this very thing, that he which hath begun a good work in you will perform it until the day of Jesus Christ. For it is God which worketh in you both to will and to do of his good pleasure" (Phil. 1:6, 2:13, KJV). God is willing and working in us of His good pleasure. We are no more the creatures we were before our rebirth in Him than a gorgeous butterfly was when it was in its cocoon. Like the butterfly, we are new creatures in Christ. And this, my friend, is enough to make us all marvel at the works of God.

280 I ONCE KNEW A MAN WHO ADMONISHED PEOPLE TO take note of the fact that the people then assembled in that particular place would never be assembled exactly the same way again. His point was to challenge his audiences to seize the day—carpe diem. I don't know the effects his urgings had on his audiences, but I do understand the point he was making. It is a point well worth taking, but I wonder if any of us really comprehend it. If we did, then it would seem our lives would drastically change. No longer would we take any moment lightly. We would relish it, lap it up, nourish it, hold it close, and give it up once it is gone. We would garner from our moments what is there for us in them, learning from them and taking heart in them. No longer would we look back on them wistfully, wishing we had them once again so that we could relive them, because we would know they were there only for that moment, and if we lived the moment to its fullest, that would be enough for us. "To every thing there is a season, and a time to every purpose under the heaven" (Eccles. 3:1, KJV). Our challenge becomes knowing and being aware of what season we're in with a willingness to relinquish a season once it has gone. We cannot fully embrace or become fully conscious of a new season until we bid the old one adieu. Perhaps if we allowed ourselves to become aware of the uniqueness of each moment of the day with the realization that it will never return in the exact same way again, then we would understand the message of the person who tells us we will never assemble the same group of people in the same way again.

Already Ours, Every Day of the Year

281 NOT TOO INFREQUENTLY THE MEDIA REPORTS ON AN elderly person dying almost destitute, with people later finding a wealth of monies hidden throughout the elderly person's home. When this happens, we wonder why the old person didn't buy food and clothing or spend money heating or cooling their houses and meeting the necessities of their lives rather than doing without and stashing away their wealth. We cannot help our disbelief at such senselessness and wonder what prompted such a person to do such a thing.

The seemingly destitute elderly who would not spend their money knew of their financial resources and chose to hide them. They knew what they had, but chose not to use what they had. On the other hand, all of us have garnered some insight and knowledge in our lifetimes. Within each one of us lies a wealth of resources available to us, but somehow we ignore what is there, not heeding that still, small voice from within us that prompts us to use what is there that could sustain, benefit, or encourage us. If we don't know we have something, we don't search for it. If we don't search for it, we won't find it. If we don't find it, then certainly we cannot use it.

Far better to have something, know we have it, and choose not to use it than to have something and not search for it so that we can use it—that which is in us that is already ours.

282 IN THE FIRST BOOK OF SAMUEL, WE READ ABOUT Hannah, Samuel's mother. She was one of Elkanah's two wives, and she was barren. Elkanah loved Hannah dearly and knew it grieved her heart that she had no children. On one of their yearly trips to Shiloh to worship and sacrifice unto the Lord, Hannah went to the temple area where she communed in prayer with God. Weeping, she made a vow to God, saying, "O Lord of hosts, if thou wilt indeed look on the affliction of thine handmaid and remember me, and not forget thine handmaid but wilt give unto thine handmaid a man child, then I will give him unto the Lord all the days of his life, and there shall no razor come upon his head" (1 Sam. 1:11, KJV).

Eli, the priest, sat nearby on a seat by a post of the temple and saw Hannah's lips moving and assumed she was drunk. He reprimanded her for her drunkenness and when he did, Hannah said, "No, my lord, I am a woman of a sorrowful spirit: I have drunk neither wine nor strong drink, but have poured out my soul before the Lord" (1 Sam. 1:15, KJV). She went on to tell Eli she wasn't a wicked woman but a woman seeking God out of a grief-stricken heart. Eli then blessed Hannah, telling her that the God of Israel would grant her her petition. Later, Hannah bore a son and named him Samuel because she had asked God for him.

Hannah did not return for their yearly trip to Shiloh for worship and sacrifice until she had weaned Samuel because she knew at that time she would take Samuel to "appear before the Lord, and there abide for ever" (1 Sam. 1:22, KJV).

"And when she had weaned him, she took him up with her, with three bullocks, and one ephah of flour, and a bottle of wine and brought him unto the house of the Lord in Shiloh: and the child was young. And they slew a bullock, and brought the child to Eli. And she said, Oh my lord, as thy should liveth, my lord, I am the woman that stood by thee here, praying unto the Lord. For this child I prayed; and the Lord hath given me my petition which I asked of him: Therefore also I have lent him to the Lord; as long as he liveth he shall be lent to the Lord. And he worshipped the Lord there" (1 Sam. 1:24–28, KJV).

And then Hannah prayed a beautiful prayer and in it said, "There is none holy as the Lord: for there is none beside thee: neither is there any rock like our God" (1 Sam. 2:2, KJV). Imagine such dedication and gratitude. A woman longed to have a child, and God gave her a child. The woman then turned that child back over to the Lord, and the whole nation of Israel benefited from the ministry of Samuel, Israel's last judge and first prophet.

Would that every child born to a child of God were dedicated by his mother to God and given back to God for God to use to bless us all.

283

SEVERAL YEARS AGO, A POPULAR SONG CARRIED THE words, "Don't worry. Be happy." I sang the song along with others, perhaps even you. It was a cheerful little tune, and one that captured the fancy of many of us. The apostle Paul wrote much the same thing, admonishing us not to fret, not to worry. He said, "Be

Already Ours, Every Day of the Year

careful for nothing: but in everything by prayer and supplication with thanksgiving let your requests be made known unto God" (Phil. 4:6, KJV).

The road leading from worry to happiness is an easy road to find, but a difficult road to stay on if we forget how we discovered it in the first place. A worry-free person is a person of prayer, a person willing to go to his or her knees, asking God for His help and not forgetting to thank Him for His work in us. God's work in us is often a painful path to walk, one that can lead us to anxiety and fretfulness if we allow it to. A thankful heart, even for that which we do not understand and find difficult to bear, is a heart close to the heart of God, and one God touches with His love and compassion and understanding. Take your worries to God, my friend. And in the process, don't forget to thank Him for all He's done for you.

284 WHEN I WAS A CHILD, FOR A TIME MY MOTHER AND I lived with her parents, whose house was near the Georgia Tech campus. During the fall, my young aunt, two cousins, and I used to make our way to the streets surrounding several fields near our home and not too far from the football stadium, where we would offer our services to watch the cars of the those going to the football game. We'd sit around the cars parked on the street and talk, play, and have fun until the game was over. Then the fans would return to get into their cars to go home, but not before tossing us a nickel or a dime or a quarter for our services.

I don't know which one of us kids thought up this idea, but it was a good one. On game days, we thought we were rich, and we were, but not materially. Our wealth came not in the coins tossed our way but in just being who we were—poor children out on a Saturday afternoon, drinking in the aromas of fall, bantering with each other, talking and telling tales and not even aware we were poor at all.

No matter how little we have, we always have more than we think we do.

285 WHEN I WAS A CHILD, I LOVED GOING TO THE MOVIES. Back then in Atlanta, Georgia, neighborhood theaters played a double bill each Saturday, and I usually managed to see those double features each week. One Saturday I decided I liked the movies so much I stayed through a double showing of each of them. My mother was frantic with worry when I didn't return home at the appointed time. I, on the other hand, couldn't understand what all the hullabaloo was about when I finally did get home. I got the only spanking I ever got in my entire life, and to this day I remember it vividly.

It was not until I had my own children and sat waiting for them to return home from one activity or the other that I finally understood my mother's anxiety. As a child, I could not walk in her shoes because they would have been too big for me. I didn't have enough life experience to comprehend her fear. And it was not until I experienced love for my own children that I began to get a glimmer of understanding of God's love for me and all of His children. Just as my children will always be my children, no matter what they say or how they act, I will always be God's child no matter what I might say or what I might do. God loves me, and He loves you. We might disobey Him, and we might grieve His Spirit, but He loves us, and we can never do anything or say anything that would separate us from His love.

286 CHILDREN ARE BUSY CREATURES, INVESTIGATING FIRST one thing and then another, but on occasion some children just become too busy. They flit here and there, bouncing between one activity and another, becoming dissatisfied and restless at the least provocation. When this happens, a parent usually shouts, "Be still!" The child's overactivity not only wears out his caregiver, but it isn't good for the child either. Children learn self-discipline through loving parents willing to teach it to them.

God, our heavenly Parent, does the same with His children. He commands His children to be still because He knows if we don't cease from our busy and often meaningless activity, we won't learn self-discipline. God can only instruct His children if they're still long enough to hear His instructions. When we sit still as God commands us, we can hear His still, small voice within us, and when we do, we exalt Him among the heathen and exalt Him in the earth. "Be still and know that I am God" (Ps. 46:10, KJV). It is through stillness in Him that we come to know, "God is our refuge and strength, a very present help in trouble" (Ps. 46:1, KJV), and when we apprehend this, then we know without a shadow of doubt there is no need to fear, "though the earth be removed, and though the mountains be carried into the midst of the sea; though the waters thereof roar and be troubled, though the mountains shake with the swelling thereof" (Ps. 46:2–3, KJV).

Just as an earthly parent expects her child to be still when she tells him to, so too, does our Heavenly parent expect us to obey this command also. Be still!

287 ASK. SEEK. KNOCK. A-S-K. GOD PROMISES US THAT AS we ask Him, we will receive. In seeking, we will find. When knocking, a door will open. What a simple acrostic. Ask. Seek. Knock. We've all had experiences, however, when we've asked people for help and had them turn their backs on us, seemingly paying no attention to our pain or our plight or our neediness. We become confused, thinking our Lord will do the same thing. God never turns His back on us—not one of us.

Not only does God not reject us or our pleas, but He comforts us as no other can comfort us. He acts on our behalf as no other will act on our behalf. God will never abandon us or forsake us. People can and sometimes do turn away from us. God never leaves us without help.

Ask God. Seek His face. Knock on the door to His throne. Keep asking, keep seeking, and keep knocking. God always hears. If there is a delay in a response from Him, there is an excellent reason for it. Persist in approaching God. Persist in asking for His help. God will never turn you away empty handed.

288 THIRTY YEARS AGO, MY HUSBAND AND I BOUGHT TEN acres of land outside the city limits. Our children were small then, and we planned to build a house when we got enough money together to begin building. Finally we were able to clear a part of the land for a house, and we began the ordeal many people endure of erecting a structure that eventually becomes a home. Years have come and gone since this time. Only my husband and I now occupy a house once filled with the laughter and tears of children romping about, investigating first one thing and then another, sometimes whispering, sometimes screaming, sometimes crying, sometimes taunting. The only noise now made in this house is that which we make, and I've discovered we don't make that much.

But I don't long for what was and no longer is. I don't long for it because those days, as awesome and spectacular as they were, are still inside me. They are in my heart and in my memory, and they are wonderful memories indeed—some joyful and some not so joyful. All I have to do to recapture one of them is close my eyes, concentrate hard, and envision what we were like as a family in this room or that room or outside the house. And then I thank God that He gave us this land where we could build a home and raise three lovely children, and I thank Him that He has taught me to embrace every moment, culling from that moment what is in it. Even though my husband and I don't make much noise in this house, the noise we do make is quite enough. And this is enough for me because it is the moment I now am in.

289 I LIKE THE SILENCE AND STILLNESS OF OUR HOUSE when no one is at home but me. I like it when the only noise I hear is the rustling wind or a bird's song or the roar of a car passing by or a dog barking or my scraping an Irish potato to cook. I like to roam throughout the house, inspecting each room and reminiscing about events occurring in each one. I like sitting on the sunporch, watching the pines sway in the wind, and catching a glimpse of hummingbirds as they flitter around a feeder prepared just for them. I like to study the sun's rays making their way through the windows and bringing light where once there was darkness. I like the ticking of our grandfather clock and the toll of its Westminster chimes.

I like the silence and stillness of our home, but more than this, I like the sound of the carport door opening and hearing the pitter-patter of small feet making their way inside, breaking the house's silence and stillness with gleeful cries, for nothing is better than a grandchild's small voice calling out, "Gamma. Gamma. Where are you? Where's Paw Paw?"

In such moments I eagerly relinquish the silence and stillness, for I know such moments are fleeting. Before I can turn around, the carport door will open once again, but this time there will be no soft pitter-patter of tiny feet. There will be two grown men or two grown women standing in the doorway asking, "What's up, Grandma? Got anything to eat?" And I know when these young people leave from their visit, I will once again make my way through the house, reminiscing again about the time when they used to burst through the door shouting, "Gamma. Gamma. Where are you? Where's Paw Paw?"

And life goes on.

290 SITTING ON THE SUNPORCH TODAY, I NOTICED THE PINE trees in our backyard and was almost struck dumb with wonder at how tall they had grown in the twenty-nine years since we became acquainted. They are robust and sturdy-looking and sway with the wind. As I busied myself with the chores of everyday living, being a wife and mother and a professional, doing the things one does, I marveled at my own growth as well. Over the years, the pines lapped up the sweet drops of rain and endured the harshness of the cold and grew and grew until today they are giants. So too have I lapped up the sweetness of life and endured the harshness of it and grown in God's grace. Swaying with the winds of life has now become a daily occurrence for me too. And for this I count myself blessed by God and thank Him for the sweetness in life, the ability to endure its trials and the growth each one has produced in me.

291 WHILE DRIVING TO THE POST OFFICE TODAY TO PICK up the mail, I listened on the radio to what I call high church music. I haven't heard choral singing like this in a long time, and the music captured my heart. Then I wondered where on earth I got my liking for this kind of music, for certainly I wasn't brought up on it. Then I remembered how as a child I once heard such chords echoing from the halls of a church I walked past. I immediately went home and begged my mother to enroll me in the school at that church, thinking I could perhaps hear the music once again. I didn't get to go to school there, of course, but I have been fortunate to hear that kind of music over and over again.

Not too many churches today offer such a musical diet, but I always have my tapes and CDs, public radio, and my memories of passing by a church and soaring to the heights of the universe, carried by voices of singers praising God and His work in man in such an awesome and glorious way. And then I wonder what will happen to today's child if he or she is not exposed to such musical glory? How will he or she touch the hem of God's garment without exposure to what I call high church music? And then I cease from wondering. With God, nothing is impossible.

292 God sent the prophet and judge, Samuel, on a mission. Saul was king of Israel at that time, and once again Saul disobeyed God in a specific command God had given him. God told Samuel to fill his horn with oil, go to Bethlehem, and seek out Jesse because God would appoint one of Jesse's sons to become the next king of Israel. Samuel separated Jesse and his sons from the others and had Jesse parade his sons before him so that he could select the one God had sent him to select. Samuel looked first at the oldest son, Eliab, and said to himself, "Surely the Lord's anointed is before him" (1 Sam. 16:6, KJV).

God told Samuel not to be so taken with Eliab's looks and height, and so Jesse's second son passed by as did his third. When Jesse had presented seven of his sons to Samuel with no selection being made, Samuel asked Jesse, "Are here all thy children? (1 Sam. 16:11, KJV). The youngest boy, David, was out watching the sheep. Samuel ordered Jesse to send for David, so that he could get a look at him. David was "ruddy, and withal of a beautiful countenance, and goodly to look to" (1 Sam. 16:12, KJV). God didn't select the one we might have chosen; instead He chose the one we might think of as still being wet behind the ears.

"The Lord seeth not as man seeth; for man looketh on the outward appearance, but the Lord looketh on the heart" (1 Sam. 16:7, KJV). I am grateful that when God looks at me, he sees what is inside in my heart. I am thankful that God sees us as He sees us and not as man sees us. May we strive to disregard outward appearances and see with a Godly vision that which dwells in the hearts of the men, women, and children whom we meet each day.

Already Ours, Every Day of the Year

293 A NUMBER OF YEARS AGO, I HAD THE PRIVILEGE OF going to Seoul, Korea. I traveled with a group of Texans with the mission of witnessing to these people. At the last minute, my husband was unable to go with us, and I found myself in a foreign country, a very strange land indeed, and I was alone. Yes, there were at least a hundred others with me, but as far as I was concerned I was alone, and I quickly became homesick for my beloved. I not only wanted him there with me, but in my heart I believed I needed him there with me. Everything was so strange, so foreign. I hadn't realized until then how much I counted on him, depended on him. I had to see to my luggage. I had to go through customs without his aid. I had to exchange American money for Korean money by myself, and still to this I day I wonder if I did it correctly. I had to stay in a hotel room without him, and all this in a country with curfews, and Korean soldiers barking out what I perceived as orders to people on the streets below. The trip became one of my most unusual and exciting experiences.

When God gives us life, He sends each of us on a mission. He puts us in the foreign environment we call earth or the world. He is not with us physically on our journey, but He is ever close by, watching over us and taking care of us, because we do nothing without Him. We are here with millions of others, and yet, so often we feel alone. Not so. My husband wasn't with me physically in Korea, but his spirit permeated everything I did, said, and saw. The same is true with our Lord. We might not be able to see Him with our human eyes, but we always experience Him in our hearts. He is always with us. He hasn't left us alone in this foreign land we call home. Nevertheless, we, like the apostle Paul, wrestle with homesickness for heaven and to be with our beloved Lord and to nestle in His loving arms.

294 GOLIATH LOOKED AT DAVID AND MADE A JUDGMENT about him because of what he looked like and because he was young; so young that when Saul put his own armour and helmet and coat of mail on David and gave him his sword, David must have looked laden down and somewhat pathetic and inept.

David may have been young, but he wasn't inexperienced. A lion and a bear took one of the sheep out of David's flock. He chased after and killed the predators, bringing the sheep back to its flock. David may have been young, but he had faith that if his God saved him from the lion and the bear, then He certainly would save him from Goliath. David went out to meet a man nine feet and nine inches in height with nothing more than faith in God and a slingshot and five smooth stones he picked up out of the valley.

If one so young can do such a thing, then what prevents us from doing likewise? What keeps us from shouting with David, "the battle is the Lord's" (1 Sam. 17:47, KJV)? For whatever battle in which we might happen to be at any given moment is the Lord's. Let us pray we stand as did David when he was taunted and cursed and threatened by a pagan giant. Giants surround us and are on every side of us, but they don't always look like menacing giants. Sometimes our giants are heartaches and distresses, or envies and jealousies, or hatred and meanness, or any spiteful event or circumstance that might enter our lives. We might feel overwhelmed at the sight of our giants' armour, but let us always remember: With God at our side, all things are possible, and if God is for us, who can be against us?

295 Our older grandson loves ice cream from a particular fast food restaurant. He never goes there that he doesn't beg his mother or father to buy him an ice cream cone. Sometimes they give it to him and sometimes they don't. Of course he's pleased when he gets one, and he's learning not to throw a fit when he doesn't get one. Our daughter and son-in-law give our grandson such a treat when it doesn't interfere with his appetite or encroach on a mealtime. These parents don't bother to explain to him in great detail why he can or cannot have what he wants. The child asks and sometimes he begs, but he either receives or doesn't receive at his parents' discretion. This is the way parenthood is designed.

Such is God's prerogative with His children. God instructs us: "Ask, and it shall be given you; seek, and ye shall find; knock, and it shall be opened unto you. For every one that asketh receiveth; and he that seeketh findeth; and to him that knocketh it shall be opened" (Luke 11:9–10, KJV). But we all know that we haven't always gotten from God what we've asked of Him, and far too often we wonder why and become angry at our heavenly Father for denying us what we know He can give us and not explaining to us why he's denied a request.

"If a son shall ask bread of any of you that is a father, will he give him a stone? or if he ask a fish, will he for a fish give him a serpent? Or if he shall ask an egg, will he offer him a scorpion? If ye then, being evil, know how to give good gifts unto your children: how much more shall your heavenly Father give the Holy Spirit to them that ask him?" (Luke 11:11–13, KJV).

Parents don't always give their children what their children beg to get for the same reason God doesn't always give us what we want. As I am quite sure our daughter and son-in-law hear our grandson's plea for ice cream, so too does our Lord hear our prayers and supplications and pleas for whatever it is that we long to have. If earthly parents know how to be discriminating and wise in granting their children's wishes, then, dear friend, how much more discriminating and wise is our heavenly Parent in granting to us our heart's desires.

296

HAVE YOU EVER BEEN LISTENING TO A FRIEND AS SHE talked with you about a problem and asked her point blank at some point in your conversation what she wants, and find she is unable to tell you exactly what she wants? I have, and if I'm really close to such a friend, I won't let her off the hook until she can state what it is she's after, because I know if she can clarify what she wants regarding her problem, then she's well on the way to resolving it.

There have been times in my life when I've been plagued with some problem or other and have floundered around and wallowed in my misery simply because I didn't know what it was I wanted in a particular situation or from a particular person. Whenever you have a problem, regardless of the lightness or seriousness of it, sit down, be quiet, and then ask yourself: What do I want? Your answer will determine the outcome of your problem, and whether you resolve it or leave it hanging about your neck like an albatross.

What do you want?

297 King Saul wanted to get rid of David any way that he could. On two different occasions he threw his javelin at David, hoping to pin him to a wall and kill him. He ordered his servants to kill David, but his own son, Jonathan, warned David of the plot, sparing David's life. Saul sent messengers to kill David, but once again a member of Saul's family, Michal, who had married David, warned him and helped him escape her father's wrath. Saul even tried to kill David at the prophet Samuel's house. When this scheme also failed, Saul once again tried to enlist the aid of Jonathan to help him kill David. This plot also failed. Saul even said to the priests of God, "all of you have conspired against me, and there is none that sheweth me that my son hath made a league with the son of Jesse, and there is none of you that is sorry for me, or sheweth unto me that my son hath stirred up my servant against me, to lie in wait, as at this day" (1 Sam. 22:8, KJV). Saul then had Ahimelech the priest and all except one of his sons killed, forty-five people in all. Not only did Saul do this, but he also went to Nob, the city of the priests, and killed all the men and women and children and babies and oxen and asses and sheep.

Afterward David had two opportunities to kill Saul, but he didn't, saying, "I will not put forth mine hand against my lord; for he is the Lord's anointed" (1 Sam. 24:10, KJV). What finally felled King Saul was an arrow from the bow of a Philistine soldier, and when Saul perceived he was mortally wounded, he asked his armour bearer to draw his sword and finish the job. When the armour bearer wouldn't do this, Saul took his own sword and fell on it, dying. David then became Israel's second king.

Few Bible stories intrigue me as does this one, for through it I gain the courage to continue on with God's mission for my life regardless of the obstacles that might surround me. As far as I know, no one has tried to kill me. I have not had to flee for my physical life. But all of us have people who don't like us, some even hating us and wishing us harm. Others come after us not with swords but with their tongues, and the effects of such attacks are as devastating and debilitating as if others sought to physically kill us. Sometimes we have opportunities to get back at our enemies, with the threat of harming them with our own tongues in return.

Already Ours, Every Day of the Year

Let us guard our tongues, remembering that the God who has numbered the very hairs of our heads is our shield and defender. God avenges the wrongs inflicted on us by those who want to take us down.

298 GOD CREATED US SENSUAL BEINGS. WE SEE, HEAR, smell, taste, and touch the world in which we live. At any given moment, however, we cannot process everything that bombards us because of the enormity of it all. We can't drink it all in, so to speak, so we end up processing only a fraction of what comes our way through our five senses.

God is everywhere, and His presence is with us in every event we experience, everything we see, everything we hear, every odor we sniff, everything we taste and everything we touch with our hands or our bodies. God is in everything.

Perhaps we don't comprehend this because we focus our attention too much on the temporal—what our eyes can see and what our ears can hear or what we smell or taste or how our skin feels when it is brushed by an object. Too many of us use our God-given senses to explore the temporal alone—that which is actually present and in front of us. How much more enriched our lives would be if we allowed our senses to enter the spiritual realm, that place where we are conscious of God's work in the world and in mankind. It is in that place that we sense God and can see Him in everything—a raindrop, a snowflake, an airplane in the sky, the giggle of a child, a sigh of sorrow or relief, a tragedy, or any of the hundreds of everyday mundane events and happenings of life.

Being able to feel God's presence in everything that comes to us through our five senses is a magnificent gift, but in order to possess this gift we first have to receive it and then open it up.

299 ATTENTION-DEFICIT DISORDER IS A CONDITION THAT prohibits the sufferer from being able to process the world in which he or she lives like the rest of us. Such people often have difficulty listening when spoken to directly, paying attention to what has been said, or organizing tasks or activities. They are often easily distracted by extraneous stimuli and forgetful in their daily activities. For such people, to be able to walk into a room to retrieve a specific object and come out of the room with the object in hand, without first investigating and becoming absorbed in other objects in the room, is nothing less than phenomenal.

Many sufferers of ADD take a drug called Ritalin that enables them more effectively to process the information that comes their way. Those with ADD also have to learn to calm down and pay attention to the tasks at hand, and this is not easy for a person with such a condition. It isn't impossible, however. It just takes training, hard work, and time.

All of us have what I call spiritual ADD, meaning unless something intervenes, we will short-circuit ourselves and have difficulty seeing God around us, in every event that occurs, in every sound we hear, in everything that happens to us. We don't have to take a drug like Ritalin to calm us down so that we can operate more efficiently, but we do have to ingest into our systems the Word of God as revealed in the Bible by God's Holy Spirit. We do have to avail ourselves of communing with God on a regular basis, for it is only through talking with Him and listening to Him in return that we remain in tune with Him. When we aren't in tune with God, then we become disconnected from our source of power, short-circuiting ourselves, unable to see God in every event and in every place.

Not only must we keep ourselves in spiritual condition by reading His word, we must also teach ourselves to sit still and be quiet, for in so doing our spiritual senses are liberated, enabling us to see God everywhere and in every event. It is at such times that God whispers magnificent words into our ears—words that enable us to see Him more clearly and to smell the sweetness that is there for us, tasting His spiritual world and reaching out to bring it in to ourselves.

All of us are afflicted with spiritual ADD, but we can live with the condition and tolerate it better once we recognize it for what it is and then submit to God's treatment for it.

300

I WAS IN A SCHOOL SITUATION ONE TIME WHERE ONE OF my friends sabotaged me, stealing what I considered a profound thought I'd shared with her regarding the

Already Ours, Every Day of the Year

subject we were studying, and then passing it off to our professor as her own. I had a leader of a seminar in which I'd been asked to participate make copies of my presentation without asking my permission to do so. I've been in work situations where coworkers and friends, in order to further their own agendas, smashed me to smithereens. I've turned around in a crisis, expecting a friendly face to be there to offer encouragement, sympathy, and compassion only to find nothing but empty space. I've shared deep secrets with some only to discover they've set my words free to roam and land where they would.

Nothing can seem to disquieten our spirits and bring us to the depths of despair as does betrayal by a friend. Nothing can cause us to want to throw up our hands and surrender to the demands of the terror of an invisible knife piercing the ribs in our backs. To be done in by an enemy is one thing. To be done in by a friend is quite another. At one time or another, or to one degree or another, it has happened to all of us.

We are not alone when betrayal comes. When it happens to us, we do what the God-Man did, and we do what a man of God did. When King David felt betrayed, he poured out his heart to God, telling Him of his pain, his fears, and the trembling and horror that had overwhelmed him. David even confessed to God that what he wanted to do was run away from his problems. David confessed that he could have borne attacks from those whom he knew hated him, but he just could not bear betrayal by a friend—someone who had guided him in the past and counseled with him and even been in the house of God with him. It cut David to the quick that a friend's words were softer than oil and smoother than butter, yet eager to harm him.

When the religious leaders of Jesus' day plotted to kill Jesus, one of Jesus' disciples agreed with the chief priests to find an opportunity to betray Jesus. In the garden of Gethsemane, after He had been in prayer, Jesus prepared to leave the garden with Peter and James and John and the rest of the disciples. Judas appeared on the scene with armed men at his heels. He betrayed Jesus with a kiss, signaling to Jesus' enemies He was the man to arrest. Every disciple fled, with even one young man dressed in a loin cloth scurrying naked from the scene when his cloth was snatched from him as he hastened to get away. One whom Jesus called friend betrayed Him. It was then as it so frequently is today: Every man for himself. Every woman for herself.

Our friends can and sometimes do walk out on us and turn their backs on us. When they do, we can let our spirits become embittered and sour, or we can take our pain to God, process our feelings with the great Counselor, and work through our grief. As we cast our burdens on God, He will sustain us. As we process our pain, we can finally reach the place where we can join Jesus in saying, "nevertheless not what I will, but what thou wilt" (Mark 14:36b, KJV).

301 WE HAVE PICTURES OF OUR OLDER GRANDDAUGHTER sitting in her high chair with a small birthday cake in front of her on the chair's tray. The one-year-old toddler has icing and cake crumbs smeared all over her mouth and chin, and she's managed to decorate her bib and the chair handles with the same substances. It's her first birthday celebration, and she's never tasted cake before. It's obvious by the twinkle in her eyes and the delightful grin on her face that she likes what's in her mouth. Her mother was adamant about restricting refined sugars in her diet and had kept our granddaughter sugar-free for the first year of her life and is even limiting the amount of it in her second year. Alas, our granddaughter has finally tasted sugar, and she likes it. But, our daughter doesn't always give her child what she wants. She's picks the times and the places to treat her child, and she does this because she wants her child's nutritional needs met. Our granddaughter doesn't always get what she wants, but she always gets what she needs.

In the same way, God doesn't always give us what we want either, but He always gives us what we need.

302 FALL IS MY FAVORITE TIME OF YEAR. I ANTICIPATE ITS arrival the moment I catch a glimpse of the first leaf slowly drifting downward to a resting place on the ground. Each approaching season, my husband and I tell ourselves we'll travel into nearby Arkansas to view God's glorious array of brilliance or perhaps catch a plane for Vermont and experience what New England has to offer. These plans usually fall through. This year was no different, or so I initially thought.

Already Ours, Every Day of the Year

At the precise moment I realized we would not have time to go to Arkansas or travel to New England for the season and once again we would miss God's glory revealed in nature, God opened my eyes to what surrounds me — what is at my very fingertips. My home rests on the fringes of town, out in the country. All I ever need to do to witness His spectacular seasonal performance is look at what is beneath my nose. Burnt oranges, flaming reds, and brilliant yellows dot the highway leading to my home. The acreage surrounding my house abounds with autumn brilliance. Everywhere my eyes rest they drink in God's glorious display of His season. I don't have to travel elsewhere to witness it. It is beneath my nose.

This is the way it is with God's bountiful gifts for us. His blessings are already ours, but we're so preoccupied with looking for them exactly the way we want them to be or expect them to be or in the place we think they ought to be that we often miss them altogether. Let us pray that God will open our eyes that we will see what wonderful things he has given us — what is already ours.

303 THE SOUNDS OF THE HARD DRIVE OF MY COMPUTER intrigue me. Sometimes they tick away smoothly with a definite rhythm to them, and at other times they click away and then pause as if they're having a petite seizure of sorts, only to take up once again when the seizure has passed. At such times the computer's hourglass cursor sits on the lighted monitor screen and seems to hang in that position, threatening, it seems, not to move and turn once again into an arrow so that progress can continue inside the hard drive. This scenario reminds me of how we humans process the multitudes of feelings and thoughts that are fed into our minds. Our mind can assimilate a limited amount of material and can deal with just so much, then we hesitate in our normal rhythms and sounds before we can move on and process that which has come in. Just as my computer hesitates from time to time and I fear the computer might freeze up, so too do we sometimes become overwhelmed with situations and events in our lives, those things that jam our receptors, threatening to shut us down. Just as I never demand from my computer more than it can give me, God never puts more on our shoulders than we can bear.

304

Manna is whitish in color, and it is sweet, and when God rained it down to earth from heaven to the Israelites during their wilderness wanderings, it lay on the ground after the dew disappeared. Moses told the people that it was the bread which the Lord had given them to eat. The Israelites didn't have to work or toil for it, and it rained to earth six out of the seven days of the week. Not only this, but in the evening quails came and covered the ground. God provided for His people's nutritional needs because they didn't stay in one spot long enough to grow their own food. In supplying these kinds of needs, God also met their spiritual ones as well. In so doing, God was teaching them lessons in faith, for if the people gathered too much manna and tried to save it from one day to the next, the manna spoiled, became filled with worms, and stank. On the sixth day of the week, however, Moses instructed the people to gather enough manna for the seventh day of the week, the day God set aside for His people to rest. The manna didn't spoil from the sixth to the seventh day. Some of the people, however, went out on the seventh day looking for manna. They didn't find it, and God said to Moses, "How long refuse ye to keep my commandments and my laws?" (Exod. 16:28). Finally the people rested on the seventh day, eating nothing during their forty years of wandering in the wilderness but manna and quail. God provided for all their needs—nutritional and physical as well as spiritual.

God provides for our daily needs as well, but at times we are like the Israelites in that we fuss and complain and bellyache about what is not there for us, rather than looking at what God has already given us. In sending Jesus to us, God rained down His manna from heaven. Jesus said, "I am that bread of life. Your fathers did eat manna in the wilderness, and are dead. This is the bread which cometh down from heaven, that a man may eat thereof and not die. I am the living bread which came down from heaven: if any man eat of this bread, he shall live for ever: and the bread that I will give is my flesh, which I will give for the life of the world" (John 6:48–51, KJV).

Jesus is our manna, and this manna meets all our needs whether those needs are physical, emotional, or spiritual. Have you gone out and gathered your day's supply of manna yet? If not, I urge you to do so. God's grace is sufficient. We need nothing else.

Already Ours, Every Day of the Year

305 I NEVER STEP UP ON MY TREADMILL AND LOOK forward to taking my daily thirty-minute spin around the utility room. Never. Yet I know walking is good for me. It strengthens my bones, works on sedentary muscles, and releases endorphins into my system, which in turn gives me a euphoric feeling, and is just out and out good for me. Still I dread an encounter with the machine, often counting off the seconds until I release myself from my workout on it. I've devised many ways to get through the ordeal and the one I've found that works best for me is making up silly stories—the sillier, the better. Sometimes I talk aloud and sometimes I don't, but either way, I often chuckle at the absurdity of what comes from my mind and from my tongue.

And then epiphany made its appearance and, for the first time, I clearly comprehended the power of laughter and what benefits that emotion produces in me. I still don't relish the idea of making my way to the utility room for my daily spin on the treadmill, but I can thank my dislike for this task for the remarkable discovery of the power of laughter and how such a small and insignificant thing can enrich life.

Have you had your laugh today?

306 ONE OF THE CHARACTERS IN THE ACCLAIMED MOVIE *Saving Private Ryan* says something like "We never know what keeps someone else from acting or reacting. Perhaps we don't see their pain or plight and don't know their circumstances." This movie more than moved me to the brink of disquietude; it revived long-ago, beneath-the-surface memories—ones of my father who fought with the ninety-ninth division of the army in the Battle of the Bulge in World War II. I didn't even know what division he was in until I hastened home from the movie and looked at a picture of him, the only one I own. He is in his uniform and the ninety-ninth checkerboard patch is on his left sleeve.

I began to understand why this movie was so difficult for me to watch. Few movies have evoked such emotional responses in me, and I didn't know what to do with what I was feeling. I wanted to understand my father and to know how close to death he had walked and if he was aware a particular bullet from his weapon had killed a particular enemy soldier. Did he have to engage in hand-to-hand combat? How many of his friends did he see blown to smithereens? How terrified was he? Did he pray? How did he handle his post-traumatic stress afterward, for I was sure he must have suffered from it?

I have no answers to my questions, but I really don't need them. I just needed to hear, "We never know what keeps someone else from acting and reacting. Perhaps we don't see their pain and plight and don't know their circumstances." Of one thing I am certain: My father was in World War II and he fought with the ninety-ninth division at the Battle of the Bulge. Perhaps this helps to explain why my knight never showed up.

307

I'VE JUST HUNG UP THE TELEPHONE FROM A CALL from one of those people who make their living trying to sell a company's goods by phone. Even though I've written to the proper place to have my name removed from soliciting lists, some calls still find their way to my telephone, home, or business. It annoys me because most of the people on the other end of the line are good salespeople, knowing how to make an excellent pitch. At one time, I would listen to them, but I don't do that anymore. It's too time-consuming and sometimes, if the salesperson is successful, too expensive. I've even read stories of older people losing their life savings to unsavory telephone solicitations.

So now when such a call comes through, I say something like, "I'm not interested." And then I hang up. If I don't hang up immediately, the person on the other end of the line will keep talking and keep pitching. They've been trained to do this. Once such a call comes through and I answer the phone, if I want to be rid of the caller, then I will have to hang up immediately.

The same principle holds true when ungodliness comes knocking at our door. As we all know, it makes a fantastic sales pitch. "Did you know so-and-so did so-and-so last night?" a friend might say.

"Really?" we respond.

"And do you know what else?" the friend continues.

"No. What?"

And on and on the conversation goes, and before we know it, we've assassinated another person's character. The moment we

Already Ours, Every Day of the Year

respond to ungodliness when it enters our lives is the moment we get hooked, and once we're hooked we get reeled in like a fish from a pond. Telephone solicitors are pretty crafty, and they depend on our manners and our willingness to be polite. It is never impolite to say no to something we don't want. We teach our children this, and yet when sinfulness enters our lives, as in the above example, most of us are too polite and too mannerly, and we hesitate to say no. We dare not say, "I'd rather not talk about this. Say, what did you think of that movie on television last night?" And we don't do this for the same reason we allow a stranger on the other end of a telephone line to encroach on our time and our privacy.

It not only is mannerly and polite to say no, but it is also acceptable. Ungodliness comes in a myriad of enticing and fascinating forms, and even though we've removed our names from its list, it still knocks at our doors. It is never improper to say no to something we do not want. It just takes courage to do it.

308 IN OLD TESTAMENT TIMES DURING THE REIGN OF KING David, "the king of the children of Ammon died, and Hanun his son reigned in his stead" (2 Sam. 10:1, KJV). Out of kindness, David sent some of his servants to comfort Hanun as he grieved the loss of his father. Some of the princes of Ammon, however, told Hanun they believed David had ulterior motives in sending these servants to comfort him and had sent the men only to spy out their land so that David could overthrow it. At that point, Hanun took David's servants and shaved off half of their beards and cut their clothing in the middle "even to their buttocks, and sent them away" (2 Sam. 10:4). Word got back to David what had happened to his servants, and David sent an envoy out to meet the men "because the men were greatly ashamed" (2 Sam. 10:5). David instructed the men to wait at Jericho until their beards had grown back and then come home.

David wrote in Psalm 31, "In thee, O Lord, do I put my trust; let me never be ashamed" (v.1, KJV). He ended this beautiful song saying, "Be of good courage, and he shall strengthen your heart, all ye that hope in the Lord" (v. 24). Yes, my friend, regardless of what comes in your life that brings shame to you, remember David's words and take courage, for God will strengthen your heart as you hope in the Lord.

309 SOMETIMES WE GET SO CAUGHT UP IN THE MOMENT and the frustrations that frequently fill them that we forget about God's goodness and his continual watch care over us. We hone in on what we don't have or what is absent from our lives, so much so that we develop a kind of spiritual dementia. We ruminate about our present troubles and fret and fume over them, thinking God has somehow forgotten about us or even abandoned us. We let ourselves get so worked up that often we can't hear God's still, small voice from within us, calling us to remembrance. We temporarily forget His mighty hand that brings us joy and peace and love and kindness. So caught up are we in what is absent from our lives that we forget what has been, what is, and what forever will be—God granting blessing after blessing to us and loving us with a love so superior to what the world offers us that it sometimes seems unreal. No matter how complex a problem might be or how agonizing and draining it is, a ray of sunshine always rests on our heads once we remember God's goodness, His love for us, and the bountiful blessings He's poured out on us.

310 SOMETIMES WHEN I BEGIN TRANSFERRING A LOAD OF wet clothes from the washing machine into the dryer, I discover a load of dried clothes not yet taken out of the machine and put away. I then have to interrupt what I am presently doing, take the dried clothes out of the dryer, fold them, and put them away before I can continue my routine. When this happens, I am reminded of my relationship with God, especially my prayer life.

Just as dirty clothes go into the washing machine for cleaning, I also go to the Lord in prayer for cleansing, rejuvenation, and help. Once clean clothes go into the dryer, moisture is removed from them, and the clothes are ready to put away until they become dirty again. In the same way, once my prayer sessions have ended with God wiping away my tears, the people and issues we discussed in our talk also need to be put away and left with God, so that when I once again return to the Lord for cleansing, rejuvenation, and help, I won't have to deal with a load of unfinished business before proceeding.

The process of cleaning and drying clothes chugs along more smoothly and orderly if the task is viewed as having a beginning, a middle, and an end. So does our prayer life. It has a beginning, a middle, and an end. We seldom have trouble beginning a prayer, and often we linger around the middle of it, but frequently we forget to leave our troubles and requests and anxieties with God, instead letting them linger in our minds. Then when we begin a new prayer, we're hindered in it by this load of unfinished business—those thoughts and troubles and anxieties that don't belong in our minds, a place readily accessible for rumination. Once a prayer is completed, it belongs to God, but we have to put the prayer with Him. That's our job, not His.

311 ALL OF US HAVE UTTERED WORDS THAT WE WISH WE had not spoken. Sometimes we can go back and rectify these kinds of errors. Often we cannot. Sometimes we wait for the right time or the right place to repair the harshness of our words, and sometimes we dawdle in giving breath to words of love or hope or healing or encouragement. Either way, we lose because we never know how much time is available to us or to others.

May the words of our mouths and the meditations of our hearts be acceptable in God's sight. Let us guard the words we speak or the words we refuse to speak, for we will pass this way but once.

312 THE BEST MOMENT TO BE IN IS THE PRESENT MOMENT and what that moment brings us. Some people hover around the past, never daring to get too far from it, somehow believing the past is all there is to life, and if it can be conquered then so can life. Others spend inordinate amounts of time speculating about the future, convincing themselves that if they can get a handle on it or prepare for it well enough or worry about it enough, then life will be better. Few of us invest our time and energies in routing out the intricacies of the present moment. Stop what you're doing right now. Close your eyes and take a deep breath. Listen to the sounds around you. Sniff the air. Identify the aromas. Smack your lips and swallow several times. What do you taste? Is there a breeze blowing over your body? How do your clothes feels against your skin? Now open your eyes and let your soul absorb what is in front of them. Even concentrating hard and paying rapt attention to the messages your senses relay to your brain will not make it possible for you to process everything surrounding you. Too much is going on at the same time. Our brains can't absorb it all. There's not enough time or energy to dwell in the past or ruminate about the future. We waste time and lose energy agonizing over the past or fretting about the future. What do you suppose would happen if we took a fraction of the time we invested in these endeavors and instead put them to better use by drinking in and absorbing what we can of the present moment, whatever that moment might bring our way? No matter how painful a moment might be, it is always wrapped around a lesson of growth and in God's love.

313 LAST WEEKEND WE WENT TO DALLAS TO VISIT SOME OF our children and grandchildren. As we approached the city, we ran into roadwork on the interstate, and traffic snailed along. My husband, impatient with the whole process, whipped our vehicle off at the next exit, entering yet another line of cars waiting to get around the mess on the highway. He realized he had not taken the correct street, but rather than backtrack, he proceeded onward, not really knowing where he was. I blurted out, "What have you learned in all this?"

I hoped he would say, "Patience," but I didn't get a response at all. He was oblivious to everything but the task at hand—maneuvering the car in a northwesterly direction, hoping to find the street he originally wanted to be on. I chuckled inwardly, thinking he'd gotten himself in some fine pickle and that sooner or later he'd have to admit his impatience. But he never did because before I could bat an eyelash, an arrow pointing to the right indicated we were near an on-ramp for LBJ freeway, the way we needed to go. He still didn't say anything, but his look was emphatic. "Told you!" it shouted. He was clearly pleased with himself.

Already Ours, Every Day of the Year

And then insight came. I was operating under my own agenda for my husband, not God's. I had thought this would be a perfect time and place for God to teach him a lesson in patience. Instead, God used the incident to teach me a lesson on self-righteousness. It was I, not my husband, with whom God was dealing. I needed to learn to keep my mouth shut and let him steer the car. I needed to interfere only in case of an emergency. This was not an emergency. It was simply a lesson in humility, and the lesson was for me.

314 IN OLD TESTAMENT TIMES, THE KING OF BABYLON, Berodachbaladan, heard that Hezekiah, the king of Judah, had been sick. Berodachbaladan sent letters and a present to Hezekiah. Hezekiah then did a foolish thing. He showed the messengers all his precious things: silver and gold, spices, precious ointment, and all his jewels. Hezekiah opened up all his treasures and showed them off. "There was nothing in his house, nor in all his dominion, that Hezekiah shewed them not" (2 Kings 20:13, KJV).

The prophet Isaiah came to Hezekiah and asked him what the men had said and where were they from. Hezekiah answered "They are come from a far country, even from Babylon" (2 Kings 20:14, KJV). Isaiah then wanted to know what they'd seen in the house. Hezekiah had to confess, "All the things that are in mine house have they seen: there is nothing among my treasures that I have not shewed them" (2 Kings 20:15, KJV).

Isaiah predicted the day would come that everything the men had seen in Hezekiah's house, everything he had inherited from his fathers, would be carried away into Babylon. Isaiah also foretold that the sons of the sons of Hezekiah would be taken into captivity by the Babylonians and they would be "eunuchs in the palace of the king of Babylon" (2 Kings 20:18, KJV).

Something from within me would like to shout at Hezekiah, "You idiot," but I don't. I don't because I know pride exists in all of us, in all of humanity. Hezekiah's folly serves only to remind me that we are prideful creatures, creatures prone to imitate the peacock—displaying our feathers so others can see what beautiful and wonderful creatures we are.

Betty McCutchan

315 One of my favorite Bible characters is King David. From the time he is introduced in the first book of Samuel until his death is recorded in the first book of Chronicles, I read about him with rapt attention. His life story far surpasses any novel or biography I've ever read, and I never tire of reading it. In my mind's eye, I can see that young teen approaching Goliath with nothing but a slingshot. I envision his multiple escapes from the wrath of Saul, and I gallop along with him as he fights battle after battle with Israel's enemies. My heart sinks as I read of David's lust for Bathsheba and his sins of adultery and murder because of it, and I rejoice when he admits his sins and repents of them. I'm fascinated with Jonathan's love and loyalty to David and his to Jonathan in return. I cringe when reading about Amnon committing incest with Tamar and wonder about David's thoughts concerning this. I agonize with David as he mourns the betrayal and death of his son, Absalom, and cheer his determination to carry on in spite of it. My heart skips a beat as I read about David's sin in numbering the people of Israel and God giving him three choices regarding atonement for that sin. I grieve along with David as he makes a choice, for none of them are good. On and on his story goes until he is an old man, one who cannot escape the coldness of aging, a coldness that no clothing can eradicate. I weep over the words of Adonijah's rebellion and Joab and Abiathar helping Adonijah, but rejoice when reading David's charge to Solomon as Solomon prepares to take the throne and David's final prayer of thanksgiving as recorded in 1 Chronicles 29:10–20. After a forty-year reign over Israel, David died. But he left a legacy for us, a marvelous legacy.

Were it not for King David, I wouldn't know that God is my shepherd and I will never want for anything. Were it not for his words, I wouldn't know God makes me lie down in green pastures and leads me beside still waters or that God restores my soul and leads me in the paths of righteousness. I hug his words: "Yea, though I walk through the valley of the shadow of death, I will fear no evil for thou art with me; thy rod and thy staff they comfort me" (Ps. 23:4, KJV). I am encouraged to know that even though God prepares a table before me in the presence of my enemies, He anoints my head with oil with my cup running over. Nothing soothes me more than David recording

Already Ours, Every Day of the Year

God's promise of, "Surely goodness and mercy shall follow me all the days of my life: and I will dwell in the house of the Lord for ever" (Ps. 23:6, KJV).

Jesus came from the lineage of David, a man of God, a man with a song in his heart, a man after God's own heart. I never tire of reading his story as recorded in the Bible, for in it I take hope not only for myself but for every man, woman, or child who walks on the face of the earth. In Christ, God incarnated Himself and provided a way for everyone to come into His presence with praise, thanksgiving, repentance, and joy.

316 IN DISCUSSING WITH FRIENDS MY DAILY EXERCISE ON A treadmill, one of them shook her head from side to side, sighed and exclaimed, "I can get on the treadmill, but I just can't stay on it for longer than ten minutes."

One of the ladies responded, "Why not?"

"Oh, I don't know," she said. "It's so boring, and I just can't stay with it for long. I can't make myself do it."

I almost bit my tongue to keep from blurting out, "Cannot or will not?"

There is a difference between not being able to do a thing and a refusal to do it or to try to do it. This is true in everyday life situations and it is true in our dealings with God. Our Lord is explicit in what He asks of us: forgive, trust, repent, do good, witness, ask, seek, knock, love, delight, commit, rest, wait patiently, and on and on. God never asks without empowering, and He never requires of us what we can't do, yet when His command comes, all too often we shake our heads and sigh, "Oh, I can't do that," thinking we're released from God's appeal to us.

We make excuses instead. "I'll never forgive that deed," or "What's the use of asking. It won't happen," or "I'm tired of being patient with him," or "Doing good to others just leads to my being used," or "Love my enemies? No way!" or "Turn the other cheek? Get real," and on and on.

What is God asking of you today? What is your response to Him? Cannot or will not? Or is your answer, "Yes. In His grace and by His power, yes."

317 ON A RECENT TELEVISION NEWS PROGRAM, I LEARNED about video and still cameras so small they can be hidden so well others can't know they're being filmed. It doesn't matter where we are, what we're doing, or who we're with, someone can record our actions and sometimes even our words. This is a chilling thought and one that incenses us. Most of us value privacy and balk at having it invaded. I don't want someone to snap my picture or film my words and actions on tape without my knowledge. I don't want another person to spy on me, and I'm sure you don't either. And yet God used this news story to remind me that He is omniscient. He is everywhere, sees and hears everything, knows everything about me and my world. I find this thought comforting as well as distressing. Distressing in that I'm not always on my best behavior with my mind filled with positive and helpful thoughts. Comforting in that God is with me everywhere I go, knows me better than I know myself, and still loves me in spite of myself.

I'm still not too keen on the idea of people being able to catch my every move on film, but I'm eternally grateful for being reminded of God's omniscience by such invasive acts of mankind. Mankind sees, hears, broadcasts, and frequently condemns. God sees, hears, loves, and forgives. God is omniscient, and I'm grateful that He is. I want Him to be everywhere I go and see everything I do and hear all my words because He never condemns or judges me. God reprimands His children, but He does not condemn or judge them. God is love, and my heart praises His name because He is.

318 INJUSTICE SURROUNDS US. EVERY MOMENT, EVERY day, someone somewhere encounters injustice, often without recourse. When it comes knocking at our doors, all too frequently we can't do anything about it but endure, and then endure some more. Yet, for the child of God, all wrongs are eventually set right. Sometimes we know when they are righted and sometimes we don't.

In Luke 16 we read about a rich man who dressed royally and ate lavishly every day. A beggar full of sores by the name of Lazarus was brought to the rich man's gate in hopes of the rich man feeding him from the crumbs of his table. While the beggar sat there, dogs came and licked his sores. Finally, the beggar died and "was carried by the angels into Abraham's bosom" (Luke 16:22, KJV). The rich man also died and was buried. "And in hell he lift up his eyes, being in torments, and seeth Abraham afar off, and Lazarus in his bosom. And he cried and said, Father Abraham have mercy on me, and send Lazarus, that he may dip the tip of his finger in water, and cool my tongue, for I am tormented in this flame" (Luke 16:23–24, KJV). Abraham reminded the rich man that during his lifetime he received good things and Lazarus evil things. Lazarus now received comfort while the rich man was in pain. The two men's roles were reversed.

During life, Lazarus didn't raise a hand against the rich man, and he didn't curse him or lash out at him in anger. Lazarus simply sat at the rich man's gate, hoping against hope the rich man would have mercy on him and feed him with leftovers from his table. The only comfort Lazarus received as he sat at the gate came from the tongues of the dogs.

For the child of God, all wrongs, all inequities, all injustices are finally set right. Sometimes we know when it happens and sometimes we don't, but it doesn't matter if we know or not. What does matter is our knowledge and belief that God takes care of His children and He rights the wrongs done to us.

319 AT ONE POINT DURING THE LIFE OF JESUS, SOME people brought their infants and children to Jesus so that He could touch them. When Jesus' disciples saw what was happening, they reprimanded the people, but Jesus said, "Suffer little children to come unto me, and forbid them not: for of such is the kingdom of God. Verily I say unto you, Whosoever shall not receive the kingdom of God as a little child shall in no wise enter therein" (Luke 18:16–17, KJV).

Children are delightful little creatures. They reach out to touch and explore what is around them, they hop and skip and jump, they giggle, they cry, they chuckle, they laugh, and they love without question and are fiercely loyal to those whom they love. If they haven't been abused or neglected, or abandoned, they also trust, knowing those charged with their upbringing always act in their best interests.

We, who are God's children, are the same. We want to explore the world God has given us; we work and we play and we laugh and we cry; we love and we trust our Godly Parent to act in our best interests.

When we exude the very nature of our beings, our childlikeness, and come to our Father in this state of love and trust, others sometimes chide us, even scoffing at us. But it doesn't matter what others say or what they do. A child of God must have the heart of a child—loving and trusting and resting in the knowledge that God, the Heavenly Father, loves His children and is forever working on their behalf, leading them, healing them, encouraging them, and growing them into His image.

320 It used to be when an itemized bill came in for services from the various companies with which we do business, I'd sit down and write out a check for the billed services. I can't do this anymore because some of these companies now tack on various kinds of surcharges, some reliable and some not so reliable. Now I scan every bill that comes into the house for any kind of erroneous charge. This task takes time away from my already busy schedule, especially if I have to call the company and inquire about a particular item on the bill.

If I can take time out of an already involved and overloaded schedule to pore over a bill to ferret out errors in it, then I certainly can devote as much time to broadening my spiritual horizons by sitting still long enough to be able to drink in and absorb God, Who cultivates my spiritual sight that I might see Him in everything that surrounds me. Sometimes an error on a bill is so small as to be insignificant and not worth the bother, but no revelation from God is ever insignificant. I find the more I invest in furthering my spiritual sight, the more God reveals to me and the more I see His hand in everyday and commonplace happenings and events and words that are spoken.

321 At some time or another I hear people lamenting the state of affairs regarding this nation's children. The phrase "children killing children" frequently blares through the airwaves of our radios and television sets and is proclaimed

Already Ours, Every Day of the Year

in newspapers and magazines. Local, state, and national government seem at a loss to know what to do regarding this matter. I offer no solutions—only observations.

I've heard people blame such behavior on our so-called affluent society, with today's children having too many things, yet the vast majority of children coming from homes of abundance don't kill other children and neither do children from poorer homes. Others point the finger at too many children growing up in single-parent homes, yet I can rattle off more than a bucketful of names of children from such homes who are good kids, as well as names of good kids from two-parent homes. Many accuse the media, especially moviemakers and television producers, for cranking out violent film after violent film, but would the makers of such films produce them if they didn't make money off them? Still others blame neglect of children on working parents who are too involved and too busy, yet the vast majority of such children from such homes don't kill other children. The list of possible causes is unlimited.

I grew up in a poor home with only one parent, my mother, who was so inundated with problems that she had little time to invest in anything but keeping herself together. I watched movies with the Three Stooges in them and never emulated their behavior. My parents were divorced, and my mother was an alcoholic and a working mom, and I was a latchkey kid. I wasn't exposed to formal religion, but the society in which I lived was bathed in it and it rubbed off on me, making my pathway to God plain. Unfortunately, today's society is not an overall spiritual one, and if we want to look for a solution to this national crisis of ours regarding our children, it would seem the first place to start would be our national lack of belief in what is embossed on our coins, "In God We Trust." We have gotten away from our spiritual roots and abandoned trusting God to supply our daily needs.

It is not the fault of the government, the schools, the teachers, the filmmakers, or the parents that we've become a society in which children kill children. It is each and every individual American's fault that our nation has gotten to be where we now are. We have abandoned God en masse, tipping our hats to Him only now and again, visiting Him occasionally on a Sunday morning and giving God lip service contrary to what is in our hearts. Our children have been short-changed. Hillary Clinton believes it takes a village to raise a child, and it does, but it takes a village of individual people willing to make their pilgrimage of repentance and dedication back to God, the only One who can save us from ourselves and redeem our children and give back to them joy, good heritage, and a pleasant place in which to live.

322 King David sang a song, and in it he lets us know that "The earth is the Lord's, and the fullness thereof; the world, and they that dwell therein" (Ps. 24:1). The world and everything in it belongs to God, and every person on the face of the earth belongs to God. Those of us who can approach God, who can draw near Him, are those of us who have become His children. The finished work of Christ on the cross cleans the hands of God's children and bestows in them a pure heart. God's children are the ones who receive His blessings and the ones who are bathed in His righteousness.

David sings, "Lift up your heads, O ye gates, and be ye lift up, ye everlasting doors, and the king of glory shall come in" (Ps. 24:7, KJV). And who is this king of glory? "The Lord of hosts, he is the king of glory" (Ps. 24:10, KJV).

Were it said of our generation, "This is the generation of them that seek him, that seek thy face, O Jacob" (Ps. 24:6, KJV).

323 Every penny, nickel, dime, quarter, or any denomination of paper money in America carries this imprint: "In God We Trust." Our nation is built on trust in God. Long ago the prophet Isaiah said, "Thou wilt keep him in perfect peace, whose mind is stayed on thee, because he trusteth in thee. Trust ye in the Lord for ever: for in the Lord Jehovah is everlasting strength" (Isa. 26:3–4, KJV).

Cause us to return to You, O Lord, to be a nation that trusts in You and You alone, and lead us to a return to the ways of the people who built this nation of ours on a trust in God.

324 Several Sundays ago as I seated myself in a church pew, I scanned the bulletin and discovered to my chagrin the sermon topic. Our pastor would

Already Ours, Every Day of the Year

preach on the parable of the talents. Remember that one? A landowner goes away on a journey and leaves three servants five, two, and one talent respectively. When he returns, he quizzes the men on what they've done with their talents. I groaned. Our church was in the middle of a building campaign, and I didn't want to hear about money, and I wrongly figured that's what this sermon would be about. I've seldom heard this Bible Scripture preached when it wasn't connected to raising money for something or other.

I'm a pretty good listener to sermons, however, and try as I would, I was unable to block out the words spoken so that in my mind I could travel somewhere far off. Once our pastor finished reading the parable from Scripture, he cut loose on what I thought was another topic altogether. He prefaced it with telling us to think about what the parable was saying to us individually. I thought perhaps he might have changed his mind about what he wanted to preach, abandoned it, and instead selected another topic. Midway through the sermon, however, I understood his message, what he was doing. This was the Sunday before Thanksgiving, and he was preaching a Thanksgiving sermon—four things for which we need to be thankful. He planted the seed of the parable of the talents, preached, and then left the rest up to God, knowing that our Lord would implant an individual message in the minds of each member of the congregation if that member would open herself up to the message.

What was my message, you ask? What are you doing with what God has given you? For me that's what this parable is all about. It doesn't have to apply to money or possessions or abilities or whatever else might be out there. It simply means: what are you doing with what God has given you? That's a good question, don't you think?

325 A NUMBER OF TIMES, ONE OF OUR CHILDREN HAS approached me with a request, hoping I would grant it. More often than not, the child received what he or she wanted. But, a number of times, I have denied a child's request, even as the child pleaded with me. These incidents were especially difficult if my child knew it was in my power to grant what he or she wanted. Our children are now grown and as far as I know have forgotten about the times when they wanted this or that, or if they have not forgotten they understand the reasons more clearly now, being parents themselves.

Many times God's children approach Him in the same way, asking the Heavenly Father for this or that, knowing it is within their Father's power to grant their petition. More often than not, God grants the request, but sometimes our Father denies a plea. It is at such times that I remind myself of the words of Jeremiah: "Ah Lord thou hast made the heaven and the earth by thy great power and stretched out arm, and there is nothing too hard for thee" (Jer. 32:17, KJV).

Nothing is too hard for God. Nothing is hidden from Him. When God tells us no, He has good reasons to do so. Just as we hope our children will trust us to act in their best interest, so must we trust our heavenly Father as He wills and works in us of His good pleasure. We may never know why God refuses a petition. Our only responsibility is to trust Him, even as he says, "No."

326

As I prepared to attend church services this morning, I did so with a heavy heart. I had been waiting for God to respond to a prayer request, one left hanging in the air for quite some time. God's answer came yesterday and His answer was no. I tried to pretend, mostly to myself, that I was all right with God's response, but I wasn't. My heart ached, and I wanted to do nothing but cry. I couldn't even muster tears though, only another prayer: "Speak to me in today's service, Lord. Give me something to hold on to," and of course He did, not only through the sermon but through the words of the congregational singing and response reading as well. I voiced in song with others such words as: "Let's just praise the Lord!; Bless the Lord, O my soul, and all that is within me, bless His holy name; He has done great things; Great and mighty is the Lord our God; Shine, Jesus, shine, fill this land with the Father's glory; Majesty, worship His majesty, Unto Jesus be all glory, honor, and praise . . . So exalt, lift up on high the name of Jesus . . . Jesus, who died, now glorified, King of all kings." I even sang the words as I've never been able to sing them before, being able to reach even the highest notes and being surprised with the way my untrained voice sounded as I sang. The music ended with a piano and organ rendition of "Be Still, My Soul." I stood with the congregation and responded with them, "Lift up your heads, O ye gates, even lift them up, ye everlasting doors; and the king of glory shall come in" (Ps. 24:9, KJV). And to top off God's response to my recent prayer, our preacher's sermon topic was, "Can You Hold, Please?"

Yes, God denied one of my prayer requests, but as He did so, He took me in His loving arms, comforted me, and dried my tears. I continue to trust God to know what is best for me, His child.

327 REGARDLESS OF WHAT MIGHT COME INTO OUR LIVES seeking to rob us of joy and a peace of mind, we must join Habakkuk the prophet in saying, "Yet I will rejoice in the Lord, I will joy in the God of my salvation" (Hab. 3:18, KJV), and we can proclaim this message of assurance because, "The Lord God is my strength, and he will make me to walk upon mine high places . . ."(Hab. 3:19).

Regardless of what this day may bring our way or what yesterday brought or what might lie ahead for us in the future, we can rejoice because God is our strength, and He is forever walking with us as we travel the road leading to those high places, the ones so near to God that we can reach out and touch Him, and the ones that are near His heart.

328 TWENTY-FIVE YEARS AGO, MY HUSBAND TRANSPLANTED a young maple tree from his parents' yard to ours. It was small and somewhat scraggly when it went into the ground, but over the years, it blossomed into a gorgeous sight in the fall. I soon began calling it Glory Tree because of its awesome and splendid seasonal elegance. After the death of my in-laws, the tree took on more significance for me. It came to represent them. I often talked to the tree as if I were addressing them, especially around Thanksgiving. Traditionally, our family celebrated this day with his parents. After their homegoings, we could no longer do this of course, but in my mind and heart Glory Tree became their substitute. If she peeked to her splendid seasonal display on Thanksgiving day, I considered myself blessed indeed, convincing myself they were here celebrating the day with us. Seldom did Glory Tree honor me in this way, for she often shed many of her leaves before

Thanksgiving. The height of her beauty seldom coincided with the day.

This past Thanksgiving, however, Glory Tree outdid herself. Never had I seen her look so splendid. She was magnificent and rained her golden leaves to the ground, littering it with a dazzling array of awesome charm. My father-in-law especially loved babies and little children, and I had thought earlier in the week how sad for both my in-laws that they could not see their four young great-grandchildren—would never know them. How they would have enjoyed being around these babies. And then I realized a truth, one brought to my attention by Glory's fantastic autumn display. The spirits of my in-laws had always permeated the festivities of the day. Were not Glory Tree's seasonal and timely display a testimony to this? Were not her golden leaves falling on the very tops of the heads of their great-grandchildren as they romped and played on the ground beneath the tree? My in-laws might not have been here physically, but they were here in spirit, and they were present in all our hearts. Would I have come to this knowledge if Glory Tree hadn't all but knocked me down with her splendor this year? I don't think so.

329

GLORY TREE'S LEAVES RAINED AN AWESOME DISPLAY of golden warmth to the ground on this particular Thanksgiving Day. I could hardly keep my eyes off her and what lay beneath her on the ground. I romped with one of my grandchildren beneath her limbs, scooping up handfuls of dry leaves, tossing them in the air to watch them fall to the ground once again. It was then I noticed one of our children's cars parked a short distance from Glory Tree. There were no leaves beneath the car. An ample supply of them dotted the car's hood and top, but there was nothing but bare ground underneath it.

The next day, after all our company returned to their own homes, I looked at the spot on the ground that had been void of leaves the day before. It now was covered with Glory's golden leaves. Another moment of epiphany occurred. It was as if my in-laws said, "We were here. We have always been here. We will always be here. We have such lovely great-grandchildren." A covering of the once vacant spot on the ground was for me their seasonal farewell to us until next year, when they once again would join us for Thanksgiving day.

Already Ours, Every Day of the Year

330 ONCE THERE WERE TWO PREGNANT PROSTITUTES WHO shared a house, and the time came for them to deliver their newborn babies. No doctor, in fact no one at all, assisted in these deliveries. The baby boys came three days apart. Soon thereafter, during the night, one woman rolled on top of her baby and accidentally smothered him, woke up at midnight, and discovered her baby dead. She then took her dead child and placed him in the arms of the other woman and took the other woman's live baby back to bed with her. The next morning, the woman with the dead baby beside her awoke and prepared to nurse him, but she discovered the baby at her side was dead, and it was not her child. She immediately confronted the other woman, who denied the dead baby was hers, saying the live one in her arms was her baby. The women argued and argued, getting nowhere to a resolution to their dilemma. Finally they came to the king of the land in which they lived and pled their case before him.

"And the king said, Bring me a sword . . . Divide the living child in two, and give half to the one, and half to the other" (1Kings 3:24–25, KJV).

And then the woman whose child it was said, "O my lord, give her the living child, and in no wise slay it" (1 Kings 3:26a, KJV).

The other woman would have none of it for she said, "Let it be neither mine nor thine, but divide it" (1 Kings 3:26b, KJV).

This was not a matter of "If I can't have it, then you can't either." The woman who accidentally smothered her baby could have walked away with the other woman's child, but she didn't. Why? She could have confessed her plot to the king, but she didn't. Why? She could have taken the baby home and then given him back his mother, but she didn't. Why? Why did this woman want this baby dead? Why was she so eager to sacrifice him? I don't know. I can only speculate, but I do know the characteristics of love. Love is long-suffering and it is kind. Love isn't envious or full of pride and it isn't selfish. Love is not easily provoked; it is unsuspecting of evil and doesn't rejoice in evil but rejoices in truth. Love bears all things, believes all things, hopes all things, and endures all things. Love never fails. The greatest gift we can give another is the gift of love.

King Solomon said, "Give her the living child, and in no way slay it; she is the mother thereof" (1 Kings 3:27, KJV). How did Solomon know who the real mother was? He knew by her love as demonstrated by her willingness to give up her child in order to save his life. We are known by our love or by our lack of it. The proof is in the pudding.

331 PRECIOUS GEMS AND STONES AND GOLD AND SILVER coins lay at our feet, begging us to pick them up, admire them, and put them to use. An abundance of wealth surrounds us, but unfortunately most of us are unaware of it. God is forever willing and working in us of His good pleasure to bring us into the image of His Son, Jesus Christ, and in doing so, He takes mundane things and works them together for our overall good.

Far too many of us are unaware of God's work in us and the great lengths He employs to educate us and grow us. God speaks to us continually. Every moment of every day His still, small voice echoes from the far distances of the world to that which is beneath our very noses. God's essence is everywhere and it is in everything. So vast is His work in us that, as humans, we're unable to take it all in. Our problem is not an inability to absorb it, but, rather, not paying attention to His work in us, not allowing ourselves to be conscious of more than a small measure of what is going on around us. Every second we experience, God is in it. All we have to do is reach out and take the treasures He has dropped at our feet. They are already ours. Be still, my friend. Absorb the moment you are in, for God is there with you, willing and working in you of His good pleasure. It matters not whether the moment is one of joy or one of sadness—God is in that moment, completing His work in you.

332 I TAKE COMFORT THAT THOSE WHO HAVE GONE BEFORE me have fought the same battles I have. They have wrestled with the same problems and agonized over the same decisions and struggled with the same dilemmas. They have prayed the same prayers and shed the same tears. And our God has recorded it all, and He has taken all of our tears and put them in His bottle, for our tears are precious to Him.

Those before me have prayed, "Mine enemies would daily swallow me up: for they be many that fight against me, O thou most High" (Ps. 56:2, KJV). They too have fallen back on the words, "What time I am afraid, I will trust in thee" (Ps. 56:3, KJV). They too have thought, "Every day they wrest my words: all their thoughts are against me for evil" (Ps. 56:2, KJV). Other generations have experienced their enemies gathering "themselves together, they hide themselves, they mark my steps, when they wait for my soul" (Ps. 56:6, KJV).

With the psalmist each generation can proclaim: "In God I will praise his word, in God I have put my trust; I will not fear what flesh can do unto me. In God will I praise his word: in the Lord will I praise his word. In God have I put my trust: I will not be afraid what man can do unto me" (Ps. 52:4, 10–11, KJV).

333 THERE WERE TIMES WHEN DAVID FELT WHAT YOU AND I have felt: "Oh that I had wings like a dove! for then would I fly away, and be at rest" (Ps. 55:6, KJV). He wanted to run away from his problems too. He wanted to put distance between himself and his "windy storm and tempest" (Ps. 56:8, KJV). David experienced a broken heart, one greatly pained. He felt a fearfulness and he trembled because of it. Horror overwhelmed him, but he came to the same conclusion we must: "Cast thy burden upon the Lord, and he shall sustain thee: he shall never suffer the righteous to be moved" (Ps. 56:22, KJV). Yes, my friend, cast your burden on God. He will sustain you.

334 THE MOST DIFFICULT PART OF MY DAILY TREADMILL walk occurs at midpoint. Because I know I have as far to go as I've already been, I often groan, wishing my task were over. The easiest part of my walk occurs exactly two minutes before the end of it. At the twenty-eighth minute, I begin to count off seconds, an easy task because my cadence is in rhythm to them. A minute passes quickly. During the twenty-ninth minute, I slow my pace in order for my body to cool down. That minute seems no more than the twinkling of an eye because the end of my task is in sight.

It is much the same way when problems and trials and difficulties appear on our horizons. It is at the midpoint of trials that most of us want to throw up our hands and quit and walk away. It isn't until we see the light at the end of our troubled tunnels that we take heart because we know an end to our distress is in sight. All problems, troubles, and difficulties have a beginning, a middle, and an ending to them. Hold on, my friend. There is always a light at the end of any tunnel.

335 AS I DROVE TO THE POST OFFICE, A FEW CAR LENGTHS in front of me a squirrel darted across the road. I spied the squirrel's companion several feet behind it, but instead of continuing to follow after the first squirrel, the second one paused momentarily, turned around, and scurried back in the direction from which it had come.

"Thank goodness," I said, because I knew if the squirrel had continued on its path, I couldn't have avoided hitting it. That little creature felt the road's vibrations, heeded them, and took cover.

Would that we were as wise as that squirrel. If you know trouble's coming your way, my friend, then exercise prudence and good judgment and rush into the arms of our Lord, Who is ever there watching over His children and taking care of them.

336 GEORGE FREDERICK HANDEL COMPOSED *The Messiah*, one of the most noble oratorios ever written. Even though he was German, Queen Anne of England gave him a pension, and Handel settled in England, becoming head of the newly founded Royal Academy of Music. *The Messiah*, Handel's chief work, came out in 1742 for the benefit of the Foundling Hospital in Dublin. At first, the work was not well received. Today *The Messiah* is considered one of the greatest oratorios ever written. It is next to impossible for me to read portions of chapter forty in the book of Isaiah that I don't sing the words: "Comfort ye my people . . . Every valley shall be exalted . . . And the glory of the Lord . . . and He shall feed his flock like a shepherd."

337 IN THREE OF THE GOSPELS IN THE NEW TESTAMENT, we read about a time in the life of Jesus when he was by the seaside, teaching a great multitude of people. The crowd was so large, Jesus got into a boat and the boat became the podium from which He related many parables to the people. When evening came, Jesus sent the people away, gathered His disciples into the boat with Him, and set sail for the other side of the sea. Jesus then went to an area near the back of the boat and fell asleep. "And there arose a great storm of wind, and the waves beat into the ship, so that it was now full" (Mark 4:37, KJV). This storm was so fierce that "the ship was covered with the waves . . ." (Matt. 8:24, KJV). The disciples were terrified, fearing their vessel would sink. They ran to Jesus, found Him sleeping and shouted Him awake with an accusation: "carest thou not that we perish?" (Mark 5:38, KJV). And they screamed, "Lord, save us: we perish" (Matt. 8:25, KJV).

Jesus immediately got up and rebuked the wind and commanded the sea, "Peace, be still . . ." (Mark 4:39, KJV). "And the wind ceased, and there was a great calm" (v. 39). Jesus then asked the disciples, "Why are ye so fearful? how is it that ye have no faith?" (Mark 4:40, KJV).

Our Lord continues to ask this question of us. Why are we so afraid? Where is our faith? God is in control and He is forever with us. When the winds of troubles blow into our lives, and the storms of sufferings seep through the cracks, God is forever there. He is not asleep, for He dwells in our hearts. His words will come: "Peace, be still." When they do, we will say as did His disciples: "What manner of man is this, that even the wind and the sea obey him?" (Mark 4:41, Matt. 8:27, Luke 8:25, KJV).

338 Jesus said, "Is a candle brought to be put under a bushel, or under a bed? and not to be set on a candlestick?" (Mark 4:21, KJV). "No man when he hath lighted a candle, covereth it with a vessel, or putteth it under a bed, but setteth it on a candlestick, that they which enter in may see the light" (Luke 8:16, KJV).

This parable conveys the meaning of God's children being lights and our allowing our lights to shine so that others can more readily see the way. Whether we're conscious of it or not, everyone sees us for who we are. If we allow ourselves to become chameleons—blowing with the wind depending on whose company we're in—we fool no one but ourselves, and we immediately cover our lights, hiding them. God's children belong on candlesticks. Our lights are not for our benefit alone. Our lights are to brighten the darkness around us, not only for ourselves, but for others as well.

339 KING SOLOMON MADE POOR MARITAL CHOICES. HE was a wise man, and yet his wisdom failed him concerning women. He made marital alliances with the daughter of Pharaoh and some of the daughters of the Moabites, Ammonites, Edomites, Zidonians, and Hittites—people God forbade the nation of Israel to marry. Solomon's wives turned his heart away from God, as God predicted they would. Not only did Solomon follow after Ashtoreth, the goddess of the Zidonians, and Molech, whom the Ammorites worshipped, but he built a pagan shrine in honor of Chemosh, pagan god of Moab, and yet another shrine to honor Molech. Solomon had seven hundred wives whose gods and goddesses he honored as well. For all of his wisdom, "Solomon did evil in the sight of the Lord, and went not fully after the Lord, as did David his father" (1 Kings 11:7, KJV). As a result of his idolatry, at Solomon's death God stripped ten of Israel's tribe from him, dividing Israel into two kingdoms.

What a pity, and all because a very wise man disobeyed God and did the very thing God had forbidden him to do. And yet today we continue to worship at pagan shrines, although these gods are not as blatantly clear to us. They are as numerous as the sand in the seas, and they are called by many names: money, pride, fame, prestige, beauty, honor, and glory being only a few of them. Any person, any place, or anything that means more to us than God does becomes a pagan god for us.

340 OUR ALMOST TWO-YEAR-OLD-GRANDSON CAME bounding from around the corner of his house. Apparently, he had heard his father, as had my husband and I, when he had said, "Here come Gamma and Paw Paw." Our grandson, mouth curled downward, a frown on his face with his eyes on the ground, plowed as fast as his legs would carry him in my direction. He didn't look upward or hold out his arms in a gesture to be picked up, but I scooped him into my arms, greeted him, and gave him a hug and kiss. He wrapped his arms around my neck and held on for dear life. Apparently, something had just happened to hurt his

Already Ours, Every Day of the Year

feelings, and he came running to Gamma for comfort.

When it came time for our visit to end, our grandson was busily playing chase with his older brother and one of the older boys who lived next door to him. Usually, whenever we tell our grandsons goodbye, they and their parents walk us to our car with a lot of hugging and kissing and verbal demonstrations of love going on. When we called out a goodbye to our grandsons, the younger one smiled and waved to us, but made no attempt to quit playing. No longer were his feelings hurt. He had been comforted, and now he busied himself with the task at hand.

The same thing happens when we run to our heavenly Father for comfort, reassurance, and help for those hurtful and painful situations that occur in our lives. He takes us in His arms, talks to us, and soothes us, and then, just as my grandson did, we jump down and busy ourselves with the goings on around us.

No balm is as soothing as the balm of Gilead. Nothing calms when we're upset or when we're hurt as does an encounter with our heavenly Father.

341 SOMETIMES WE BELIEVE NO ONE CARES ABOUT US OR what happens to us. We are not alone in this kind of thinking. Millenniums ago, King David cried out, "no man cared for my soul" (Ps. 142:4, KJV). David was hiding in a cave, and he was overwhelmed with thoughts of being ensnared and trapped with nowhere to go, nowhere to turn, no refuge in sight, believing nobody cared what happened to him. At this moment he cried out to God for help: "Thou art my refuge and my portion in the land of the living" (Ps. 142:5, KJV). "Listen to me," he pleaded. "I am brought very low; deliver me from my persecutors, for they are stronger than I" (Ps. 142:6, KJV).

When you're feeling nobody cares about you or what is happening to you, follow in David's footsteps and pour out your heart to God and know as did David, "for thou shall deal bountifully with me" (v. 7). God cares what happens to us, and that's what counts and that's what sustains us.

342 IT COMFORTS ME AND IT ALSO ENCOURAGES ME TO know that others who have gone before me have felt overwhelmed, experiencing troubles and problems that lead to a desolation of spirit. I need to know that when the going gets tough, others resort to some of the same kinds of defense mechanisms I employ, one of which is thinking about the good old days and how simple life seemed in them. Unlike David who sang, "I remember the days of old . . ." (Ps. 143:5, KJV), when nostalgia comes knocking at my door I don't take it far enough. Unlike David, I don't move quickly away from my thoughts about the good old days and rush headlong into meditations regarding God's work in me during them.

It comforts me and also encourages me to know that if David can think about yesterday in terms of God's work in him, then so can I. I can confess to God as did he: "my spirit faileth: hide not thy face from me, lest I be like unto them that go down into the pit" (Ps. 143:7, KJV). I can pray these words with him: "Cause me to hear thy lovingkindness in the morning; for in thee do I trust: cause me to know thy way wherein I should walk; for I lift up my soul to thee" (Ps. 143:8, KJV). And having done so, I can freely ask God: "Teach me to do thy will; for thou art my God: thy spirit is good; lead me into the land of uprightness" (Ps. 143:10, KJV).

Having finally reached this plane, I can then join with David proclaiming: "for I am thy servant" (Ps. 143:12, KJV).

343 GOD IS GOOD. HE IS OUR FORTRESS. HE IS OUR HIGH tower. He is our liberator. He is our shield. We can trust Him. Knowing this, I ask along with King David, "What is man, that thou takest knowledge of him! or the son of man, that thou makest account of him!" (Ps. 144:3, KJV).

Happy are those who know the Lord as their heavenly Father. God loves each and every one of His children, and He is a fortress, a high tower, a liberator, and a shield for them. God's children can trust Him in everything and for everything for "happy is that people, whose God is the Lord" (Ps. 144:15, KJV).

344 NO MUSICAL INSTRUMENT TOUCHES MY SOUL OR reaches the depth of my being as does the pipe organ, especially when it groans a classical piece of sacred music. Hearing such notes and drinking them in is the next best thing to heaven itself. I have somehow convinced myself that when I enter those pearly gates, my entrance into heaven and into God's presence will be accompanied not by a heavenly being alone but by the music of a pipe organ, throttles open full, and sounding out sacred notes that I've never heard before. And then as I fall prostrate before the Lord paying homage to Him, God will say, "Well done, thy good and faithful servant."

And I will respond, "This is what I wanted."

345 "The Lord is my light and my salvation; whom shall I fear? The Lord is the strength of my life; of whom shall I be afraid?" (Ps. 27:1, KJV). I know that God is my light, and I know He is my salvation, and I understand He is the strength of my life, and yet there are times when I am terrified in spite of what I know about God.

Isaiah wrote: "Fear thou not . . . for I am with thee: be not dismayed; for I am thy God: I will strengthen thee; yea, I will help thee; yea, I will uphold thee with the right hand of my righteousness" (Isa. 4:10, KJV). God, Who is our salvation and our strength, is with us always. As God walks along beside us every step of our way, He holds our right hand as He whispers into our ear, "Fear not; I will help thee" (Isa. 41:13, KJV). And then He says, "Wait on the Lord: be of good courage, and he shall strengthen thine heart: wait, I say, on the Lord" (Ps. 27:14, KJV).

Fear not. Be of good courage. God is our strength. He is our light and He is our salvation. Wait for Him. And in the meantime, let's hold up our right hands, for our Lord God is reaching out for them. Don't be afraid.

346 When my children were growing up and they fell and scraped a knee or injured themselves in some other way, I would scoop them into my arms and kiss away the pain. When they were teenagers, I would listen to their tales of woe, empathizing with them. My spirit marched with them throughout their college days, again lending an ear to troubled words. Today I'm only a telephone call away and available with a salve for their injured spirits. As long as I am alive and my mental capacities are intact I will bind up their wounds the best I can, and I will do this because they are my children and I love them.

It is the same with God. "He healeth the broken in heart, and bindeth up their wounds" (Ps. 147:3, KJV). There is a difference, however, between an earthly parent and an Heavenly One. Humanity limits our abilities to heal or comfort or control events. God has no limits, so when He tells us that He heals our broken hearts and binds up our wounds, then we can rest assured He will do just that.

347 Sometimes we feel alone and we believe no one cares about us. At such times, it would serve us well to remember the psalmist's words: "As the mountains are round about Jerusalem, so the Lord is round about his people, from henceforth even for ever" (Ps. 123:2, KJV). God is with His children— He always has been and He always will be. We are never alone. Others may forsake us, but God never will. God cares about us and what happens to us. He invites us to commit our burdens to Him and to trust Him to work on our behalf. He always has worked for us and He always will work for us.

"Cast thy burden upon the Lord, and he shall sustain thee . . ." (Ps. 55:22, KJV).

348 There are twenty-six verses in Psalm 136, and God has the writer of these words repeat twenty-six times, "for his mercy endureth forever." In four of those verses, the psalmist urges, "O give thanks unto the Lord," and he enumerates solid reasons for so doing: God is good; God performs great wonders; God created the heavens; God divided the land from the seas; God created the planets and the moon and sun and the stars; God rescued His people from Egyptian bondage; God divided the Red Sea so His people could flee on dry land in order that He might guide them during their wilderness wanderings; God then rescued His people from wicked kings and gave them a promised land. God redeems and God continually provides for His children. Let us sing along with the psalmists, "O give thanks unto the God of heaven: for his mercy endureth for ever."

Forever is a mighty long time. God's mercy endures forever. We are never without it.

Already Ours, Every Day of the Year

349 SOMETIMES WE GET SO CAUGHT UP IN A MOMENT'S happenings or a situation threatening to engulf us that we don't pause long enough to take inventory of God's mighty acts, especially those initiated on our behalf. We become spiritually nearsighted and somewhat pessimistic in attitude. Some are even bold enough to shake their fists heavenward, accusing God of not being there for them, completely ignoring the multitude of times God has reached down from heaven and rescued them from danger or trouble or trials or distress. God has done great things for each of His children.

At some point of each day, I try to pause and reflect on God's mighty acts on my behalf and either silently or aloud thank Him for the numerous blessings He has granted me. Our heavenly Father continually wills and works in our lives to bring us into the image of His Son. We, His children, are more than millionaires. We are more than conquerors. We are His heirs, the recipients of everything that belongs to Him. He never forsakes us. He never turns His back on us. He is forever in our corner. God has done great things for us.

How does it make you feel when you give a splendid gift and the receiver accepts it with the unspoken question lingering in his or her mouth: "Is this all?"

350 UNFORTUNATELY WE ARE A JUDGMENTAL LOT. SOME OF us pride ourselves on not being judgmental, but nevertheless, we are. It is our nature. Another's dress is inappropriate or speech is inadequate or manner is weird or house is tacky or car is old or hair is outlandish. We might not verbalize it, but we think it. Whether we admit it to ourselves or not, we continually make judgments on people and places and things and situations. We judge everything, and since we do, then it would seem wise for us to raise our voices heavenward and request along with the psalmist: "Teach me good judgment and knowledge . . ." (Ps. 119:66, KJV). Yes, Lord, teach us good judgment.

351 SOMETIMES THE SKIES SEEM TO OPEN UP AND RAIN down troubles by the dozens on our heads. We mumble above the rumble of the racket engulfing us, "Help!" but no help comes—not from mankind anyway. God, however, hears our plea, and He is quick to act on our behalf. No call to Him for help ever goes unheeded. Look not to man to save you, dear friend. God is ever there, watching over you and taking care of you. Know that "Through God we shall do valiantly: for he it is that shall tread down our enemies" (Ps. 108:13, KJV).

352 WHO AMONG US HAS NOT OPENED HIS OR HER MOUTH and then put his or her foot into it? If David, the king and ruler of Israel, sought help from God for this kind of dilemma, then what prevents our doing so? Let us also cry with David, "Set a watch, O Lord, before my mouth; keep the door of my lips" (Ps. 141:3, KJV).

353 THE PSALMIST WROTE, "I THOUGHT ON MY WAYS, AND turned my feet unto thy testimonies" (Ps. 119:59, KJV). It would serve us all well to take stock of our behavior and monitor our words. From time to time, we need to ruminate on what it is within us that drives us and, as we do so, remember that "Thou art my portion, O Lord: I have said that I would keep thy words" (Ps. 119:57, KJV). In so doing, we can voice with the psalmist, "I made haste, and delayed not to keep thy commandments" (Ps. 119:60, KJV).

354 TODAY IS THE ANNIVERSARY OF THE DEATH OF THE SON of a dear friend of mine. Even though this event occurred many years ago, deep anguish and pain still resides in her heart. I don't think anyone ever gets over the loss of a child. I called her this morning to check to see how she was weathering the day. She sounded sad, but did say she and her husband were going out of town to visit a nearby city that was decked out with Christmas decorations and lights, eat lunch there and perhaps dinner, and then return home. She told me, however, that two days ago, she'd spent the day crying, and since doing this was feeling somewhat better.

My prayer for her and her family today is: Lord, may joy come into their lives today through what their eyes behold in the lights of Christmas. May her tears serve as a balm for her deep sorrow. "They that sow in tears shall reap in joy" (Ps. 126:5, KJV). May it be so for my friend, Lord. May it be so.

355 TODAY, MY HUSBAND'S EMPLOYEES BROUGHT ALL kinds of delicious covered dishes to work, celebrating the Christmas season. This has become an annual affair for them and some of them had their families with them. In the midst of waiting on customers, everyone managed to pile up a plate of food and scurry to find a place to eat the feast. One almost two-year-old boy caught my eye and attention. He is the grandson of a retired employee. He took all of this hullabaloo in stride and gave me the impression that he thought these goings-on were not out of the ordinary at all. He just waited for his grandmother to fix him a plate and then sat down to eat what she had prepared for him.

Is this not the way it is for us who are God's children? He goes to great lengths to prepare many feasts for us. All we have to do is what this little boy did: just sit down and wait for God to bring what He has prepared for us to us. He always does. And, my friend, it's well worth the wait.

356 HAS ANYONE EVER ACCUSED YOU BY SAYING, "A promise is a promise is a promise?" From time to time, all of us are prone to renege on a promise, perhaps one we've made in haste or without thought. God never goes back on His word. God says, "Great peace have they which love thy law: and nothing shall offend them" (Ps. 119:165, KJV).

Great peace is a gift of God. He promises it to those who love His law. As we love God's law, nothing comes along that shall offend us — nothing. This is God's promise to us, and He always keeps His word.

357 KING DAVID UNDERSTOOD THAT GOD KNEW EVERY- thing about him. He acknowledged that God took note of when he went to bed and when he got up. He understood that God knew his thoughts and his words even before he spoke them. And he said, "Whither shall I go from thy spirit? or whither shall I flee from thy presence" (Ps. 139:7, KJV). Eons before Francis Thompson even thought about penning the words to *The Hound of Heaven,* David knew there was no place under the heavens or the sun that he could flee without God being where he was. It was with such knowledge about God that David could sing, "Search me, O God, and know my heart: try me, and know my thoughts: And see if there be any wicked way in me, and lead me in the way everlasting" (Ps. 139:23–24, KJV).

Once we understand that God is everywhere and knows us even better than we know ourselves, we, too, can invite our Lord to search us and know our hearts and to try us by knowing our thoughts. It is with such knowledge that we can rest in God, knowing it is more than safe to invite Him to sit a spell with us because we have nothing to hide from the One who already knows all there is to know about us and loves us still.

358 CHRISTMAS EVE MY HUSBAND AND I SAT IN THE FLOOR trying to assemble a wagon for our grandson. We got the wheels on and the sides, and then we turned our attention to attaching the handle to the front of the wagon. This meant inserting a rod through eight separate holes. Sound easy, right? Well, it wasn't. There was no way to see the holes once we entered the first one, and we unsuccessfully worked and worked, trying to get the rod to navigate all eight of them. Finally, in desperation, my husband threw his hands up and asked me to try to do it. I began the task, but I couldn't do it. I worked and worked, managing to pass by several of the openings, but my frustration level began to rise sharply.

"Lord, I know this is such a small thing to ask," I silently prayed, "and I know there are a lot of really big things out there, but it seems if we get this handle on this wagon, then you're going to have to do it for us because we can't do it."

The rod immediately slid through all eight holes and my husband secured its ends with the equipment provided for the task. Mumbling, "Thank you, Lord," I set about with other chores.

Nothing is too great and nothing is too small to bring to the attention of our Heavenly Father. He is ever willing and He is ever able to assist us. Our dilemma is not whether we are able to accomplish something, but

Already Ours, Every Day of the Year

whether we trust in our own strength or knowledge to do it. Blessed are we if we understand that God is in everything and is always there for us. All we have to do is turn it over to Him and let Him lead the way to the path He's opened for us.

359

A LONG TIME AGO, THERE WAS A YOUNG GIRL ENGAGED to marry a young man. She lived in a small town and when she became pregnant during her engagement period, the people in her town gossiped about her, rumors clicking on many tongues. As she passed down a street, people stared at her, and gave her condemning glances. Little children made fun of her and some of the elders of the town sighed and shook their heads from side to side as she brushed past them. Her fiancé wanted to break his engagement to her because he knew he was not the father of her child. He loved her, however, and he wanted to do this in such a way that she wouldn't be shamed. As the young man thought on how he might accomplish this, he had a dream, and a man appeared in his dream and told him not to be afraid to marry the young girl. The man went on to tell him the young lady would have a boy, and then the man told the young man what the child's name would be. When the young man awakened from his dream, he went and married the young lady.

Before the young lady knew the heart of the young man regarding her condition, however, she left town and went to visit a cousin in another town. The moment the young lady entered the house of her cousin and greeted her, her cousin said to her, "Blessed art thou among women, and blessed is the fruit of thy womb. And whence is this to me, that the mother of my Lord should come to me? For, lo, as soon as the voice of thy salutation sounded in mine ears, the babe leaped in my womb for joy. And blessed is she that believed: for there shall be a performance of those things which were told her from the Lord" (Luke 1:42–45, KJV).

By now you have guessed the identity of the young woman and young man. We have no written record of how people responded to Mary's pregnancy, what was said to her, if anything, or how she responded to the way the people might have treated her. We know the fruit of her womb was Jesus, and we know He was miraculously conceived. And Mary's response to receiving the news of her pregnancy from Gabriel is recorded for us: "Behold the handmaid of the Lord; be it unto me according to thy word" (Luke 1:38, KJV). Mary's beautiful discourse delivered to her cousin, Elisabeth, is also recorded with her saying in part of it: "My soul doth magnify the Lord. And my spirit hath rejoiced in God my Saviour" (Luke 1:46–47, KJV).

Through the ages, among the many things that can be said about us, one of them has not changed: We are a judgmental lot. It doesn't matter who it is or what the circumstances might be, far too many of us jump to wrong conclusions about others and, in so doing, heap coals of sorrow and pain and condemnation on the heads of those whom we think are not as good as we are, who in our view don't live up to our standards. From time to time all of us are guilty of this kind of thinking.

Let us now focus on the little Boy, the One who "grew, and waxed strong in spirit, filled with wisdom: and the grace of God was upon him" (Luke 2:40, KJV). There is no doubt in my mind that as this little Boy made His way about the streets of Nazareth, tongues clicked and heads wagged and gossip filled the air. Some people have long memories indeed.

Lord, help us not to be judgmental. Help us to leave all judgment in Your hands, and in so doing stretch out our own, offering love and help and guidance to those whom the world has turned their backs on.

360

LAST NIGHT I WATCHED A TELEVISION ADAPTATION OF Truman Capote's book, *A Christmas Memory*. The bond between the young boy, Buddy, and maiden older cousin, Sooky, tugged at my heartstrings. I knew exactly what Sooky felt when she had to tell Buddy goodbye. Unfortunately, one of Sooky's sisters decided Buddy needed to be in a military academy rather than living at home with four people over the age of fifty.

I had a brother who was thirteen months older than I, and his name was Buddy. When he was about six, my divorced mother sent him away to live with my paternal grandparents. Mother and I remained with her parents. I was too young at that time to understand grief and my need to mourn, so I did nothing more than a day's worth of tears and clinging to a lifelong memory of a boy who had meant the world to me. It wasn't until years later, when Buddy died in adulthood, that I finally comprehended my early loss and my deep need to mourn

Already Ours, Every Day of the Year

life without him. I did more than a day's worth of tears then. They lasted almost a year, but the tears healed me and helped me through not only my current loss but that long ago and faraway one—the one that happened when I didn't have the skills to deal with it.

If Jesus wept, then why is it so many of us refuse to do so or are ashamed to do so? Our Heavenly Father collects our tears. They are precious in His sight. Cry, my friend. Tears will cleanse your soul. They will heal your sorrow.

361 NOT TOO MUCH IS MORE ELECTRIFYING THAN DECOrating a Christmas tree, placing each ornament just so and arranging the lights and garland in such a way that those who see it gasp at its loveliness. And nothing is more unexciting than taking down that same tree and placing those same ornaments, lights, and garland in their resting places, awaiting another season and another tree to adorn.

As I undecorated this year's tree, I began to wonder what the new year would bring my way. As I put away each ornament and tucked the lights and garland in their boxes, I prayed that whatever happened this new year, I would turn my eyes heavenward and look into the face of my Heavenly Father, who is willing to guide and direct my paths and enable me to choose wisely. He's never failed me yet, and He never will. And He will never fail you either. How blessed we are to have such a loving Father.

362 MY MOST VIVID MEMORY OF EARLY CHILDHOOD IS ONE of uncontrollable, unrelenting weeping. At that time, my divorced mother lived with my six-year-old brother and me in a house with her parents. My grandfather struggled financially trying to make ends meet and to provide food, clothing, and shelter for not only my mother, brother, and me, but also for my uncle and three aunts, one the same age as I was. About the only thing my grandfather had going for him was that his other grown daughter was married and, at that time, didn't live with the rest of us.

For many decades after this time, I thought my tears were prompted by my brother threatening to pack a few duds and run away from home.

I adored my older brother. I envisioned him as my protector, thinking he stood between me and the rest of the world.

Gobs of time passed before I remembered my weeping was the result of my mother sending my brother away to live with my other set of grandparents. It wasn't until my brother died in adulthood that I recalled the events of that day differently than I had remembered them. My brother wasn't going to run away. My mother was sending him away.

The more I cried, the more my mother threatened me with a spanking if I didn't hush. The more she threatened, the more I wept. Try as I would, I couldn't quit sobbing. I had worked myself into such a state that it frightened me out of my wits I would never be able to hush. If I didn't shut up, I erroneously believed my mother just might send me away too. I couldn't get my mother to understand this. I couldn't get her to see that I was trying to quit crying. Somehow I finally managed to quell my sobs. Unfortunately, after this episode, I only allowed myself to cry when I was alone. Even then, I tried to squelch my tears.

Not only did I seldom cry, I divorced myself from the feelings that produced tears. I shed none at the age of twelve when my maternal grandfather died or at the age of sixteen when my maternal grandmother also died. I never allowed myself to feel my anguish at losing my brother because I shoved him out of my mind. I was too busy protecting myself from also being sent away from home. I seldom acknowledged my brother was gone.

Once I rediscovered feelings of sadness over the loss of a father who would never be a part of my life and an adored brother who was snatched away from me, I located a well of uncried tears. I cut them loose, releasing the dam holding them back, and cried until my sorrow abated.

My husband and I recently saw the movie *Hope Floats*. In the scene where the little girl expects her father, who is separated from her mother, to take her back to his home with him and he doesn't, the child cuts loose in a fit of screaming and heart-wrenching sobs. I immediately thought of the time when I was five, and I couldn't quit crying. I felt the same sensations coming over me that I had had then, and I knew if I didn't breathe deeply, I would begin wailing. I also knew I wasn't suppressing my tears to please a mother who might send me away. I kept my emotions in check because I was in a movie theater, sitting by a husband who loved me and would understand, but I was also surrounded by strangers who wouldn't understand.

Jesus wept. He modeled this healthy behavior for us. Let us go and do likewise.

363 A WOMAN ONCE ASKED ME HOW I COULD BELIEVE A virgin could conceive and give birth to a baby. She was referring to the miraculous conception of Jesus. She went on to say such a thing is impossible. I was struck dumb by her question and didn't reply because I was unprepared to give her an answer. Later I pondered God parting the Red Sea and also the Jordan River — miracles indeed. Then I thought about God raining manna from heaven and quail from the sky so His people wouldn't starve. Other miraculous events. God spared David from Saul's wickedness and wrath on a number of occasions. Either David was quick-footed or Saul was a slow javelin thrower or God performed a miracle. I choose miracle. And then my thoughts turned to the multiple raisings from death recorded in the Bible — the widow's son and child in the Old Testament, and another widow's son, Jairus's daughter, Lazarus, Dorcas, and Eutychus in the New Testament. How, except for a miracle, were the five loaves of bread and two fish enough food to feed five thousand people? What about stories of the lame walking, the blind seeing, and the deaf hearing? All miracles, every one of them.

How could this woman question the miraculous birth of Jesus? And how could I not have been prepared to give this woman an answer to her question? "Preach the word; be instant in season, out of season; reprove, rebuke, exhort with all long-suffering and doctrine" (2 Tim. 4:2, KJV). We are to witness any time and any place. Let us pray today that we are instant in season and out of season. We never know when an opportunity will come our way to witness to others about Jesus.

364 EVERYBODY HAS DAYS WHERE THEY WOULD LIKE nothing more than to pull the bed covers up over their heads and stay put, not venturing out of bed at all. Sometimes life has a way of crashing down on us, causing us to wonder what life is all about anyway. The psalmist wrote, "Thou art my hiding place and my shield: I hope in thy word" (Ps. 119:114, KJV). Others who have gone before us have wanted to hide too. Other have felt helpless and hopeless. Others have felt defenseless, not knowing where to turn or what to do.

God is forever with His children. He is our hiding place. He is our shield. We can forever hope in Him, for He's never failed us yet—He's never let us down. We who belong to God don't have to resort to bed covers or caves or dungeons in which to hide. We don't have to shield ourselves. Our hope has been, is, and always will be in God's word—His promises as revealed to us by those inspired by Him to write the Holy Bible. "Thy word is a lamp unto my feet, and a light unto my path" (Ps. 119:105 KJV).

365 During the writing of this book, I painfully became aware of many of my shortcomings. My loveless behaviors became all too apparent to me. In the writing process, it was as if I journeyed to the core of my being, and in so doing saw myself in the raw, not painted up or covered over with the illusions we all carry around about who we are. I caught a glimpse of the real me, and in so doing could have hit rock bottom were it not for the book of Job, what our Lord recorded for us about him, and the knowledge of my standing before God.

Job was a good and upright man, a man who avoided evil and a man who loved God. Nevertheless, calamity struck him. His seven sons and three daughters were killed in a freak accident; he lost his seven thousand sheep, three thousand camels, five hundred yoke of oxen, and five hundred she asses. And on top of all this, God allowed Satan to inflict Job from the soles of his feet to the crown of his head with boils. Job's wife told him, "What are you waiting for? Curse God and die."

Three of Job's good friends came along to comfort him, telling him he must have some sort of secret and horrible sin in his life to cause such disasters to befall him.

The Open Bible tells us that no book "has wrestled so earnestly with the problem of suffering and evil as does the book of Job." I think we can all agree on this. But do we also understand, as is pointed out in the Open Bible, "the book of Job calls men to unreserved consecration to

Already Ours, Every Day of the Year

their sovereign Lord"? This is what writing *Already Ours, Every Day Of The Year* has done for me. During the work, I ventured inward, and I didn't like some of what I uncovered about myself, but this now-conscious personal knowledge about myself is that which calls me to an unreserved consecration to my sovereign Lord. Job was a righteous man. Because of God's finished work on the cross, I, too, am made righteous by the blood of the Lamb. With all of my failings, with all of my warts, with all of my shortcomings, with all of my weaknesses and flaws, I stand righteous before my King.

Would I have gotten to this point of understanding in my spiritual walk with God had I not plunged inward and then looked at what I saw there? I don't think so. I needed to do this so that I could hit the road with the good news of God's love for His children and His assurance that all of His promises and all of His blessings are already ours. We don't have to wait for them. Let's open God's gifts and see for ourselves what magnificent and glorious things are inside. The journey is well worth it. Let yourself see God in everything that happens to you, in every event that occurs, in every person you meet or see. Pray without ceasing. God's speed on your inward journey.

366 WHEN I FIRST BEGAN WRITING *Already Ours, Every Day Of The Year,* I didn't know the energy, the inspiration, or the toil and hard work it would take for me to get from Day 1 to Day 366. There were times when I didn't know if I'd be able to continue from one day's writing to the next. My spirits frequently sagged, especially around midpoint of the work, and it was at this time that I realized the enormity of this undertaking.

As I trudged along, however, the thought came that when the work was over it really wasn't going to be over at all. It was just beginning, for the words that came from the tips of my fingers clamored for an additional hearing. *Already Ours Again* is now knocking at the door demanding a hearing, and I will give it, but first I will rest. When my rest is over, I will once again remind readers that God's great gifts to us are already ours. We don't have to wait until we see Him face to face to get them — they are already ours.

Hallelujah and amen!